CUTTING EDGE

MY AUTOBIOGRAPHY

JAVED MIANDAD

with Saad Shafqat

Foreword by
Tony Greig

OXFORD
UNIVERSITY PRESS

OXFORD

UNIVERSITY PRESS

Great Clarendon Street, Oxford OX2 6DP

Oxford University Press is a department of the University of Oxford.
It furthers the University's objective of excellence in research, scholarship,
and education by publishing worldwide in

Oxford New York

Auckland Bangkok Buenos Aires Cape Town Chennai
Dar es Salaam Delhi Hong Kong Istanbul Karachi Kolkata
Kuala Lumpur Madrid Melbourne Mexico City Mumbai Nairobi
São Paulo Shanghai Taipei Tokyo Toronto

Oxford is a registered trade mark of Oxford University Press
in the UK and in certain other countries

ISBN 0 19 579918 6

Cover photographs courtesy: Iqbal Munir

Typeset in Times
Printed in Pakistan by
New Sketch Graphics, Karachi.
Published by
Ameena Saiyid, Oxford University Press
Plot No. 38, Sector 15, Korangi Industrial Area,
Karachi-74900, Pakistan.

For my Father,
the Late Miandad Noor Mohammed

*You left me long ago, but your memory
has nourished me at every step.*

And for my beloved Mother

*It is your wishes and prayers that have taken me
wherever I have managed to go.*

Contents

Foreword

I t is not easy to do adequate justice to the cricket career of Javed Miandad. Let us in the first instance, study his figures. Javed's batting average and strike rate are exceptional— there are only seven other test cricketers, Donald Bradman, Len Hutton, Walter Hammond, Ken Barrington, Gary Sobers, Greg Chappell and Sachin Tendulkar who have averaged over 52 and scored over 8,000 Test runs. Now, that is a very exclusive group!

One should also consider his contribution on and off the field—he has captained and coached his country with distinction.

Then there are the special moments in Javed's career of which there are too many to document here but include the endless occasions when Javed stamped his class and sense of adventure on the game we love so much. As far as I am concerned, it is his all-encompassing sense of enthusiasm and fun that sets Javed Miandad apart from any other player. In my capacity as Sussex captain, I was charged with the responsibility of seeing to it that my county had the best possible overseas players. I recall making the decision that I needed four players; two of whom would be South Africans. The reason for this was simple: South Africa was banned from Test cricket at the time, and their players were therefore always available to play county cricket. This did not apply to the other cricketers all of whom rightly had to put their own national tours of England ahead of all other cricket commitments.

I wanted the two best available fast bowlers and the two best young batsmen in world cricket. I think I achieved that with Javed and Kepler Wessels—they were by far the two best young batsmen around at the time and Imran and Garth Le Roux, the two best available fast bowlers.

I am not going to dwell on the talent that Javed displayed on the field because we all know he was a great player. It was his attitude to the game and for that matter, to life itself, that I just loved. He was positive and aggressive in his approach and the tougher the situation the more he seemed to revel in the challenge. His enthusiasm was extremely infectious which made him one of the best team men I have ever had the pleasure to play with or against. During his time with Sussex he was the one Sussex player my young kids wanted, more than the rest put together, to be with. You see, status did not really matter to this great Pakistani cricketer—life was meant to be fun and he shared his enthusiasm with absolutely everyone. There were plenty of occasions when Sussex were in trouble and it would be Javed, at the time the 'new boy' in the team, who would approach me, the captain, with an idea, more often than not, a good one. But better still, if one did not adopt his recommendation, it did not make the slightest difference to him, as he never took umbrage. I do not think there could ever have been a cricketer with a better temperament.

Thanks mate, for your friendship. For me, it has been a privilege to have crossed your path. May the rest of your journey bring you ongoing good health, happiness and more of that wonderful Javed Miandad sense of adventure and fun.

Tony Greig

Acknowledgements

I have been blessed with a wonderful family and have been extremely fortunate in the friends and elders who have helped me, and watched over me at every stage of my life—my gratitude to these individuals is recorded in the forthcoming pages. Here I would like to acknowledge the assistance I have received in the writing of this book.

Over the years, there had been quite a few tempting invitations and offers to help me write and publish my autobiography. Writing an autobiography is, of course, a time-honoured cricket tradition and I was grateful to see that people seemed interested in what I might have to say about my life and career.

I was always very clear that mine is, foremost, a Pakistani story and it was very important to me that my autobiography should be co-authored by a Pakistani writer and published in Pakistan. I was on the lookout for a Pakistani who could write with skill and clarity and knew the game well. It would also help if he or she were a Miandad fan.

I was very glad to have found Dr Saad Shafqat, who took time out from a demanding life as a physician in Karachi to help me write this book.

I am also grateful to my sister-in-law, Mrs Yasmeen Bashir Miandad, for helpful comments on the manuscript.

I would also like to acknowledge Ameena Saiyid and her team at Oxford University Press, Pakistan, who are thorough professionals at their job and are doing a great service for the publishing industry in Pakistan.

Co-author's Note

J aved Miandad's cricket career was the stuff of genius, and for a cricket devotee like myself to participate in putting that career into words has been a privilege of the highest order. For this opportunity of a lifetime, I will always be indebted to Javed.

I am also grateful to Raju Jamil—my mentor in the art of being a cricket fan—without whose encouragement I would not have dreamt about this project in the first place.

Several cricket-mad friends read parts of the draft and gave constructive feedback. I would especially like to mention Saleem Islam, Muzaffar Qazilbash, Nadeem Mustafa Khan, Afzal Ahmed, and Salman Hussain.

Kamran Abbasi of *Wisden Cricket Monthly* was a valuable resource throughout the writing of this book. Dr Andrew Hignell, official historian of Glamorgan County Cricket Club, was kind enough to meet me at short notice and provided important figures and references. Abid Ali Kazi, author of the definitive work on first-class cricket in Pakistan, was invaluable in compiling the statistical details of Javed's career, done in collaboration with Philip Bailey. Sports photo-journalist Iqbal Munir was most generous in sharing his treasure of cricket photos. Special thanks are also due Omar Noman, whose *Pride and Passion: An Exhilarating Half-century of Cricket in Pakistan* (Karachi: Oxford University Press 1998) is inspiring many of us to add to the literature on Pakistan cricket.

My parents and sisters—Miandad fans all—found reason to be even more generous with their love. And finally, I must acknowledge the love and support of my wife, Dr Anita Zaidi, who always knows what to do and when exactly to do it.

Saad Shafqat
Karachi, March 2003

CHAPTER 1
An Early Start

As far back as I can remember, I have been crazy about cricket. My father loved cricket and he passed that love on to his sons, all but one of us going on to play first-class cricket.

I have six siblings, four brothers and two sisters. Two sisters and two brothers are older than I am. The eldest is Farzana, who is married to a chemical engineer and lives in Karachi. Then my brother Bashir, followed by my brother Hanif Miandad who is a graphics artist settled in Canada. Bashir played first-class cricket but Hanif gave up after participating at the inter-collegiate level. After Hanif comes my sister Safia Iqbal, whose son Faisal Iqbal has also become a Test player for Pakistan. My two younger brothers Anwar and Sohail have played first-class cricket; both now manage a sports goods business in Karachi. Our father died in 1976 and my brother Bashir, who owns an import-export business in Karachi and does a lot of volunteer work with social organizations, now heads the clan.

My family comes originally from India. My father's side of the family is from the Indian cities of Bombay and Ahmedabad. My mother's family is from a small state called Palanpur, one of several princely states that flourished under British colonial rule.

In 1947, my parents joined the wave of immigrants from India that accompanied the end of British rule and the creation of Pakistan. They made their new home in Karachi, the sleepy port town that was destined to become the young country's nerve centre. I was born in Karachi ten years later, on 12 June 1957.

My father's name was Miandad Noor Mohammed. He loved all sports, but most particularly cricket. He used to play cricket in India and after 1947 continued to play in Pakistan. While he never played at a professional level, he nevertheless approached the game with the commitment of a professional. In India, my father had been an intelligence officer in the police department, posted mainly in the Ahmedabad-Baroda area. Because of his love of sports, he used to oversee the sports activities in nearby Palanpur, managing cricket, hockey and soccer teams that were patronized by Palanpur's Nawab.

My father's involvement in sports administration continued in Karachi, where he became Secretary of the Muslim Gymkhana, a popular sports club, and also became an office-bearer of the Karachi Cricket Association (KCA), a statutory body managing the city's cricket affairs.

In Pakistan, my father earned his living as a cotton expert and grader at the Cotton Exchange, a cotton-trading centre located in the heart of Karachi's business district. His job was to grade and price all the cotton produce that was brought to the Exchange for trade. The cotton would come in from the farmlands and Pakistan's big textile houses—the Adamjees, the Bawanys, the Dawoods—would line up to buy it. As a little boy, I would sometimes be taken to the Cotton Exchange and I came to revere these visits as a matter of great privilege.

The Cotton Exchange was a busy place and my father immersed himself in his job there. He would deal with several people at once as he looked over the cotton that had come in from all over Pakistan. He was a humble, kind-hearted and scrupulously honest man. He had a sensitive and powerful position at the Cotton Exchange but he always discharged his responsibilities with the utmost devotion and sincerity. God-fearing and very upright, he never indulged in any frivolous activities—a perfect gentleman. He never spoke ill of anyone, always preferring to remain silent rather than say something negative. He had a simple routine that involved his work, his family, a handful of close friends, and his sports affairs, and it all kept him happy and content. His memory means everything to me.

My father's greatest contribution was to the KCA. In later years this became the Karachi City Cricket Association (KCCA). He used his position as Secretary of the Muslim Gymkhana to provide an office and an available playing area for the KCA.

In those days, a number of remarkable individuals were involved in running the KCA's affairs, people like Muzaffar Hussain, Essa Jaffer, Adam Ali Alvi, Sirajul Islam Bokhari, Muneer Hussain, Noorul Harmain, Dalpat Sonavaria, Saifuddin Valika and M.S. Baloch. These illustrious gentlemen have all contributed in a major way to making Karachi one of Pakistan's great cricket nurseries and venues.

In the 1960s, my father was at the height of his involvement with the KCA. I was very young then and insisted on accompanying him everywhere, like children often do. In those days, in addition to organizing the city's internal cricket activities, the KCA also handled arrangements for Test matches that were assigned to Karachi. I would follow my father everywhere as he helped out with the Test match preparations. I remember being struck by how very dedicated everyone seemed and how everything managed to go smoothly. Each official would be assigned a specific task, like catering, seating, transport, etc., which was always discharged with great responsibility.

To help out with manpower, club-level players from all over Karachi would be recruited to help in the holding of these Karachi Test matches. When a Test match was in session, all the KCA officials—my father included—could be seen in their finest suits, working efficiently and harmoniously. At the end of the day, everyone assembled for a meeting to review the day's activities as they pertained to the administration and handling of the Test match. Whatever problems came up—and they always did—they were dealt with right then and there. No loose ends were left that might prove disruptive later. It was an older, purer time and everyone did what they had to do and were accountable for any failures. It was a unique atmosphere, and it made the cricket very charming and enjoyable.

So I inherited my love for cricket. In those early days, though, I had no idea where this would take me. I had developed my zest for the game, but my father believed that our eldest brother Bashir was the one with the real promise and the one who would one day rise to great heights in cricket.

My father loved sports, of course, and wanted all of us to play, but he had a certain outlook in this regard. He saw sports as something very constructive, good for character-building, forbearance and moral uplift. He would tell my mother that he wanted us to stay busy with sports so that we did not fall into other harmful pursuits.

Although my father wanted me to play cricket as well, I believe he had no serious ambitions for me back then. One hears of parents single-mindedly planning their child's cricket training and exposure, aiming for the big time, obsessed that their child should play for Pakistan. It was nothing like that with my father. He enjoyed the game, and he enjoyed us enjoying the game. He was not just all about sports, though. The atmosphere in our house was serious, though not oppressive or imposing. Both my parents also emphasized schoolwork and academics. All their other children graduated with degrees. (I would have, too, but I had neither the time nor, frankly, the inclination.)

My mother stressed schoolwork even more than my father did. She is a plain, soft-spoken woman of simple tastes who's never indulged in extravagance of any kind and has never traded on her son's celebrity status. She is, by far, the most unpretentious and unassuming person I know. Whenever I visit her, she fusses over me and insists on cooking for me and indulging me. To her, I will always be her little boy—and I would not have it any other way.

My father has had a very deep influence on my life, and he has certainly shaped my cricketing ethic, always urging me to strive harder, aim ever higher. He followed my cricket closely. Back in the days when I was playing club cricket, he would ask me after each match how I had done. If I had got out after a big score, he would chide me for getting out after I had become set. If I told him I had made a hundred, he would ask why I had not made a double hundred. He would urge me to always return not out. These exhortations kindled my hunger for long innings and big scores.

He would particularly berate me if I got out for a moderate score, in the 30s or 40s. He argued that getting out for a low score was understandable because very early in the innings the eye is not set. But if you got out for a moderate score, it basically meant you had thrown your wicket away and all the groundwork towards a large score was wasted, and that was just unacceptable. His admonishments never hurt, though. I understood that he and I were focused on the same goal, which was to help me elevate my game, so I always took his remarks positively. I did my best to play according to the standards he was setting for me, and it helped me tremendously.

Another very special influence in my early life was Mr A.R. Mahmood, my father's best friend who treated me like his own son. He would reprimand me for getting out cheaply or rashly. He regarded the cut as an especially vile stroke and would urge me to use it very sparingly and judiciously, and then too only after I had been in for a while and made at least 30 or 40. If he learnt I had lost my wicket while playing the cut, it invariably left him incredulous at my impetuosity and lack of judgment. He felt the same way about the hook and the sweep. He found the hook shot unsubtle, and compared it to swatting a fly with an oar. It was a blind shot, he would say, and urged me to use it with restraint.

Mahmood Sahab understood batting and coached me on how to pace my innings and vary my repertoire of strokes according to how set I was at the crease. In this way, he taught me about the sensible use of risky shots. He would instruct me on how to start an innings by playing straight. Until I had passed 30, my strokes had to be strictly within the 'V', the area between cover and mid-wicket. Beyond that, I was encouraged to play my shots.

A.R. Mahmood and my father influenced me in different ways. The reason for Mahmood Sahab's impact on me was that I was actually a little afraid of him. With my father it was different; he was a mild-mannered man who was lenient with me and, of course, I was family. But with Mahmood Sahab it was a different dynamic altogether. He was a seasoned cricketer from the old school with very exacting standards for everything. Having played his best cricket before the creation of Pakistan, he had seen a different and more severe time and so possessed a stern and unforgiving outlook, in which anything short of excellence was an unpalatable compromise. Even though Mahmood Sahab himself did not play top-level cricket, he understood the game deeply and I consider him one of my primary formative influences.

I attended the Christian Mission Society School in Karachi, located on what is now Nishtar Road (the thoroughfare is still also referred to by its colonial name, Lawrence Road). Cricketers like Haroon Rasheed, Intikhab Alam and Aftab Saeed are also the products of the Christian Mission school, as was Quaid-i-Azam Mohammed Ali Jinnah, Pakistan's founder, who was a student there in the late 1800s. By the time I had reached the seventh standard, aged 12 or 13, I was playing for the school cricket team and participating in inter-school tournaments. It was a very competitive school side and I was proud to be a part of it.

In school, I used to do everything in cricket—batting, bowling, and even wicket-keeping. I would bowl leg-breaks and also bowl with the new ball. In batting, I would come in at many different positions, as an opener, in the middle-order, or sometimes even in the lower order. Cricket consumed me.

In fact, as a schoolboy I was crazy about all sports and played a great deal of hockey, soccer and athletics as well. Our school was top in athletics and I took part in the 50 yards (no 100 yards for us as we were just little kids), the high jump, and the broad jump. Anything to do with sports, and I was right there in the thick of it, taking part with intense enthusiasm, trying to nourish a raging, insatiable appetite for competitive sport that has never showed the slightest sign of abating.

Our home was just a few blocks from my school. We lived in a fourth floor apartment, behind Karachi's Civil Hospital, in an area called Ranchore Lines. This is an old part of Karachi, located in the heart of the city, and thickly criss-crossed with narrow lanes and by-lanes. Then, as now, the area residents were mostly middle-class businessmen who ran shops on nearby Burns Road or M.A. Jinnah Road, or were traders in consumer goods in Karachi's commercial markets.

Like the other children in my neighbourhood, I used to play a lot of cricket on the streets around my house. With no parks or other open spaces in the area, and not wanting to venture too far from our house, there were few other options. In nearly forty years, things have hardly changed. You can still drive through the main thoroughfares in Ranchore Lines and find many cricket matches underway on the streets. The kids are a variety of ages, the bat is made of light wood, and the ball is a tennis ball wrapped, for extra bounce and swing, in plastic insulating tape. The roads continue to be used by vehicular traffic and, over the years, the cricketers and the traffic have reached an uneasy peace as they weave in and out of one another. Apart from the streets, the one other place one could knock a cricket ball about was on the roof of our apartment building. My brother Bashir and I would often go up to the roof's relative serenity and enjoy hours of batting against each other. This was a crucial time in the shaping of my cricket instincts and Bashir played a big part here. I credit him with taking away my fear of the ball, which is probably the single most important contribution anyone has ever made towards the evolution of my batsmanship.

There was very little room up on the rooftop where my brother and I used to play. He would bowl at me with a cricket ball while I stood in a cramped part of the roof with hardly any room to move, ungloved, unpadded, and unprotected, but for the bat in my hands. I was barely nine or ten then and Bashir, a few years older, would bowl his best at me, and mix it up good. A flighted off-break could immediately be followed by a nippy inswinger that stung my knee-caps. I would bat long periods like this. Each time the ball escaped my defenses, it inflicted pain, thus it was an even greater incentive to learn to make better contact with the bat. I had no place to run to, nowhere to hide, and using the bat well was my only viable option for self-preservation. Desperate to rise to Bashir's challenge, I never flinched. I was like a tiger, he would say. It did wonders for my hand-eye coordination.

I never received much in the way of formal coaching. There was the occasional short camp organized by KCA that I attended, but nothing on a regular basis. When I was a little older, I joined a club called the *Aik Lakh* CC. It was a very good club and its affairs were managed by a certain Mr Haroon, ably assisted by Mr Sakhawat. Both gentlemen were proprietors of a successful drugstore selling traditional medicines on Burns Road. Managing and maintaining the club side was an expression of their love for cricket. They looked after me well and never tired of giving encouragement and support. During my days with *Aik Lakh* CC, I had no worries other than doing well at cricket. We would play teams from all over Karachi. I remember going to what appeared then to be far-flung areas of the city—Landhi, Nazimabad, Korangi, Clifton, to all the four corners of Karachi. Then there was no hint of the heavy construction and the population that would come to these areas in later years. They were mostly just quiet, deserted stretches of open space, with a modest urban development.

Sometimes we would play matches at the Karachi Polo Ground, which used to be a vast open dirt field but has since been developed into a lovely manicured park in the city's hotel district. The polo ground was far from ideal. There would be literally scores of matches going on at the same time, within the same playing area, and you considered yourself lucky if you were able to even spot your own fielders in the crowd.

For the most part, then, *Aik Lakh* CC did not have access to any proper grounds. More often than not, we would simply find a naturally flat spot, mark out the area of the pitch and pick it clean of rocks and pebbles, then roll out a matting surface. To a degree, the outfield would also get tidied, the boundary would be defined by using natural landmarks identified by mutual consent, and the stumps were homemade, fashioned out of scrap wood. Occasionally, we would come across a manual roller left about by a road crew working in the area, and this would be 'borrowed' to smooth out the playing surface.

Around this time, I started going to the Muslim Gymkhana, ostensibly to be with my father who was part of the club management, but really to be part of the club's cricket activities. The place had reasonable cricket facilities and hosted unofficial matches. The games were played in a friendly atmosphere but many of the teams would often have one or two first-class players, and the cricket was competitive and of high quality.

On Saturdays, the KCA officials used to play a half-day game at the Muslim Gymkhana in which my father was a regular participant. In fact, being a member of the KCA as well as the club Secretary for Muslim Gymkhana, he was responsible for arranging the ground facilities. I was 13 or 14 at the time and would frequently be recruited as twelfth man, getting called upon to field when a senior player wanted a break. The matches would start at 2:30 or 3:00 in the afternoon and usually be twenty-five overs-a-side. Afterwards, high tea would be served in a relaxed, cordial atmosphere in which the conversation never strayed very far from cricket.

My life as a club cricketer did not last very long as I soon became a regular in the Muslim Gymkhana team. My captain was a jovial fellow named Masood Mirza, who was friendly with the Test-playing Mohammed brothers Hanif, Mushtaq and Sadiq, Pakistan's elite cricketing family. Every now and then, Masood would get one or more of the Mohammed brothers to come play with us at Muslim Gymkhana. Whenever they were around, I yearned to impress them and hoped they would notice my talents.

One day I learned that Mushtaq Mohammed had predicted to my father that I would some day play for Pakistan. You can't imagine how much that pleased me. Mushtaq also gifted me one of his bats—a fine English make he had played with in Tests—and I used it with a great sense of privilege.

Around this time, it was announced in the newspapers that trials were being held for the formation of provincial teams of players under the age of 19. Being from Karachi, capital of the

Sindh province, I was eligible to try out for the Sindh team. Sindh and Punjab are Pakistan's two largest provinces and selection into the Sindh or Punjab Under-19 sides held the promise of exposure at the national level. The trials were well attended, with hundreds of boys showing up. I had hoped I would make the cut and when I learnt that I had been selected, it brought great relief and gratitude.

I played several matches with the Sindh Under-19 side and performed well enough to earn a spot in the national Under-19 team for Pakistan. With the Pakistan Under-19 side, I later undertook two tours, to Sri Lanka in 1973-74 (as captain) and to England in 1974 (as vice-captain). Pakistan's national Under-19 side has generally been seen as a reflection of the country's future Test side. In addition to myself, several of my teammates went on to play Tests for Pakistan including Mudassar Nazar, Ejaz Faqih, Qasim Omar and Mansoor Akhtar.

Along with selection into the Sindh Under-19 team, I was also honoured by selection into a special Pakistan Cricket Board XI comprising promising youngsters from schools and colleges throughout Pakistan.

I understood the significance of getting a place in the Sindh Under-19 team. From leisure cricket with club sides, I was now moving into organized, representative cricket at a competitive level. It was a serious transition, and it had opened up all kinds of possibilities, including perhaps one day even playing for Pakistan.

CHAPTER 2

Promises to Keep

B y the early 1970s, the city of Karachi had become a huge metropolis. To accommodate the large amount of talent emerging from the city, the Karachi Cricket Association (KCA) had to organize four representative first-class teams. During the 1973-74 season, I made my first-class debut for one of these teams, the KCA Whites.

My cricket career was taking off and I was clearly rising through the prescribed system, but I wasn't self-conscious and certainly had no defined expectations. I was just happy to be playing all the time, and playing well. I was grateful to have broken into first-class cricket, and the KCA Whites cap represented a great honour for me.

First-class cricket in Pakistan was seen differently in those days. It represented quality and value, and therefore a certain amount of exclusivity. By the 1990s we had literally hundreds of first-class cricketers in Pakistan, but in the 1970s there were very few first-class teams and therefore very few first-class cricketers. Becoming a first-class cricketer was considered a very big achievement, and those of us who aspired to its ranks always looked up to first-class players as people of great importance.

I got exactly 50 in my first-class debut innings, playing at the Karachi Gymkhana ground, for KCA Whites versus Pakistan Customs. It was an exciting day for me and I remember it clearly. On the morning of the match, I rode my motorcycle to my friend Sikander Bakht's house, from where his father drove us to the Karachi Gymkhana. Like me, Sikander too had been hoping to play for KCA Whites and made his own first-class debut shortly after that. He went on to take many Test wickets for Pakistan with his nippy medium-pace.

Later that season, I also played in first-class matches for Sindh, and had the honour of representing Pakistan in an Under-19 cricket 'Test' at Multan. We were playing competitive first-class cricket, but there was also a strong social side to it. I developed close friendships with a number of other players during this period, including Nasir Valika, Humayun Dyer, Farooq Kirmani, Khalid Irteza and Arifuddin, all of whom became very accomplished first-class cricketers, and enjoyed careers of distinction in Pakistan's domestic cricket.

At the start of the next season, 1974-75, I was seventeen years old. I had now begun to dream about playing for my country. That season, events unfolded that confirmed my batting had been noticed at the highest levels of the game in Pakistan. As captain of the Sindh Under-19 team, I had led my side to the final of Pakistan's National Under-19 tournament. Predictably, we were going to meet Punjab in the final, to be played at Gaddafi Stadium, Lahore, in late November 1974. It was being seen as a high-profile match and a showcase for future Pakistan players. The press as well as Pakistan's cricket administrators and selectors were expected to give it close attention.

That match went well for me. Batting first, Sindh Under-19 made 254, of which I contributed 135. Punjab Under-19 replied with 221 and then, in our second innings, I returned unbeaten with 225 in a total of 392-9 declared. Punjab managed only a token resistance and we took the title. I was pleased with our victory, and even more pleased that I had not just come into runs, but had pulled off a century and an unbeaten double-century. It was a well-timed performance, in more ways than one. One of the spectators had been the late Abdul Hafeez Kardar, at the time president of Pakistan's cricket board. Kardar's figure dominated Pakistan cricket like none other, being a superb tactician who had led Pakistan to some stirring performances in the inaugural Test years and later, as president of the Pakistan Cricket Board, had been the architect of a comprehensive domestic cricket structure that endures to the present day.

At the end of that match on that late November day in 1974, the president summoned me. I was well aware of Kardar's formidable stature and bearing, and I remember feeling a sense of awe, mixed with intense anticipation, at the thought of meeting him.

I was led into the president's box and there I was—face to face with Mr Kardar. The sort of man who prides himself on an economy of words, Kardar was brief yet highly effective.

'Well played and keep it up,' he told me. I can't remember how I answered. I may well have said nothing. I just know that my head was spinning with delight. The next day, a statement from Kardar appeared in the newspapers in which he had called me the 'find of the decade.' I felt I had been handed the moon.

That performance in the National Under-19 final ignited my cricket career and thereafter things started happening at a rapid pace. The previous season, while I was waiting to make my first-class debut, I had been made twelfth man for several matches. After my fourth straight match as twelfth man, I had begun to despair and expressed my frustrations to my father. He had simply urged me to be patient and to have faith in Allah, and the opportunity had eventually come. Now, after my performances in the Under-19 final and the endorsement by A.H. Kardar, I felt I had really moved on to the fast track.

I sensed that I was about to live out a dream. In the following two years—1975 and 1976—I would make my One-Day International debut for Pakistan in the inaugural cricket World Cup, win a contract from Sussex to play in the English county championship, and then finally play my first Test for Pakistan.

I had performed creditably in first-class cricket for two regular seasons in Pakistan, and the effort was good enough to earn me the twelfth man spot with the Pakistan Test side, which hosted the West Indies for two Tests in 1974-75. I was so close to Test cricket now that I could almost touch it. I desperately wanted the selectors to give me a chance. I wanted to show them what I could do for Pakistan.

My best cricketing moment, however, came towards the end of the season. In April 1975, a special domestic tournament called the Kardar Summer Shield was organized in Pakistan in which the country's leading first-class teams participated. I made 311 in the tournament final playing for the KCA Whites against the National Bank of Pakistan at Karachi's National Stadium. It would be the only triple-century of my first-class career, but it couldn't have come at a better time. The following month, Pakistan's team for the 1975 World Cup was named, and I was included in it.

I was thrilled to be in Pakistan's squad for the inaugural World Cup, to be played in England in 1975. From being a little-known first-class cricketer in Pakistan, I now found myself walking alongside star players with world reputations. I was like a boy in a candy store, overwhelmed at the excess of goodies in front of me. I was now rubbing shoulders with players who were international mega-stars, whose cricket I had followed on radio and television with admiration. I was not yet eighteen, barely out of school, and I remained in a constant heightened state of excitement.

I was the youngest member of the Pakistan team, and was unofficially designated the baby in the squad. Everyone encouraged me and looked after me. This was my second trip to England, having earlier toured in 1974 with the Pakistan Under-19 side, and I was enjoying my return visit.

I was also getting accustomed, on this trip, to the ways of the English. I was contemplating part-time employment as a county cricketer during the English summer and I began to observe things from the eyes of one who may be spending the coming summers in England.

On one of our free evenings during that trip, I received an invitation to go out for dinner from Tony Smith, the baggage master assigned to the Pakistan team. Tony had been to Pakistan in the previous season in some capacity, and I had met him during the Test match against the West Indies at Lahore in 1974-75, for which I had been twelfth man. Tony was an amiable fellow and he and I had struck up a friendship. His dinner invitation sounded like a fine idea; I enjoyed his company and I thought it would give us a good chance to catch up with each other's news.

The problem, though, was that Sirajul Islam Bokhari had also invited me out for dinner for the same evening. Mr Bokhari was Secretary of the Karachi City Cricket Association and had come to England to follow the World Cup. He was a friend of my father's and a senior figure in Karachi's cricket administration whom I respected. I couldn't say no to him, nor could I to Tony, as nice a fellow as you can imagine. So I decided to have dinner with them both. I asked Mr Bokhari to come join us for dinner, and I told Tony that I would be bringing along a guest.

Tony said that would be fine. In the evening the three of us met and we went to a fashionable Indian restaurant in London's Soho district. After a hearty meal, it was time to settle the bill. My cultural background led me to expect that Tony would take care of it. He had invited me and I had told him that I would be bringing along a guest, which he had said was fine. Besides, he was an Englishman and we were two foreign guests in his country, which I thought made him the natural host.

Tony, apparently, saw it differently. When the waiter brought the bill, Tony took it and studied it; he laid it out between the three of us and started trying to figure who had eaten what and how much they owed. I was deeply embarrassed. Nit-picking with invited guests over the cost of a meal was something completely alien in my own culture, and I was mortified at having to sit through it with Sirajul Islam Bokhari. Tony seemed to be managing just fine. In the end, I paid for Mr Bokhari and myself and Tony paid his share. When the acute embarrassment wore off, I finally saw the experience for what it really was—an interesting education in understanding another culture.

The cricket experience on that trip provided an even greater education for me. The 1975 World Cup was the first of its kind—never before had all the elite of international cricket gathered together in one place for a tournament. It was my great good fortune to get my first exposure to international cricket at this super-festival.

We were a much better side in that tournament than our performance showed. While we lost two of our three group matches and could not proceed beyond the league stage, we came within a whisker of knocking out the West Indies, the eventual World Cup winners.

I didn't play in our first match, which we lost to Australia by 73 runs. The second match was played on 11 June 1975, a day before my eighteenth birthday, and it marked my One-Day International debut. These were the earliest days of the one-day game and the genre then was nothing like the craze it would later become. But the tournament had been marketed well and national prestige was at stake, so the competition was intense.

In my first international limited-overs innings, I was run out after contributing 24 (with two 4s), in our team's score of 266-7. It was an imposing total in those days and it almost won us the game, but for a fairy tale tenth wicket partnership between Derryck Murray and Andy Roberts that gave the West Indies a one-wicket victory with two balls to spare.

It was a terrible, devastating loss; our team was in a state of shock. I was overwhelmed by grief and cried for hours. It was the first time I was representing Pakistan in international competition and the match should have fond memories for me, but instead it is associated with a permanent bitter aftertaste.

Our third and last match was against Sri Lanka. The game generated little interest as Sri Lanka were not yet a Test side and the outcome of the match had become irrelevant to the tournament. Nevertheless, the game mattered to us because we were playing for pride. Zaheer Abbas, Majid Khan and Sadiq Mohammed made big scores, with Zaheer falling just three runs short of a century. I made 28 not out and our total of 330-6 proved decisive.

As a team, we left the tournament feeling depressed and demoralized. In terms of personal performance, I felt I had done well. I had fielded with enthusiasm, and was delighted to have taken three wickets with my leg-breaks. While I hadn't made many runs, I had also not had that much opportunity as I had been coming lower down the batting order when not many overs were left to be bowled.

After the World Cup ended, I stayed back in England to play English League cricket for a club called Daisy Hill, in the city of Bolton. There I began a long and dear friendship with the club's captain, Jimmy Irani, a Pakistani expatriate settled in England. My association with Jimmy has stood the test of time and I count him amongst my most special friends. Jimmy's son Ronnie Irani, whom I used to bowl to in their backyard when he was just a toddler, has gone on to become captain of Essex and has played for England.

My real purpose in staying back in England that season was in fact not to play League cricket but to find professional employment as an overseas player for one of the English county teams. Increasingly, successful Pakistan Test players had been taking this career route and had begun to command great respect on the county circuit. The rewards were obvious, and included remuneration as well as a chance to learn the finer points of the game by playing with the world's leading cricketers, most of whom spent summers in England in those days.

I had yet to play my first Test match, but this didn't deter me in my search for a county contract. Pakistan's impressive performances during tours to England in 1971 and 1974 had opened the county doors for our players. By 1975, Sadiq Mohammed was established at Gloucestershire, Asif Iqbal at Kent, Intikhab Alam at Somerset, Mushtaq Mohammed and Sarfraz Nawaz at Northamptonshire, and Imran Khan at Worcestershire. Zaheer Abbas had become an absolute star for Gloucestershire, where the locals had started to compare him to W.G. Grace. All these players were my teammates in the 1975 Pakistan World Cup squad and they encouraged me and tried to attract a county contract on my behalf.

My first opportunity was at Kent, where Asif Iqbal had managed to arrange a couple of matches for me with the Kent Second XI. While I did very well in those games, the club management politely explained that there were no openings in the main Kent team. Word must have got out that an enthusiastic young Pakistani was looking for a county job, because soon afterwards I received an expression of interest from Derbyshire.

That club, however, was struggling in the championship table and Mushtaq Mohammed gently suggested I may be better off looking elsewhere.

It was then that Mushtaq's brother Sadiq conveyed a message to me from the Sussex captain Tony Greig expressing an interest in my services. Apparently Tony had noticed me during the World Cup games and had been asking after me; he was now offering me a trial match with the Sussex Second XI to prove my potential.

I was still playing League cricket for Daisy Hill but the following day, I took the train from Bolton and reached the Sussex home ground at Hove on the eve of my assigned match, which was to be played against the Hampshire Second XI. I hadn't been very organized about my travel plans and realized on arriving in Hove that I had made no arrangements for the night. The head groundsman at the Sussex County Cricket Ground came to my rescue and offered to put me up in his quarters. He was a warm and entertaining fellow who knew how to tell a good yarn, and we struck up a friendship right away.

The groundsman told me that Peter Kirsten, elder brother of South African opener Gary Kirsten, was also being tried in the match that I had come to play. He said word was that Sussex were very close to signing on Peter. This piece of information motivated me even more to excel in the upcoming game.

Peter did play well in that match and got a 50, but I think it is fair to say that I stole the show with what ended up being a double-century. I also did well with my leg-breaks. Soon afterwards, Sussex offered me a contract for 1976. I was clueless about contract negotiations and asked Sadiq to help me work out the details, which he did to my great advantage and for which I remain extremely grateful. (Peter Kirsten did also go on to play for Sussex and in fact did very well in his first-class career. His Test career, of course, was a victim of the international boycott prompted by apartheid.)

I was still committed to Daisy Hill in the English League for 1976, but we worked out an amicable arrangement whereby I would be able to share my time between both clubs, spending most of the week with Daisy Hill and travelling to Sussex on the weekends.

Pakistan had no Test commitments in 1975-76, and there was no opportunity to make my Test debut that season. In the spring of 1976, I turned up at Hove to take one of the overseas spots at Sussex, not yet having played Test cricket. I didn't play my first game for Sussex until July, when I was included in a game against Middlesex at Lord's. I was disappointed to get out cheaply in both innings, and was determined to do well the next chance I got.

My second county game was against Hampshire at Hove, where Sussex were set 311 in the fourth innings to win. I returned unbeaten with 135 and ensured victory. When the season ended, I was top of the Sussex batting averages.

I played for Sussex for another three seasons, until 1979. Imran Khan became my Sussex teammate in 1977 and we had some good times, often socializing and spending our evenings together. The other overseas players in that Sussex side were the South Africans Kepler Wessels and Garth Le Roux, both formidable talents.

My days with Sussex are a happy memory. The club enjoyed a wonderful atmosphere with great harmony and congeniality amongst the team members. And playing at the seaside ground at Hove was always a real pleasure.

One of Sussex's best assets was our captain Tony Greig, who was also captain of England. Tony really went out of his way to promote me. He was a generous and supportive captain, and an inspiring influence on me. Back in 1976, I was just an inexperienced youngster; Tony watched over me like a big brother.

Taking employment in England wasn't easy for me. I was required to qualify for the Sussex team to play in the 1976 season and had been advised to show up by April, which I did, but found a depressing atmosphere dominated by cold, gray skies and incessant rain. To make things worse, I hardly knew anyone and felt socially isolated, but Tony sensing my alienation took care of me.

'Don't worry, Javed,' Tony would say. He exuded warmth and reassurance, which I found extremely heartening. The dismal weather and unfamiliar surroundings had made me very homesick and it was Tony's affection in those early days that kept me from running back to Pakistan. Whenever we had to travel to a county game away from Hove, he would often ask me to accompany him. And there we would be, thundering down the motorway in his Jaguar, chatting, laughing and watching the world go by.

A couple of years later, Tony was also responsible for getting me a contract with Kerry Packer's World Series Cricket. Tony was very kind to me and I owe him a great deal going back to those early days.

After the English season ended, I returned to Pakistan to play the 1976-77 season at home. This time round New Zealand were due to tour for what had become a much anticipated three-Test series. The last Test series Pakistan had played prior to playing New Zealand that season had been against the West Indies in 1974-75, when I had been twelfth man. Now, after representing Pakistan in the World Cup and playing for Sussex in the county championship, I was finally hoping to enter Test cricket.

CHAPTER 3

Dream Debut

B y the beginning of the 1976-77 domestic season in Pakistan, I had left the KCA Whites and had started playing for Habib Bank. I had, in fact, joined them the previous season, in 1975-76, after they had made a persuasive offer. Habib Bank is one of the large state-owned banks in Pakistan and they were financing a first-class cricket team as part of an intelligent scheme that was the brainchild of Abdul Hafeez Kardar. According to this system, large corporations such as banks, airlines and railway companies were given ownership of first-class teams with a view to ensuring steady livelihood for the cricketers. The corporations fielded these teams in our domestic tournaments and enjoyed the ensuing exposure; in the process, a pool of professional cricketers were nourished and maintained as a nursery for the Pakistan Test side. While the system has had its critics, it has served us well (discussed in Chapter 21).

Habib Bank was a very good team, with many promising youngsters, including names like Mohsin Hasan Khan and Mudassar Nazar, who went on to become a successful Test opening pair for Pakistan. Also in that Habib Bank team were people like Arshad Pervez, Agha Zahid, Azhar Khan, Abdur Raquib and Liaqat Ali, who may not have shone in Tests but were acknowledged stars on the domestic circuit.

The New Zealand team arrived in Pakistan in October 1976, captained by Glen Turner. The team also included a young Richard Hadlee, whose career was then only a few Tests old. I was named in the side for the opening tour match, a three-day affair between New Zealand and a Chief Minister's XI, to be played in Peshawar, the capital of the North West Frontier province. Hoping to get the nod for Test selection, I was anxious to do well. Though I managed only 27 in the first innings, I made 138 not out in the second, coming in to bat when the score was an anxiety provoking 3 runs for 2 wickets.

I was very pleased with my performance in that side game and felt certain I would be selected for the first Test. Sure enough, I was picked, but if you see the competition I was up against, I was in fact lucky to have made it into the side.

Pakistan boasted a solid batting line-up in the 1970s. A middle-order packed with Zaheer Abbas, Mushtaq Mohammed and Asif Iqbal was not an easy one to break into. Even a gifted batsman like Majid Khan had to move up the order to become an opener because there was no room for him in that middle-order. Talented players like Wasim Hasan Raja, a breathtaking strokemaker, and Imran Khan, who was always a solid bat, were available to bat in the lower middle-order. I felt I certainly deserved a chance in that team, and I was extremely grateful for being selected, but I also knew I could take nothing for granted. There really was no room in that Pakistan middle-order and if I wanted to keep on playing Test cricket, I would have to make room for myself.

Prior to playing in Tests, I had already accumulated a reasonable amount of international experience, having played in the 1975 World Cup and the English county championship. I was coming into Test cricket along the precise path that the system had prescribed for me: school, Under-19, regional first-class team, limited-overs international, and English county.

I should not have felt overawed, but I did. It was not that I did not feel prepared, far from it, but Test cricket is, after all, the ultimate form of cricket and one can never take it lightly, least of all one making his debut.

Selected with me were Sikander Bakht, who would serve Pakistan creditably with his lively medium-pace, and Farrukh Zaman, an orthodox left-arm spinner who had bowled well against New Zealand in the side match in Peshawar. At the last minute, though, their names were withdrawn because the selectors decided to go for more experience and less youth. I was disappointed to see Sikander and Farrukh go, but was relieved to have retained my own spot, and it made me value the opportunity all the more. (Farrukh made his debut in the next Test at Hyderabad and Sikander, in the one after that at Karachi.)

In those days I used to play a very attacking game. I wanted to hit every ball, punish every bowler, creating shots as needed. I have always had an aggressive attitude towards the game and it really came out in my batting in that series against New Zealand.

I made my Test debut on 9 October 1976, at Lahore's Gaddafi Stadium. Mushtaq Mohammed, our newly appointed captain, won the toss and decided to bat. I was due to come in at no. 5 and, with Majid, Sadiq, Zaheer and Mushtaq ahead of me, I was not expecting to go in for a while. But before we knew it, Hadlee had reduced us to 44-3 and I was walking out to the wicket. Soon my partner Zaheer also got out, leaving us 55-4. Asif Iqbal then joined me at the other end.

Pakistan's innings was in trouble but I did not feel any pressure. I was a rookie and played freely, as I did not yet feel the burden of having to anchor Pakistan's batting. In later years I would be burdened with the knowledge that my personal failure could well mean a batting collapse for Pakistan, and it would make my batting more circumspect.

I wasn't really troubled in my debut innings, and started going after the bowling from the outset. I had no inhibitions, and began coming down the wicket even to the quicker bowlers. I kept making my shots and the runs began to flow. Asif soon became set and our partnership quickly developed. I was eager and excited and kept chatting away. At times, more out of excitement and innocence than anything else, I would go up to Asif and point out to him when I felt he had made a technical mistake.

Asif was an international star and some years my senior, but it did not occur to me that I was being presumptuous in telling him how to go about his game. Part of the reason for this is that I have never hesitated to point out a mistake—be it my own or someone else's—if I felt one had been made. I was also very excited and hyped up, I was playing in my first Test match, the ball was coming on to the bat, and I was picking out gaps in the field almost at will. To Asif's credit, he took my pushiness in his stride. He was not only a star but also a gentleman, and he treated me like a master would an exuberant apprentice. At one point, he walked down the wicket and said 'Looks like I'm the one making my Test debut and you're the one who's been playing for years.' He was a wonderful steadying influence and it was my good fortune that he was there at the other end during my debut innings.

I eventually made 163, getting out late on the first day. We had scored rapidly and Pakistan finished the day at 349-7, Asif not out on 128. I became the second Pakistani (after Khalid Ibadulla) to score a century on Test debut. My fifth wicket partnership with Asif had been worth 281 runs, which was then the second-highest fifth wicket partnership in Test history. (It has since been surpassed by several others, but remains a Pakistan record).

Interestingly, my wicket went to New Zealand off-spinner Peter Petherick who was also making his Test debut, and who then proceeded to dismiss Wasim Raja and Intikhab Alam on successive deliveries to record a hat-trick.

Pakistani fans had become accustomed to dull home games that invariably ended in lifeless draws and all this drama on the first day of an opening Test created quite a sensation. My performance was hailed in the media as some great event. It gave me a tremendous rush, but I tried not to let the coverage and attention affect me.

My family also shared in the celebrations and received an avalanche of congratulatory messages and good wishes. My father, in particular, was feasted and feted for days. What mattered most to me was to continue doing well. I sensed I had made a connection with the fans and that spurred me on as well. We won that opening Test by six wickets after New Zealand had followed on. The fourth innings target was 101 and I was not out on 25 when we reached it. I hit a six to end the match.

We went on to Hyderabad for the second Test where I made 25 in my only innings, but found success with my leg-breaks and dismissed five batsmen in the match. Pakistan won comfortably by ten wickets.

And then on to Karachi. I was hungry to do well here, my hometown where I had learned my cricket. I was competing against our opponents of course, but in my mind I was also competing with the other Pakistan batsmen and was desperate to do better than anyone else in the team. Up until that stage in my career, I had been relaxed about my batting; but my approach now started to undergo a qualitative change. I started thinking in terms of international success and felt it a realistic ambition to try to be the best in the world. The goal gave me focus and drive.

We won the toss and batted. The series was already won and we felt relaxed and in a festive mood. Majid Khan started that match with a ferocious assault on the New Zealand bowling and recorded the rare feat of making a century before lunch on the first day of a Test. I was sent in at no. 4 and, beginning at 161-3, found myself in a partnership with Mushtaq Mohammed. As at Lahore, I batted aggressively, making all my shots. At the end of the first day, Pakistan were 338-3; I had got my second Test hundred and was batting on 110.

My debut innings had whetted my appetite for runs and a double-century was on my mind. I got to that milestone the next day. My brashness then took over. Having brought up my double-century in a flurry of boundaries, I tried to hook Dick Collinge for six. But the shot ended up finding Hadlee at long-leg, who caught me at the boundary for 206. I was 19 years, 141 days old at the time and became the youngest player to score a Test double-century.

I nearly got another century in the same match. In our second innings, I had stroked my way to 85, before being stumped off the flighted leg-spin of Derek O'Sullivan trying to hit one out of the ground.

I had made 504 in the three Tests of my debut series at an average of 126. The public response was fantastic. The print and broadcast media hailed me as some kind of phenomenon. One of the opinion columns said I was 'the best thing that's ever happened to Pakistan cricket.'

Factors other than my batting undoubtedly also contributed to this general acclaim. Success in sports has always been highly valued in Pakistan; this being Pakistan's first series win at home in over a decade, the jubilation was understandable. Mushtaq's captaincy also found favour with our supporters and he was seen as a capable man in charge of a competitive unit. The general atmosphere of celebration added to the public's appreciation of my performances.

Far from giving me a swollen head, though, the public reaction made me realize that the game is ultimately about the fans. Cricketers come and go but the game flourishes because the fans give it life. I have seen public adulation make many gifted cricketers arrogant and self-centred; these people need to realize that what makes them special is not their skill, but the fans who appreciate it. The most glorious performances, the most daring innings, the deadliest bowling spells—without the appreciation of the fans it does not mean a thing.

In that heady atmosphere of congratulations and celebration, I could never have suspected that a major life-event was around the corner for me.

After the New Zealand tour ended in late 1976, we played some unofficial matches against a visiting international team. We had finished a game in Sukkur, in the northern part of Sindh province, and were headed to the town of Mirpurkhas for the next fixture. This was around the time of Eid-ul-Azha, one of the two major annual Muslim festivals. The thought of Eid festivities made me homesick. I told our manager that instead of going to Mirpurkhas for the next match, I wanted to go home to Karachi to offer Eid prayers with my father. My brother Bashir, who was living in Bahrain in those days, was also visiting Karachi over Eid and I wanted to see him too and spend the day with my family. The team management didn't like the idea, but

I was adamant and simply refused to play the next game. Finally, it was decided that I would go with the team to Mirpurkhas but then go on to Karachi while the rest of the team stayed back and played the match.

I didn't know this at the time, but while we were en route from Sukkur to Mirpurkhas, my father had died in Karachi. In Mirpurkhas, we were received by Pir Aftab Shah Gilani, a prominent local personality. By this time, the news of my father's death had reached the Pir. As soon as he saw me, he took me aside and said that he had arranged for a car and driver to take me to Karachi right away. He said that my father had been taken seriously ill and I should leave immediately.

This was shocking news to me, my head was spinning. My father had had some chronic health problems but nothing serious. I was very close to him—a son, a friend, a private secretary and a valet all at the same time—and I feared the worst.

We sped off towards Hyderabad, from where we would take the Super Highway to Karachi. In Hyderabad, though, the car broke down, adding to my mounting sense of frustration and helplessness. Luckily, we were near the Highway, and I was able to flag down a bus whose driver recognized me. When we reached Karachi, I got off and took a taxi to our house.

It must have been around 8 or 9 p.m. when I finally got home. There was a bit of a crowd outside and right away I knew that the worst had happened. I went in and was told that my father had died earlier in the day from a heart attack. That same night, we buried him.

It was a cruel emotional blow, coming on the heels of my memorable debut series. My father had meant the world to me and I was deeply sad that he had left me when so much of my career remained to be realized. My entire family knew we were going to miss him very much. Two of my sisters needed to be married and settled, and two of my brothers were still very young. I knew I was going to miss my father in my cricket career, but at the time I did not realize just how much. In later years, I longed for my father's counsel every step of the way as my career went through its twists and turns.

Just ten days after my father died, the Pakistan team was due to depart for its most important foreign trip in decades. This was to be a three-Test tour of Australia followed immediately by a five-Test tour of the West Indies. Pakistan had tended to struggle on tour and we were desperate to prove ourselves abroad. The team was starting to mature under Mushtaq and morale was high after the thumping home-series win against New Zealand. I was now firmly in the national side and expected to go on tour. But in the aftermath of my father's death I could not think straight and didn't know what to do.

I looked to my mother for guidance. She said I should go because what's done cannot be undone. I realized too, that this is what my father would have wanted as well, and so I boarded the plane for Australia.

CHAPTER 4

Dropping Anchor

The 1976-77 trip to Australia and West Indies remains one of the most demanding tours ever undertaken by a Pakistan cricket team. It was certainly our toughest assignment up until that point in our cricket history. As I struggled with my deep sense of personal loss, the timing of that trip could not have been worse. I had to play my first major overseas tour in the wake of my father's death—and it also just happened to be a pivotal tour that had the potential to make or break my country's rising cricket stature.

Looking back, those twin tours represent an important watershed in the evolution of Pakistan's cricket psyche. Both Australia and West Indies were very much at the top of world cricket in 1976-77. We were going to be taking them on in succession: three Tests in Australia on the first leg of the tour, followed by five in West Indies. Australia were captained by the highly accomplished Greg Chappell, and West Indies by no less a figure than Clive Lloyd, who presided over West Indian cricket's greatest era. They were both imposing teams, with able leadership, solid batting and top quality fielding.

But what really gave us a genuine fright was the platoon of bowlers waiting to greet us. The list read like the fast bowling hall of fame, with names like Dennis Lillee, Jeff Thomson, Andy Roberts, and Michael Holding, who were all acknowledged match-winners. Throw in a mystifying Australian medium-pacer called Max Walker, and a couple of West Indian Test debutants named Joel Garner and Colin Croft, and you can see why we felt we were facing a firing squad.

For me personally, there was literally no time to nurse my bereavement. Fresh from what was openly being regarded as a phenomenal debut series, I now had a reputation to keep. And here, then, 22 yards from an Australian and West Indian fast-bowling artillery, it was being put on the line. I came under a great deal of pressure and didn't quite know how to handle it.

Although the trip proved unsatisfactory in terms of my own individual performance, the Pakistan team was up to the challenge in that very trying season, drawing 1-1 in Australia and losing a closely fought series 1-2 in the West Indies. We had stood up to the best in the world and it marked our coming of age.

My own form was disappointing. In Australia, I had Test scores of 15, 54, 5, 10 and 64—a clear decline in the run fest I had enjoyed at home against New Zealand. There were two problems. Of course, Australia were a much stronger bowling side than New Zealand had been; but also, I had not realized how different the playing conditions were going to be in Australia.

I had never played in Australia before. The ball came higher and quicker off the hard and bouncy Australian tracks and that took me by surprise. I did my best to adjust my batting technique to handle Lillee and Thomson thunderbolts on those firm Australian wickets, but my lack of experience showed and I struggled.

I did manage a couple of good innings, though. In the drawn first Test at Adelaide I got 54 in the second innings. It was an important contribution as we were 182 behind on the first innings and were struggling to set Australia a competitive fourth innings target. During that innings I shared a partnership with Asif Iqbal, whose heroic 152 not out saved the game for us.

My best knock on that tour was a score of 64 in the third Test at Sydney that helped us take a sizeable first-innings lead over Australia after Imran had bowled them out for 211. Sydney marked Pakistan's first Test victory in Australia and I was proud to have made my contribution. This time around the batting hero was Asif Iqbal again. Asif was a great man for pressure situations. He was rebuilding our innings when I went in at 205-5. Lillee was blazing away and it was crucial that we consolidate. I did my part and Asif made a match-winning 120 as our total reached 360 and we put Australia under pressure. After that, Imran moved in to take his second 6-wicket haul of the match and we were left with the formality of scoring 35 in the fourth innings to win, which we did for the loss of Sadiq and Zaheer.

When we went to the West Indies, I played in the first Test at Bridgetown but fared miserably, scoring 2 and 1. It was an exciting match, made memorable by inspired performances from both sides, and it ended in a tense finish that saw the West Indies holding on to a draw with just a wicket to spare. Except for getting the wicket of Joel Garner, who was making his Test debut, I could claim no part in Pakistan's creditable performance.

I was dropped after that match, the selectors' job being made easier after I had failed a fitness test because of an elbow strain.

I was disappointed with my failures, but I remained confident in my ability to make it in international cricket. In fact, even though I had been dropped for lack of form, I never really feared for my place in the Pakistan side. Prior to my Test debut, I had been anxious to get a foothold in the competitive Pakistan line-up, but things had gone so well during my debut series that I had started to feel an integral member of the team. I was certain my low scores in Australia and West Indies were little more than a transitory failure and I felt that my teammates, captain and selectors thought the same as well.

In Pakistan, some sections of the press were saying that I was only good for home wickets. Considering that I was just starting my Test career, I thought this was a little harsh and premature. Nevertheless, comments like these only strengthened my resolve to do better.

I think my difficulties on that Australia-West Indies tour were basically a case of too much too soon. My strong showing against New Zealand in the previous series had created too high an expectation from my batting. I was too inexperienced to handle the novel conditions and the high-class bowling that I was confronted with in the new arena.

Another limitation was that I was actually expected to perform as an all-rounder and I didn't have the luxury of concentrating solely on my batting.

In the first Test against Australia at Adelaide, I bowled no less than 46 overs with my leg-breaks, 25 in the first innings (taking 3 wickets for 85) and 21 in the second innings (taking 1 for 71). The spell in the second innings was especially demanding. Iqbal Qasim and I bowled unchanged for long periods as Australia chased 285 for victory. They were eventually only 24 runs short of their target with 4 wickets to spare. My bowling had been important in saving that match for Pakistan and I realized I could be called upon to perform as an all-rounder as well.

After that tour ended, Pakistan had no commitments until the start of the domestic season later that year, so I was free to play for Sussex in the summer of 1977. I had a full season at Sussex and played in each of their twenty-one matches in the county championship, averaging a reasonable 40.38 with three 100s (top score 109 not out) and seven 50s. I also managed to get some wickets with my leg-breaks, including decisive figures of 5.2-2-10-4 in the second innings of a match against Northamptonshire.

It was a fun season at Sussex even if I was not as successful with the bat as I would have liked. Imran was also playing for Sussex and I spent a lot of time with him that summer, sharing a flat in Hove and spending many evenings together. Many of my teammates from the Pakistan Test side were also playing county cricket then and it was always a joy to catch up with them on the circuit. We would get together after the day's play and enjoy each others' company over Pakistani food. It made us feel at home.

Around that time, an Australian business tycoon named Kerry Packer was involved in an acrimonious dispute with the Australian Cricket Board (ACB) over the matter of TV rights for international cricket played in Australia. When the ACB refused Packer's offer, he set up a rival international cricket extravaganza that he called World Series Cricket.

World Series Cricket would actually go on to revolutionize the sport like nothing before or since (see Chapter 23). What affected me immediately in that summer of 1977, however, was that World Series Cricket had managed to sign up four of Pakistan's best batsmen—Majid Khan, Zaheer Abbas, Mushtaq Mohammed and Asif Iqbal—who were the lifeblood of our national batting line-up.

Cricket establishments throughout the world responded to Packer's insolence—what else could you call an action that challenged a century of tradition—by banning the so-called 'Packer players' from Test cricket. So, in the time it takes to sign four Packer contracts, I went from being rookie batsman to becoming the batting anchor in the Pakistan Test side.

Our major upcoming assignments were two series against England. First up were three Tests at home later in 1977, and we were then due to tour England for another three Tests the following summer, in 1978.

When it became clear that the Pakistan Cricket Board was not going to select the so-called Packer players, public interest in the home series against England waned. I welcomed the opportunity to anchor the Pakistan batting and cement my place in the side, but I must confess that I too found the series a dull prospect.

We were going to be without Mushtaq Mohammed, who had been a brilliant and imaginative captain and had turned our talented but underachieving side into a winning outfit. Wasim Bari was made captain in place of Mushtaq but proved a total failure. Bari has been one of cricket's greatest wicketkeepers, but he knew next to nothing about captaincy and his bland management only added to the tedium.

All three Tests were drawn. I averaged 131, making three 50s and being dismissed just twice in five innings, but my batting added little to the contest and has left me with no particular memories.

The only excitement in that series happened off the field. Three members from Pakistan's Packer contingent (Zaheer, Majid and Imran) flew home in time for the third Test at Karachi and made themselves available to play. The Pakistan Cricket Board was persuaded to name them in the line-up for the Test, but the English team, backed by their cricket board, refused to take the field if the Packer players were going to be included.

England were also without a number of key players due to the Packer ban being enforced by their own board. This was, of course, their internal matter, but I thought they had no justification in expecting the Pakistan Board to act in the same way. In my opinion, our board had every right to take a unilateral decision regarding the inclusion of the Packer players. Common sporting etiquette demanded that England should have been ready to face the best side we could put together. The English team and management didn't quite see it that way and in the end the match went ahead without the Packer stars. I thought it was all a bit childish of the English, especially their captain Mike Brearley.

When we went to England in the first half of the 1978 English summer for the return visit, Wasim Bari was still captain. The Packer ban was still in force and we continued to miss the presence of key players who could have significantly altered the balance between the two sides.

Technically, I also qualified for the Packer ban. By the summer of 1978, Packer's World Series Cricket had signed three more Pakistanis in the second round of recruitment—Sarfraz Nawaz, Haroon Rasheed and myself—but the matter was not made public and we remained in the Pakistan side.

England were also minus their big names—players like Derek Underwood, Tony Greig, Bob Woolmer, Dennis Amiss, and Alan Knott were all Packer recruits—but because of the excellent health of the county system in those days, English cricket reserves were far stronger than ours.

Inevitably, we were outplayed, losing the three-Test series 0-2, including two innings defeats and a match cut short by rain.

England called on two new young players in that series whose performances made it clear that they were going to be major international stars of the future.

David Gower made 58 on his Test debut against us in the first Test at Edgbaston. He dispatched the very first delivery of his Test career to the midwicket boundary with an ease and elegance that made it clear here was a man of class. He made 56 and 39 in the two other innings he played in that series.

The other young English hero was Ian Botham. His career was only five Tests old at the start of that English summer but he tore into us in that series like a seasoned master of seam and swing, taking 13 wickets at 16.07 apiece and scoring a century in each of the two Tests that England won. He completely dominated the second Test at Lord's where, in addition to his aggressive 108, he took 8-34 in our second innings, the best bowling figures of his remarkable career.

There were suggestions that Botham's performances may have been overrated because they were made against a weak and depleted side. Regardless of the opposition, turning in a good performance at Test level is never easy. Botham's match-winning feats deserved all the praise they received. In any case, his many fine performances against other, stronger sides confirm his place amongst the game's top all-rounders.

Unlike Botham, no one in our side managed to get going in that series. We lacked experience. It was only the second tour of my Test career, but in comparison to many of my teammates this practically made me an old hand. It didn't say much for our team. I managed a miserable 57 runs from five innings, the average of 11.40 being my worst for any Test series of my career. Our most experienced batsman Sadiq Mohammed managed a respectable average of 42 and Mohsin Hasan Khan also performed creditably, consistently reaching the 30s and 40s and averaging 38.20.

The bowling fared no better than the batting, and it all made for a truly miserable series. One of the joys of touring England is the energetic crowd support our team gets from the Pakistani community in Britain. But in that wretched series, even they turned against us. They booed and heckled wherever we went. Few things could have been more demoralizing. It was a cheerless, gloomy tour where nothing was a pleasure, least of all the cricket.

Pakistan had undertaken two tours to England in the 1960s—both had proved disastrous. In particular, the 1962 trip under Javed Burki with a stinging 0-4 loss was probably the worst of the lot. Speaking for myself, I can safely affirm that 1978 series in England was the unhappiest tour of my career.

The misery of that one-sided series behind us, we had much to look forward to in the upcoming season in Pakistan.

The traditional rivalry between India and Pakistan has always generated great excitement whenever the two countries compete. In cricket, the contests are nothing less than an Asian version of the Ashes. In fact, they have even more of an edge to them because, unlike England and Australia, the Asian neighbours have actually fought each other in real wars.

India and Pakistan had last met on the cricket field in 1961 and the last time a Test had been decided between the two teams was as long ago as 1952. Now in the autumn of 1978 a star-studded Indian team boasting the likes of Sunil Gavaskar, Gundappa Vishwanath, Dilip Vengsarkar, Mohinder Amarnath and the famed Indian spin quartet, was expected in Pakistan for a three-Test tour beginning in October. And oh, yes—a promising all-rounder named Kapil Dev was going to be making his Test debut.

A series that had been anticipated for seventeen years was not going to let anything stand in its way, and the nagging matter of the Packer players was quickly resolved. Mushtaq returned as captain and we came out with our finest batting line-up with Majid and Sadiq as openers, Zaheer at 1-down, and Mushtaq, myself and Asif in the middle-order.

Imran, the hero of Sydney, was back to take the new ball. He had bowled well in Packer's World Series matches and was now regarded as a major international fast bowler, really the first bowler from the subcontinent to be so recognized.

For the cricket-starved fans in Pakistan, the build-up to that series must have been unbearable. On 25 September 1978, the

Indian team was received at Karachi airport with tremendous fanfare. An electric atmosphere prevailed throughout the tour. A host of public and private social functions were held in addition to the cricket, and the media spotlight never left the Indian team, on the field as well as off the field.

The public frenzy put us under great pressure to win, but with the home advantage, a winning captain back in charge, and with the team full-strength again, we fancied our chances and were cautiously optimistic.

I was very conscious of the need to perform well against India. I still didn't regard myself as being permanent in the Pakistan side, especially with our star batsmen back in the fold. I was taking nothing for granted. I knew that a solid showing in such high profile a series as this one could go a long way towards cementing my spot. I decided to leave nothing to chance.

To guarantee my success, I needed a methodical approach and a plan. Taking stock of India's bowling strengths, the threat of their celebrated spin quartet loomed large. Bishen Singh Bedi was an orthodox left-arm spinner who had perfected the art of flighting the ball; Srinivasan Venkataraghavan and Erapali Prasanna were penetrating off-spinners; and Bhagwan Chandrasekhar was an unclassifiable right-arm spinner with the guile of a snake-charmer who could turn a flighted googly square just as easily as he could send down a yorker with the pace of Andy Roberts.

I had never really been troubled by spin bowling, but the Indian spinners had undone many strong batting sides and I spent many long hours in the nets trying to make sure I would be ready for them.

The central part of my plan was to face the Indians with focused mental preparation. The first step was to reject fear. Allow yourself to become afraid of the bowler, and you've already been defeated as a batsman. I simply didn't let any fear of the bowler take hold. It is easy to do if you really understand how to handle a bat. I have great respect for the highly accomplished bowlers I have faced in my career, but I have never feared them. In the art of batting, there is no room for fear.

As the Tests approached, I started disciplining myself into a routine. In the nets, I practiced particular shots for long periods. Wanting to polish my cut against spin, I would deliberately cut six deliveries in a row, regardless of where or how they pitched. Then I would do the same with another shot, then go back to cutting again. And so on and on.

I began spending evenings thinking about my batting tactics. I would eat light and sleep late. Sleeping late may not sound like the best way to prepare for a major sporting encounter (and I certainly don't advise it for young players), but it suited me. I wasn't out and about in the evenings but rather would just stay in my room, going over methods and plans in my head. By the time I went to bed, usually around 1:00 a.m., I had decided on what I would be doing the following day.

Once my mind had settled on a set of plans, I was loath to revise or rethink them. This was the logic behind sleeping late. If I slept late, I also got up late, ideally just in time for the next day's cricket activities. I preferred this to getting up early and obsessing over the cricket again. I didn't want to overthink the cricket. I have never needed more than five or six hours of sleep every night, and sleeping early would have meant getting up early and having time for the mind to wander and to brood.

I also refused to play any side matches just before the Tests. I wanted to avoid injury, of course, but more importantly, I didn't want to risk undermining my confidence with a chance dismissal against the Indians. The team management wasn't happy about my refusing to play in the side matches, but I gave them no other option.

The first Test of that series started in front of a sell-out crowd in Faisalabad's Iqbal Stadium. Mushtaq Mohammed won the toss and Majid and Sadiq went out to open our innings. It was also the first Test of Kapil Dev's long and distinguished career and he started the proceedings for India by opening the bowling.

I came out to bat at 110-3, by which stage Bedi had dismissed both openers, and Chandrasekhar had cheaply removed Mushtaq. I concentrated hard and took my time settling in. I soon realized the ball wasn't doing much and that boosted my confidence. I had been concerned about getting an outside edge off Bedi's left-arm spin, and I eliminated this possibility by keeping my right pad flush with the bat's outside edge each time I played defensively to him. Unorthodox, yes, but like I said, I was leaving nothing to chance.

At the other end, Zaheer Abbas found his touch and started batting like a well-oiled machine. He flayed the spinners and was particularly severe on Prasanna, who we soon realized was the most predictable of the lot. I also became very comfortable with the bowling and our partnership progressed. Zaheer and I both wanted maximum strike against Prasanna because he was the easiest to score off, but Zaheer pulled rank and told me to stay away from Prasanna, whom he wanted all to himself. Instead, he wanted me to protect him from Chandrasekhar, whom he was finding 'a little difficult'. Being the junior partner, I naturally had to comply.

Zaheer had come into this series with more to prove than I. His talent was unquestioned, but his performances within Pakistan had been poor. Two Test double-centuries in England and a prolific record for Gloucestershire had left no doubt what he was capable of, but his Test batting average within Pakistan prior to that series against India had been in the teens, with a top score of only 33.

All that was now remedied. Zaheer made 176 as he pushed a nail into the coffin of India's spinning quartet. I got 154, and our partnership yielded 255 runs for the fourth wicket. Faisalabad was a flat track, though, and India also batted well, with Gundappa Vishwanath scoring 145 and Sunil Gavaskar and Dilip Vengsarkar making scores in the 80s. Zaheer followed up his 176 in the first innings with 96 on the last day and the match ended in a tame draw.

The next Test, at Lahore, belonged completely to Zaheer Abbas. He was in devastating form and mercilessly thrashed the Indian bowling to make 235 not out. I went cheaply, bowled by Mohinder Amarnath off an inside edge for 35, but Zaheer's double-century helped us post an imposing 539 in response to India's modest first innings of 199. Eventually left needing 126 to win after tea on the last day, we got there comfortably thanks to some aggressive one-day style batting by Majid, Zaheer and Asif Iqbal. It was a sweet victory, and it triggered a nation-wide outpouring of joy. Acknowledging the country's festive mood, President Ziaul Haq declared the following day a national holiday.

The third Test, in Karachi, proved even more historic. India won the toss and batted first, Sunil Gavaskar topscoring with 111, the first of his two centuries in the match. In response to India's first innings of 344, we soon found ourselves 187-5. Zaheer was already gone, caught sweeping off Bedi for 42. When Mushtaq joined me for the sixth wicket, there was just Imran to follow, and then the tail.

Mushtaq and I arrested the slide of wickets. It was a measure of the depth of our batting in those days that one or two of us would invariably rise to the challenge of making a healthy score if the other batsmen failed. There was no room in that side for a batsman who could do no better than the 30s or 40s. You had to keep getting big scores to keep your selection chances alive. If the openers left early, Zaheer or I would get the runs, or Mushtaq or Asif would come good in the middle-order without fail.

You can't be a competitive Test side unless you have three or four batsmen who are routinely getting big scores. Look at any team worth its salt—the modern Australians or the West Indians of the 1980s—and you will find this formula holds true. The Pakistan team under Mushtaq Mohammed was such a side, with Majid, Zaheer, Asif, and Mushtaq himself all frequently posting large scores. My mandate for securing a permanent position in that team was clear: drop anchor, especially on a day when no one else had managed to do so.

In the first innings of that third Test at Karachi I did exactly that, and the Indians hit a roadblock in my sixth wicket partnership with Mushtaq, which yielded 154 and took us to within three runs of the Indian first innings. I was determined to secure a significant first innings lead and was eventually out for exactly 100, Mushtaq getting 78. The last four wickets also put up a fight and we declared leading India by 137.

We were already well into the fourth day when India started their second innings, and our bowlers desperately fought against the clock to leave us a feasible fourth innings target with enough time to spare. Sunil Gavaskar was a rock and made a valiant 137, but the Indian resistance ended at tea on the last day and we were left needing 164 to win in the game's final session of play—half-an-hour plus twenty overs.

By this time, National Stadium had filled to capacity. It was an incredibly thrilling and electric atmosphere. The whole nation seemed to be on the edge of its seat. Mushtaq was in his element and planned our final assault like a general at war. He promoted Asif to open with Majid and told me to pad up and be ready to go in at no. 3.

When Majid went for 14, I walked out to join Asif. We faced a daunting task but both Asif and I sensed what it would take to win and we set to work. Asif and I have built up a great mutual chemistry over the years and it was on full display during our partnership that day.

Asif Iqbal was a highly intelligent player who used his mind to extend the reach of his physical talents. I found a kinship with him through his mental approach to the game. We both realized very early after getting to know each other that our minds worked the same way. (We also shared a sense of humour, which made for some fine pranks.)

In that second wicket partnership, we quickly made 97 as the Indians did all they could to stop the runs. Bedi had set a scattered field. This being Test cricket, there were no field restrictions and no penalty for bowling down the leg side. The

Indians were bowling to their field and it forced Asif and I to come up with some creative running between the wickets.

In fact, it wasn't so much running as anticipating, because our understanding reached a level where we started to read each other's minds. It got to the point where even before Asif would play a shot, I had sensed where he would play it, how far it would go, and how many we could run for it. And I also sensed that Asif was reading me the same way.

It was the kind of understanding about running between the wickets that gets you runs out of nothing. We were routinely taking singles after the ball had missed the bat and had been collected by the wicketkeeper. Once we even got two from a delivery like that. A stroke that would typically get a single, like a push towards point, was netting us three runs. We'd run the first almost as the ball was delivered, then get the second as it went into the outfield, and then run the third if the fielder was someone like Bishen Bedi, whose arm we could chance. Three runs from a shot to point—I still think it is incredible. It put the Indians under great pressure and they started to crumble. Asif and I hardly talked during that partnership. There was no need to.

After Asif's dismissal, Mushtaq sent in Imran to use the long handle, which he did very well. Bedi came on to stem the run flow but Imran sent him off for two sixes and a four and the fate of the match was as good as sealed.

It was a truly historic match. We won by eight wickets and I was Man of the Match. It was a significant point in my career. Pakistan had turned to me and I had delivered. There can be no greater achievement as far as I am concerned. This triumph gave me the confidence that I, too, could be a frontline player for Pakistan. How I had wanted to anchor the batting for my country: now it had actually happened.

Playing the Indian spinners had turned out to be easy as apple pie. The myth of their invincibility was blown by the way we took them apart in that series. It effectively ended their playing careers. With my batting confidence restored after the failures of the foreign tours, I began looking ahead towards

settling into a career for Pakistan. Even though the success had
come on home wickets, I had discovered a new self-assurance
that made me feel I could bat anywhere, under any conditions,
whatever the odds.

After the Indian series, things moved into high gear for me.
Later in that 1978-79 season we visited New Zealand where I
got 81 and 160 not out at Christchurch. The runs were scored
against an attack that included Richard Hadlee, who had begun
to bowl beautifully and looked like a legend in the making. Our
victory at Christchurch decided the three-Test rubber 1-0.

From New Zealand we went to Australia where I made 129
not out in the second Test at Perth. This was a depleted
Australian side, lacking the players contracted to World Series
Cricket, but we were also tired at the end of a full season and
the two-Test series was tied 1-1. During that series I got my
first genuine taste of being the subject of controversy when I
ran out Rodney Hogg after he had strolled out of his wicket
(discussed in Chapter 19). Where I came from, nobody would
have thought anything of it, but down in Melbourne that run out
seemed to get everyone all worked up.

After that, the 1979 World Cup came and brought the high
drama of yet another tragic defeat against the West Indies. Then
we went to India in 1979-80 for an unsettling six-Test series
that left us bitter and battle-scarred, and which I have addressed
in Chapter 11 (*Wars with India*).

I had managed to secure a firm foothold in the Pakistan side,
but the cricket was happening too fast too soon and I longed for
a change of pace that would allow me to consolidate. How
naïve I was. In the wake of the 1979-80 tour to India, there was
a leadership crisis and before I knew it, I was captain of
Pakistan.

Things would never be the same again.

CHAPTER 5

Captain of Pakistan

Pakistan became a Test-playing nation in 1952. Twenty-eight years later, by the end of the 1979-80 tour to India, ten players had received the honour of leading the Pakistan side. It is an impressive list of captains that includes some distinguished names like Abdul Hafeez Kardar and Mushtaq Mohammed.

I, too, had hoped that one day I would add my name to this list. But I had not expected to be the eleventh.

In retrospect, my appointment to the Pakistan captaincy had much to do with the way things turned out on that ill-fated tour to India in 1979-80. Expectations from that tour had been extremely high because we had already beaten India at home the previous season. Our team had several players with world class match-winning potential, and the demanding Pakistan public was expecting them to deliver. And of course there was the usual hype that develops whenever we play India. In our first trip to that country in eighteen years, we were just not up to it and lost 0-2.

Asif Iqbal had taken on the dangerous job of leading Pakistan in that series. He was under tremendous pressure to succeed and I am sure he knew that if he faltered he would fall hard. When he returned home in February 1980 with a defeated side, he was the most obvious target for everyone's frustrations. He took it on the chin and retired from Test cricket, vacating the captaincy.

I was not the next natural choice for captain. There were a couple of players ahead of me in seniority. But the disappointing performances of these particular players during the Indian tour had left even their team selection in doubt, let alone their appointment to the captaincy.

In the climate of reform following the Indian tour, the leadership in Pakistan's cricket administration also changed and Air Marshal Nur Khan took over. The Air Marshal had become famous after overseeing Pakistan's rise to near-invincibility in world hockey in the late 1970s. He had a reputation for taking bold decisions and his first major move after becoming the Pakistan Cricket Board chief was to make me captain of the Pakistan side.

I was only twenty-two years old and the news took many by surprise, not the least being myself. I believe, however, that I was deserving of the honour. I have always believed in the value of merit and of assigning responsibility according to ability. To my mind, merit and ability are far more important in appointing a captain than his age or the length of his career.

Surely one gauge of eligibility for the captaincy is previous captaincy experience. By the 1979-80 season, I had already acquired a good deal of such experience, and had been a fairly successful captain. Early in my career, I had led the team for my home province of Sindh and had also captained the Pakistan Under-19 team. I had even captained on tour, when I took the Pakistan Under-19 side to Sri Lanka in 1973-74. The most important of all my captaincy assignments had been my leadership of the Habib Bank team, whom I had taken to the top of Pakistan's domestic first-class championships. In 1977-78, I had captained Habib Bank to the title in each of Pakistan's three major first-class tournaments—the Quaid-e-Azam Trophy, the Patron's Trophy and the Pentangular Tournament—to complete a rare grand slam.

Although there was some vocal dissent to my appointment, I don't feel this reflected the general mood in Pakistan. I believe that the majority of the cricket-following public in Pakistan were behind me and welcomed Nur Khan's daring move. I was young, but I feel the public also recognized that I knew a thing or two about captaincy.

I went on to win my first Test as captain of Pakistan. Australia visited Pakistan for a three-Test series in early 1980. Led by Greg Chappell, it was a tough Australian side that included the likes of Allan Border, Kim Hughes, Dennis Lillee and Rodney Marsh. In the opening Test, in Karachi, I put my faith in the nagging left-arm spin of Iqbal Qasim and he spun us to victory with eleven wickets in the match. The remaining two Tests were drawn and we won the rubber 1-0. I had proven that I did have the ability to lead Pakistan.

My next captaincy assignment was another home series, but I knew this one was going to be tougher than the Australian series by at least an order of magnitude.

By 1980-81, the West Indies were on top of the world. The previous season they had beaten Australia in Australia and all but beaten New Zealand in New Zealand (but for some controversial umpiring). They were coming fresh from having beaten England in England in the summer of 1980.

In November 1980, the West Indians came to Pakistan for a four-Test series under Clive Lloyd. Names like Desmond Haynes, Vivian Richards, Malcolm Marshall, Colin Croft and Joel Garner were in the ranks. We lost the series 0-1 but it was an honourable loss. A superior opponent had defeated us, but we had gone down fighting and I felt that the fans appreciated the honesty of our effort. On paper the West Indians were much stronger than we were and I am sure they had expected to win by a more convincing margin, but our dogged efforts kept the contest from being too one-sided.

I was satisfied with my leadership during that series and I credit myself with having brought out some brave performances from my team. Imran made an invaluable hundred to save the first Test and also put in some valiant bowling performances. The off-spinner Mohammad Nazir (now a Test umpire) also bowled like a champion and troubled the best of the West Indian batsmen. Of Viv Richards's five dismissals during that series, Nazir accounted for three, including twice bowling him with nippy off-breaks that nearly turned square to clip middle and off.

Next on Pakistan's Test calendar was a trip to Australia in 1981-82, for three Tests and for a triangular one-day tournament (the Benson and Hedges World Series) that would also feature the West Indies. Even though it was months away, and I had a whole summer of cricket with Glamorgan to look forward to, the idea of leading the Pakistan side on a tour of Australia excited me and dominated my thoughts.

Australian tours have always been very demanding for Pakistani sides. We have never won a series there. This particular tour was no different. We were up against a strong Australian side and lost the Test series 1-2. We also failed to reach the final of the Benson and Hedges triangular.

The lowest point of the tour came early on, in our first innings of the first Test. The match was played at the WACA Stadium in Perth, a ground famous for its lightning fast pitch. The wicket that greeted us for the start of the Test series looked hard and fast all right, but it was also green. The sight gave us pause. Our team had next to no experience of bouncy green-tops.

I won the toss and had absolutely no hesitation asking Australia to bat. For a while things went well. Imran, Sarfraz and Sikander Bakht made good use of the quick surface and Australia lost wickets steadily. We were very pleased when we eventually got them out for 180.

And then the fireworks began. None of the regular Pakistan batsmen reached double-figures and before we knew it we were 26-8, in danger of equalling the world record lowest Test innings total of 26 (currently held by New Zealand). But Sarfraz Nawaz hit out lustily at the end and we ended up with 62 as Sarfraz topscored with 26. It was Pakistan's lowest score in a Test innings at the time.

Australia made 424 in their second innings, leaving us with a victory target of 543. We fell well short by 286 runs. In our second innings, I had a physical and verbal exchange with Dennis Lillee which became instantaneously famous. (The incident is described in Chapter 19.)

I am embarrassed that we recorded one of Pakistan's lowest Test innings totals under my captaincy, but the explanation lies in the fast and slippery nature of the Perth wicket, to which we were unaccustomed. On top of that, we were up against a high-class pace, seam and swing attack from Lillee, Thomson and Terry Alderman.

Except for that forgettable first innings at Perth, though, the cricketing encounters during that tour were not entirely one-sided. In fact, there were several positive cricketing moments for Pakistan during that trip.

Overall, I felt I had been a good captain in Australia and had earned the respect of my opponents regarding my leadership. I also found encouragement from the media's comments about my captaincy in that series. During the coverage on Australian television, respected observers like Richie Benaud and Bill Lawry made many generous remarks about the quality of my captaincy, which I found extremely heartening.

I remember one match in particular. At the Adelaide Oval, during one of the Benson and Hedges World Series one-day games, we defended a total of 140 against the mighty West Indians, winning by a mere eight runs. I had put in a great deal of thought into my field settings and bowling changes in that match, and it paid off. One of the gambles had been to use Wasim Hasan Raja as the sixth bowler, and it worked beautifully as he sliced through the West Indian late middle-order with four wickets from seven overs. Richie Benaud observed during the TV commentary that the match had been won by the captaincy. Such an endorsement from a man whom many regard as the ultimate cricket personality was flattering indeed.

Another memorable match, at least from our perspective, was the third Test in Melbourne. Unlike the previous pitches at Perth and Sydney, the Melbourne wicket suited us. After making 500-8 declared, we won the Test by an innings as we forced Australia to follow-on. Test victory on foreign soil is always sweet but this one was especially meaningful, as it is never easy bouncing back from a series of defeats. In that third Test in Melbourne, we had wrought an innings victory after being, for all purposes, outplayed by the same team. This is one of the Test victories under my captaincy of which I am most proud.

In fact, our achievements during that 1981-82 tour of Australia, modest though they were, were actually quite impressive considering that our internal team harmony was not what it should have been.

Take the case of Zaheer Abbas. It was well known that he coveted the captaincy. Zaheer played his first Test for Pakistan seven years before I had, and my appointment to the captaincy ahead of him clearly annoyed him. I can understand, even sympathize, with his frustrations, but what I found incomprehensible was that he allowed his bitterness to interfere with his professional role as a core member of our team.

Zaheer's passive-aggressive approach peaked in an incident that happened during one of the side matches on that tour of Australia.

The start to the match had been delayed by rain. The downpour was so heavy it seemed likely that the entire first day would be washed out. Even though the chances of playing appeared slim, it was of course our professional duty to be available at the ground until the umpires had officially abandoned play for the day.

After a while, the most amazing thing happened and the weather suddenly turned fine. Before long the outfield had dried out and the umpires walked out to start the game. We were batting.

Soon enough, we had lost a couple of wickets and it was Zaheer's turn to go in, but he was nowhere to be found, and no one seemed to know his whereabouts. He knew he was part of the playing eleven and had, in fact, accompanied the team to the ground that morning. But, from all available evidence, he had then disappeared. It was all very perplexing.

It soon emerged that Zaheer had gone back to his hotel room. Apparently he had not been feeling well, but he didn't inform anyone—not even me, his captain. When I finally caught up with Zaheer back at the hotel, I took him aside along with the team manager Ijaz Butt and took him to task for his irresponsible behaviour. Zaheer remained an unhappy creature throughout that tour, an unnecessary distraction we could all have done without.

Press reports in Pakistan said that I was having trouble managing the senior players on that tour and questioned my management style, especially with regards to the older players. These were misconceptions. In addition to Zaheer, I had several other senior players under me on that tour, including Sarfraz Nawaz, Majid Khan and Wasim Bari. Except for Zaheer, though, none of them were any trouble.

The issue of my management of the senior players was complicated by the sense of hierarchy that dominates Eastern cultures like Pakistan's. In Pakistani society, as in most oriental cultures, seniority counts for a lot. One can command—and receive—respect simply on the basis of age. I respect this tradition and have always held my seniors in great esteem.

This traditional age-based attitude can also interfere with the relationship between a manager and his subordinates if the subordinates happen to be older than he is. While I agree that seniority commands respect, I also believe that true respect is earned, not given. If Zaheer was sensitive about being questioned by a young captain like myself, he should simply not have given me the opportunity. His behaviour was unprofessional and I had no choice but to reprimand him, respect for seniority notwithstanding.

In fact, Zaheer's behaviour on that tour exemplifies an endemic problem that has plagued Pakistan cricket for years. Many of our star players, after they have become successful on the field and have received some public recognition, develop an inordinate sense of their own importance. They cease to be team players and expect special treatment. This divisive attitude disturbs team unity and keeps us from rising to our true potential. One must always remain humble and down-to-earth. It doesn't matter what great cricketing feats we've performed, it should never go to one's head.

Above all, one must have respect for rules and regulations. The world's most successful nations are the ones where the rule of law is supreme. Cricket, of course, mirrors life, and the key to success at cricket is respect for the rules and etiquettes of the game. In a cricket team there is no room for special treatment for anyone, regardless of who they are, how well they play, and for how long they've been in the side.

I sometimes wish the Pakistan cricket team could be managed according to a code in which behaviour is strictly proscribed within clearly set limits and any infractions carry severe penalties. The team needs ruthlessly imposed discipline to get the best out of it.

However, even military-style management would be a temporary solution. Just as respect is earned, not given, so I believe that discipline ultimately comes from within and cannot be imposed. To be truly effective, discipline must be created through self-motivation. As captain of Pakistan I dearly wanted to create an atmosphere in the team that was conducive to self-discipline, but it was a struggle.

I have always had a militant approach to cricket. To me it is not so much a game as it is war. When I became captain of the Pakistan side, I saw myself as a commanding officer and expected that my judgement would be respected and my planning would be executed with enthusiasm.

The complexity of cricket makes the role of captain a very powerful one. On the field, there is very little room for the captain's decisions to be questioned. A team's best chance of success is to place their complete trust in the captain and follow his orders to the last detail, no exceptions.

My first spell as captain came to an abrupt halt after we returned from the 1981-82 trip to Australia. This happened through the players' revolt during the home series against Sri Lanka later that season, discussed in the following chapter.

I eventually captained Pakistan in 34 Tests, spread out in different spells over the course of my career. At the end of my first captaincy spell, I had led Pakistan in 13 Tests (including the Sri Lankan series), losing 3 and winning 4, and I was satisfied with the overall tally. I would eventually win 14 of my 34 Tests as captain, which is the best winning percentage amongst Pakistan's Test captains bar none.

CHAPTER 6

The Players' Revolt

As is well known, after two years as captain of Pakistan, I had to step down from the job. As we shall see shortly, circumstances had emerged that made it impossible for me to continue. My giving up the captaincy at that stage was a completely voluntary act and I did it against the wishes of the Pakistan Cricket Board, who were solidly behind me and wanted me to remain in the job.

Divisions had developed within the team, and had I continued, Pakistan cricket would have been the ultimate victim. This was unacceptable to me, and I stepped aside to make room for another leader.

As I have already indicated, my appointment to the Pakistan captaincy back in early 1980 had caused distress to some people. The grumbling had appeared in a section of the local press, but originally came from certain players who for some reason felt they couldn't play under me. Perhaps they felt they had been passed over and wanted me out of the way to satisfy their own ambitions for the captaincy.

Certainly, the issue was not my ability to captain the side. Even before becoming the Pakistan captain, I had already proved an able captain in competitive cricket. In any case, my record as captain of Pakistan is a testament in itself. By the beginning of March 1982, I had captained Pakistan in nine Tests, leading the side to victory against Australia at home; losing a closely fought series to the 1980s West Indians, probably the best team of all time; and defeating Australia by an innings in Melbourne.

My batting form had also not particularly suffered. In my first nine Tests as captain, I had scored 616 runs at an average of 41.07, including one 100 and five 50s.

So it is hard for me to accept that the people who were grumbling about my captaincy were motivated by any lack of ability in me.

It could be said that perhaps the timing of my appointment was not right. The circumstances of the 1979-80 tour to India had created a mood for radical change in Pakistan cricket and I probably would not have been made captain at that time had such a climate not prevailed and had a bold administrator like Air Marshal Nur Khan not been put in charge.

Be that as it may, the fact was that by the decision of the Pakistan Cricket Board I had been appointed captain, and that should have been that.

But it was not. We come back to the issues of discipline and professionalism. Proper cricket requires strict adherence to the discipline of the game. Someone has to be captain and he is going to call the shots and it is part of the cricketing ethic for the other players to obey him. The Pakistan Cricket Board must have had their reasons for making me captain. They must have seen something they liked, and at the same time they must have seen qualities in others that they did not like, or liked less.

Many people make an issue of seniority but I will say again that the captaincy is about more than just seniority. If you do not have the qualities of a good captain—a strategic mind, the ability to think on your feet, to stay strong under pressure, to lead by example—you do not deserve to be captain, no matter how senior you might become.

On the cricket field, in any case, seniority is meaningless for once the ball is in play, it becomes a level playing field. Everyone has to perform according to their assignment. And that is based on what you can deliver in the game, not how senior you are. In fact if there is any cricketing quality that comes with seniority it is the responsibility to be an example and an inspiration, to fight, to lead the charge, to never give up.

In the Pakistan team, traditionally seniority has been taken to mean a license to ease off, to slack, to field casually, and to tell off youngsters who start to pick up these very same habits. This kind of behaviour isn't seniority, it is a mockery of seniority. There are many great examples of senior players guiding and inspiring their teams alongside their captains—names like Viv Richards and the Chappell brothers come readily to mind—but such examples have been rare in Pakistani teams.

The events surrounding my resignation from the captaincy crystallized in a conspiracy against me during the Sri Lankan tour of Pakistan in March 1982. The principal instigators behind this action were a small group of players who created a web of intrigue aimed at destabilizing my captaincy. I know precisely who these individuals are. I am, however, reluctant to name them for it serves little purpose except to reopen old wounds.

Compared to the rest of the team, this little band of instigators was a small minority, but as their revolt gained momentum, their intrigue snared other players too, many of whom were either neutral about my captaincy or, in some cases, had even favoured it.

The Pakistan Cricket Board had made no commitment to me about the captaincy beyond the tour to Australia. So when we returned home after the 1981-82 Australian trip, the captaincy spot was technically open.

Next up on Pakistan's cricket schedule was a three-Test home series against Sri Lanka. I didn't know if I would be asked to continue as captain for that rubber.

The Sri Lankan visit was an important one and I was anxious to retain my captaincy. Sri Lanka were the latest addition to the Test club, having been admitted to full ICC membership in 1981. This was going to be their first visit to Pakistan, and the first time that the two countries would meet in Test cricket. Pakistan had campaigned hard for Sri Lanka to be given full ICC membership and Test status. The last time a new nation had been given Test-playing status was Pakistan itself, in 1952, and Sri Lanka's membership now further strengthened subcontinental representation in the ICC. This first Sri Lankan

Test tour to Pakistan was therefore associated with a lot of symbolism.

As the first Test approached, the Pakistan Cricket Board announced its decision to retain me as captain for the series. This announcement led to a public declaration of revolt, in which several players gave a written statement to the Board refusing to play under my captaincy. The signatories included Majid Khan, Zaheer Abbas, Sarfraz Nawaz, Wasim Bari, Mohsin Khan, Mudassar Nazar, Imran Khan, Wasim Raja, Sikander Bakht and Iqbal Qasim.

I had advance warning of the revolt—but only just. I first got to know of it shortly before it appeared in the morning papers.

In late February 1982, the team had gathered in Lahore for a training camp at Gaddafi Stadium in preparation for the first Test in Karachi. After the Board announced that it had retained me as captain for the Sri Lankan series, I noticed a strange attitude in several of the players. They began avoiding me and seemed in a hurry to get away if I tried to approach them. Something was definitely amiss, but what?

The training camp was well-attended, although Zaheer Abbas was prominently missing. Zaheer had been due to join the camp on time with everyone else, but his arrival had been delayed for some reason and he was now coming by a later flight to Lahore.

I soon heard that a written statement had been prepared against my captaincy for which Zaheer's signature was necessary. The statement would not be made public until Zaheer had signed his name to it. Our team hotel was abuzz with this rumour and everyone was talking about it in hushed tones. Zaheer's flight from Karachi was delayed, and the drama surrounding this 'mystery statement' was prolonged.

Eventually, Zaheer arrived at the hotel, and soon afterwards, everyone seemed to have disappeared. I didn't know what to do. I felt lonely and isolated, as if all the others were party to some secret that was being kept only from me. It was a horrible, empty feeling. I decided to leave the hotel and go to my Canal Bank residence in Lahore to stay the night. I still had no idea what exactly was going on. I didn't know who was behind the 'mystery statement' or what it said. I suspected that the statement represented a threat to my captaincy, but I also knew that I was the Pakistan Cricket Board's official choice, and that gave me heart.

At that time, I believed that I still had some friends left in the team, and this thought also comforted and sustained me.

Later that night, Iqbal Qasim turned up at my Canal Bank home along with another friend. Iqbal and I go back a long way, and I received him with all the relief and pleasure of finding an old friend in a moment of crisis.

It soon became clear, however, that Iqbal Qasim had not come to me in friendship, but had come as the spokesperson for several other players who had collectively decided not to play under my captaincy. My feelings of relief and joy at seeing Iqbal quickly gave way to bitter pangs of betrayal and rejection.

'Everyone has signed a statement refusing to play under you,' Iqbal told me.

I wanted details. Who exactly was involved, why were they doing this? Didn't they realize that they would be taking on the Board in challenging my captaincy?

They had done their homework, Iqbal assured me. 'Everyone' meant all the frontline players, including Majid, Zaheer, Sarfraz and Bari, as well as Mohsin, Mudassar, Raja, and Sikander Bakht. They also had the linchpin on their side, Imran Khan. They were reasoning that with such broad support, the Board would have to give in to their demand about replacing me.

I asked Iqbal Qasim where he stood on this, and he told me he was part of the group. He, too, was refusing to play under me. Coming from an old and trusted friend, this shocked and deeply saddened me. Then Iqbal delivered the ultimatum of the rebels: relinquish the captaincy at once, or else the revolt would make the morning papers.

How does one negotiate on an ultimatum? Knowing that I had the backing of the Pakistan Cricket Board, I told Iqbal that I would not be held hostage to the revolt. The next morning, the whole ugly mess became public.

I resented being bullied into giving up the captaincy. Even more than that, I regretted the fact that my teammates—the friends whom I trusted and the seniors whom I respected—would rather take such a hostile action against me than simply talk to me and tell me their concerns.

I was sorry that none of the team's seniors whom I so respected had talked to me about these issues personally. Had a figure with the stature of Majid Khan taken me aside and told me that I was doing something wrong and that it would be best if I stepped aside, I would have heeded his advice like a younger brother obeying his elder.

The first indication I received that something was genuinely wrong—that people were unhappy under me—was in the form of the ultimatum that Iqbal Qasim delivered to my home. Prior to that, no one had come up to me and communicated any negative feelings about my captaincy. It was underhanded and disturbing.

I cannot say with certainty what led to the revolt. I am not a mind-reader and cannot second-guess someone else's motives, although I am fairly certain that it came from a very small nucleus of players older than I who wanted me removed to make way for their own captaincy aspirations. I was only twenty-two when I was made captain, and I was doing a fine job too. So I had both time as well as ability on my side, which apparently pushed these overlooked seniors to desperation.

To make their scheme work, though, the masterminds needed support in numbers, and to get the numbers, they needed Imran Khan who had by this time become, for all intents and purposes, the Pakistan team's centre of gravity.

It was natural that once Imran was on board, several were likely to follow. Everyone realized that the Pakistan Cricket Board would think nothing of leaving out cricketers like Majid, Zaheer, Sarfraz or even Bari from the team, but the thought of leaving out Imran from the Pakistan Test side would definitely give the Board pause.

So the architects of the revolt made an all-out effort to get Imran on their side, and they succeeded. With Imran gone, other defections were only to be expected.

It still shocked and hurt me, though, to see old friends like Iqbal Qasim and Sikander Bakht join the rebellion. With an eye to safeguarding their own careers, they had cast their lot with my opponents. I felt betrayed by their opportunism.

Emotionally and mentally, the players' revolt marks one of the lowest points of my career. I was distraught and hurt, deeply hurt. It was like a body blow. The whole thing depressed me and my mind was reeling from the betrayal of close friends.

It soon became clear that the Pakistan Cricket Board was not open to blackmail. The Board's chairman Air Marshal Nur Khan was incensed that the Board's authority was being challenged. He called me on the telephone and reassured me of the Board's complete support, which gave me strength.

'We'll leave them all out, the lot of them,' the Air Marshal told me. He said he wanted to build a fresh team comprising our most promising youngsters, with an eye to the future. He instructed me to put together a team for the first Test leaving out the dissenters. I wasn't sure how deep our reserves of talent were going to be, even for playing against Test novices like Sri Lanka. I thanked the chairman for his confidence and support, and told him we would try to come up with a promising combination that would put up a good fight.

On 5 March 1982, the first Test against Sri Lanka started in Karachi's National Stadium. I was still captain, but the team was virtually a Pakistan Second XI. Four players made their Test debut for Pakistan in that match. The list of new players included the wicketkeeper Saleem Yousuf who would serve Pakistan so well in the coming years, and also the stylish Saleem Malik, whose promise had become obvious in the Under-19 matches.

Also included in the line-up for that first Test were two players—Iqbal Qasim and Wasim Hasan Raja—who had been signatories to the revolt against me. These players were forced to take the field after being pressurized by National Bank, their employers in Pakistan's domestic cricket, to cooperate with the Pakistan Cricket Board.

In the team were also some experienced players like Mansoor Akhtar and Haroon Rasheed who were given Test recalls.

Our side won that first Test by 204 runs. Saleem Malik got a hundred on debut, becoming only the third Pakistani batsman after Khalid Ibadulla and myself to do so. I partnered Saleem for most of his innings but missed out on a century myself when I was stumped off de Silva's leg-spin for 92. Haroon also got a hundred in that match, celebrating his return to the team with an imposing 153 (run out) in the first innings. Eventually, Sri Lanka were set 354 to win in nearly two days but they folded for 149. To restrict the Sri Lankan second innings, Iqbal Qasim and Wasim Raja put in inspired bowling performances, which I appreciated, given the circumstances.

The series then moved to Faisalabad for the second Test. The players behind the revolt were still deadlocked with the Pakistan Cricket Board, and we had to persist with a second-string side. I was surprised at the dissenting players' intransigence. Sri Lanka became a frontline Test side through the 1990s, but back in their early Test matches they were soft opposition. By opting to stay out of the team, players like Zaheer and Imran were missing out on turning in star performances.

Imran could easily have taken ten wickets in each of the two Test matches he sat out. As it happened, when he finally played he took fourteen wickets in the third Test alone. He could have ended up with thirty or perhaps even forty wickets in the series. I was amazed he would forego the opportunity of taking so many easy wickets.

In fact, shortly before the start of the second Test in Faisalabad, I received word that Imran was very keen to return to the team and have a bowl at the Sri Lankans, but the organizers of the revolt were putting immense pressure on him to stay put.

So the second Test also proceeded without any resolution of the players' revolt. I continued as captain as several players from the side that won the first Test were retained. We did make a few changes, though. Ashraf Ali had been a very successful wicketkeeper in our domestic first-class cricket and the occasion was used to try him out at the Test level. Also, the opener Mohsin Hasan Khan was in the side. Mohsin was party to the revolt, but like Iqbal Qasim and Wasim Raja in the previous Test, his employers in Pakistan domestic cricket (Habib Bank) forced him to cooperate with the official Pakistan Cricket Board policy.

The second Test was drawn, but Sri Lanka dominated the match from the very beginning. They batted first and made 454 with the help of an authoritative 157 from opener Sidath Wettimuny and a stylish 98 from Roy Dias. In reply, we conceded a lead of 184. Although we then dismissed Sri Lanka for just 154 in their second innings, that still left us with a fourth innings target of 339. The batting failed again, and we had our backs to the wall at 186-7 when the game finally ended.

As the third Test approached, I gave the whole situation deep thought. Our best players had declared they could not play under my captaincy and we were being forced to field an inexperienced team. It was a stark choice: I could insist on remaining in the captain's position, which would mean continuing to deprive Pakistan cricket of some of its best talents, or I could step down from the captaincy, which would end the divisiveness and allow the dissenting players to return to the team. It would have been easy for me to stay on in the job. I had the support of the Pakistan Cricket Board in this, and it was, after all, what my ego wanted.

What was the decent thing to do? Giving up the captaincy would be hard, but I ultimately decided that it was the right thing to do. I did it so that the team could be united again. The decision went against my own self-interest, but it was in the best interests of Pakistan cricket, and to me nothing matters more than that.

So I informed the Board that I wished the deadlock with our frontline players to end and had decided to relinquish the captaincy. The Board chairman Air Marshal Nur Khan told me that my wishes would be respected and a new captain would be appointed. He was concerned, though, that the leadership should not be changed in mid-series. Nur Khan said he would defer the captaincy issue until after the Sri Lankan visit, and asked me to continue as captain for the third and final Test. All these decisions were made public.

On 22 March, the third Test against Sri Lanka began in Lahore's Gaddafi Stadium. It was interesting that although I was still captain, all the dissenting players who had precipitated the revolt by refusing to play under me were now back in the side—playing under me!

It made me wonder what these players' real motives had been. The basis of their argument had been that they could not play under my captaincy; now that I had agreed to step down from the job at the end of the current series, they suddenly felt they *could* play under my captaincy. To me this confirmed that the real reason behind their revolt was not my captaincy—it had never been that at all. The problem was that the captain was not one of them.

On the field, though, it was a pleasure to lead a full-strength Pakistan side once again. I won the toss but the wicket had tufts of green so I asked Sri Lanka to bat. Imran was at his merciless best and celebrated his return with figures of 8 for 58, which ended up being the best analysis of his Test career. In response to the Sri Lankan first innings of 240, we piled up an imposing 500 for 7 declared with Mohsin Khan making 129 and Zaheer Abbas cashing in with 134. Majid Khan was also amongst the runs and contributed 63. Sri Lanka then collapsed for 158, handing us the match by an innings and some. Imran cleaned up with another 6 wickets in the Sri Lankan second innings and his tally of 14 for 116 remains the best match analysis by a Pakistani bowler in Test cricket.

I thought Imran would make a fine captain, and when the Air Marshal asked me to recommend my successor, his was the name I suggested.

There have been rumours over the years that I had threatened not to play if Zaheer Abbas was made captain. In fact, I never named any specific player that I would not play under. I did, however, tell the Board that I would only play under Imran Khan. There were reservations about Imran being captain from several quarters, but as far as I was concerned he was the most sensible choice.

The players' revolt had been a severe disappointment to me, but once I had decided to step down from the captaincy and put an end to it, I wanted to move on. Important tours and demanding cricket lay ahead, and I wanted to put the partisanship and politics behind me so we could all play our best cricket.

Naturally, I had sulked for a while, but I soon got over it. I held no grudge and sought no revenge. I just wanted to help my country reach the top of world cricket. Although I had bitterly disagreed with the architects of the revolt, nevertheless I was willing to play alongside them for the cause of Pakistan cricket. I disliked the fact that these players had rejected my captaincy, but this certainly didn't mean that I disliked everything about them. I wanted to, and did, join hands with them and we went on to win many Tests and One-Day Internationals for Pakistan together.

I also believe that the perpetrators of the revolt, in their own private and personal ways, eventually saw the error of their actions. I think they realized that I wasn't the villain they had made me out to be and that they had misjudged me.

I had been cheated out of the captaincy through an underhanded plot. I finally decided to step down because, as I have said, this pathetic drama wasn't serving Pakistan cricket. Even as I was being removed from the post, I knew I would one day be needed to occupy it again. After that Sri Lankan series, I left the captaincy but made myself available to be captain whenever my country might need me again.

CHAPTER 7

Anatomy of a Declaration

I have been fortunate to experience many joys in my career; with these joys there have naturally also been some disappointments. I have never been one to brood. My nature has always been to put frustrations behind me and look to the future. Yet one disappointment has been hard to get over. In our 1982-83 home series, I was denied a chance to score 300 and to try for Gary Sobers's record 365 because of an arbitrary declaration by my captain. Years have gone by, but it still rankles.

In the spring of 1982, after I had stepped down in the wake of the players' revolt, Imran Khan took over the Pakistan captaincy. Disillusioned and hurt as I had been with the revolt, I put it out of my mind and focused on the challenges ahead. A busy English season lay ahead for us, as we were scheduled to make a three-Test tour of England that summer, our first major assignment under Imran. I was still on contract with Glamorgan and would also be playing in the English county championship through the season, whenever I wasn't on Test duty for Pakistan.

The 1982 series in England proved a memorable one. Though we lost the rubber 1-2, it could very easily have been 2-1 in our favour. In any case, on that trip we managed to record the first Pakistani Test victory in England since 1954. That tour is described in Chapter 12, along with other tours of England.

Back in Pakistan, the 1982-83 home season also promised to be intense. First, Australia were due for a three-Test series under the captaincy of Kim Hughes, followed by a highly anticipated visit from India that would include six Test matches and four One-Day Internationals.

The Australian series was a return visit for our three-Test tour of Australia the previous season, in 1981-82, when they defeated us 2-1. Australia had played two other series after that, against New Zealand and West Indies, drawing both 1-1; in fact, they had not lost a series since the eventful Ashes in England in 1981.

The Australian side that visited Pakistan that season included several of their biggest stars, including Allan Border, Kim Hughes, Jeff Thomson and Rodney Marsh, with some promising youngsters like Geoff Lawson and Greg Ritchie. Anticipating the nature of Pakistani wickets, three spinners had also been included in the team—left-arm orthodox spinner Ray Bright, off-spinner Bruce Yardley and wrist-spinner Peter Sleep.

Australia had come prepared, but they were completely undone by Abdul Qadir, who hit a rich vein of form and took 22 wickets as Australia fell 0-3—that series victory being our first whitewash. There were some impressive Australian performances—Greg Ritchie made 106 not out as Australia followed on in the second Test, and Geoff Lawson bowled a couple of sharp spells—but thanks to Qadir it ended up being a largely one-sided series.

Abdul Qadir was a magnificent leg-break and googly bowler whom I regard as one of the truly great Test bowlers. I knew him well as he was also my colleague at Habib Bank, the team we represented in Pakistan's domestic first-class competitions. He was a genuine artist who kept the craft of wrist spin alive at a time when it had few exponents and appeared to be a dying art. Qadir deserved to be even more successful than he actually was, but he happened to be playing at a time when batting standards were exceptionally high and he had to contend with many outstanding batsmen on the Test circuit. Considering this, his 236 career Test wickets are a superlative achievement.

Qadir and I developed a close understanding over the years. He was the kind of guy who was always ready to share a joke, always good for a laugh. Whenever he bowled under my captaincy, the two of us would try and have some fun at the batsman's expense. I would make a great fuss and tell him loudly to bowl 'number 2' or 'number 3,' which meant absolutely nothing. Sometimes, after he had bowled a certain delivery, I would make a show of being displeased and tell him off for bowling 'number 5' when I had clearly asked him to bowl 'number 2.' Perhaps the batsmen caught on to this charade, perhaps they didn't, but Qadir and I used to enjoy it no end.

In contrast to Qadir, the Australian bowlers in that 1982-83 series struggled as our batting consistently came good in every Test. Zaheer Abbas, Mansoor Akhtar, Mohsin Khan and I each recorded centuries during that series, but the only Australian centurion remained Greg Ritchie. The Australians were thoroughly unsettled by Qadir and none of them managed to properly read either his googly or his flipper. They would shout expletives each time Qadir beat them in the air or surprised them off the pitch.

On one occasion, Qadir bowled Rodney Marsh for a duck off a googly that wobbled in the air and reared up from the bowlers' rough. 'Goddamitt, I just can't read 'em!' muttered Marsh in frustration as he trudged back, shaking his head in disbelief.

The 3-0 whitewash filled us with the confidence we needed to take on India during the second leg of the season.

In fact, in that 1982-83 home season, the nucleus of the Pakistan team that would go on to dominate the world in the 1980s was starting to take shape. The roots of Pakistan's most successful years in Test cricket can be traced back to this particular season against Australia and India.

The Indians arrived in late November with the usual fanfare accorded to Indian guests. Public anticipation had reached fever pitch and the team received a tremendous welcome. Under the captaincy of Sunil Gavaskar, it was actually quite a strong Indian side. Batting stalwarts like Vengsarkar, Vishwanath and Mohinder Amarnath, who had already toured Pakistan in 1978-79, were now returning. With them was the latest Indian batting sensation, Sandeep Patil. Kapil Dev was fast maturing into the superstar he would soon become, and he spearheaded the bowling. Despite Kapil's presence, though, the team's bowling resources were a little thin. Kapil's bowling partner was Madan Lal, not known for anything beyond innocuous medium-pace. Three orthodox left-arm spinners accompanied the team, but Ravi Shastri and Maninder Singh were still inexperienced and Dilip Doshi's form was too variable to be a genuine threat.

The series ended up being a Pakistan show. We dominated the contest right from the beginning and never let up. Zaheer, Mudassar, Mohsin, Imran, Saleem Malik and I each recorded one or more centuries.

Zaheer was hoping to resume his batting from where he had left off the last time India were in Pakistan. As the series approached, he openly talked of aiming for 1,000 runs in the series and breaking Don Bradman's 1930 record of 974 runs in a Test rubber. He started in dramatic fashion, posting scores of 215, 186 and 168 from his first three innings, but then trailed off.

Pakistan's bowling was equally dominant. Imran, in fact, was phenomenal and bowled some of the best spells of his career, taking in all 40 wickets for 13.95 apiece. His famous afternoon spell in Karachi during the second Test—when he brought down India from 102-1 to 114-7 with reverse-swinging boomerangs— is one of the most famous spells of bowling in Pakistan cricket. It was just out of this world.

As the series progressed, the question was not whether there would be a Pakistan victory but by how much. The eventual margin was three Test wins to none. India had simply been outplayed.

A home series as successful as this one becomes associated with many great memories in the public mind. It becomes part of cricket folklore and serves as a source of inspiration to the country's future players.

The interesting thing about that sensational 1982-83 series against India, though, is that most people remember it for something that was never intended to be a lasting memory.

They remember that series not for the emphatic overpowering wins, nor the brilliant performances, nor the margin of victory. They remember it for a declaration. Specifically, for a Pakistan declaration in the first innings of the fourth Test at Niaz Stadium, Hyderabad. It was a declaration that came out of the blue and left me stranded on 280 not out.

It was a declaration that went against the wishes and expectations of the Pakistani supporters and it has left a permanent bitter aftertaste. This is the unfortunate legacy of that otherwise highly entertaining and exciting Test series under Imran's captaincy.

Over the years, people have asked me about that declaration countless times; they want to know exactly what happened and why. It is the one incident in my career that I have been asked about most often.

It seems people still find it hard to believe that Imran declared the Pakistan batting closed when a Pakistani batsmen was within reach of a triple-hundred and when there was no pressing reason to declare as the fate of neither the match nor the series was hanging in the balance. How hard I have tried to forget that declaration and the events surrounding it but the public won't let me.

By the time the fourth Test of that series began in Hyderabad, Pakistan were already 2-0 up. Both victories had been convincing ones, the first by an innings and the other by ten wickets. Pakistan's batsmen had annihilated the Indian bowling and sapped it of any threatening qualities. Then too, the Indian batting had hardly any resolve left after being repeatedly routed by Imran. With eleven wickets in each of the preceding two Tests, Imran had simply been unplayable.

In the climate of such clearly established Pakistani superiority, the fourth Test began at Hyderabad's Niaz Stadium on 14 January 1983. We won the toss and decided to bat on a wicket that looked fairly flat and predictable. I was due in at no. 4 but judging by the slow pace of the wicket, I was not expecting to go in for a while. Then all of a sudden Balwinder Singh Sandhu took two quick wickets and I found myself walking out to join Mudassar Nazar with the score 60-2.

Haroon Rasheed had just been bowled by Sandhu for a duck, but I found the bowling quite tame. I could see at the other end that Mudassar was also untroubled by the bowling. We kept playing our shots and the runs started piling up. Before we knew it, we were both approaching our centuries.

Early on the second day, both of us got our hundreds. We continued our regular game and were soon within reach of our double-centuries. Even that didn't slow us down. We continued making our strokes, easily scoring at a run a minute.

The partnership began acquiring mammoth proportions. It went past 200, then 300. When the partnership got to 400, we knew we must have created a new world record for the third wicket. (We were right: Bill Edrich and Denis Compton had put on the previous best of 370 for the third wicket for England versus South Africa in 1947.)

And still we kept playing and kept connecting. Somewhere in our minds we must have known that we were edging closer to the highest partnership for any wicket in Test cricket. Neither Mudassar nor I, however, were consciously aware of this approaching record.

Eventually, late on the second day, with the Pakistan score at 511, with Mudassar's individual score at 231, and the partnership worth 451, he mistimed Doshi into the hands of Maninder Singh at extra-cover. We later learnt that we had equalled, though not surpassed, Bradman and Ponsford's record for the highest partnership in Test cricket, made in 1934.

It was frustrating to learn that we had missed out on making a new world record. Although I don't view records as the primary goal in cricket, they are certainly important and only a fool would say that they are not.

When the second day ended, I was batting on 238. Zaheer had joined me after Mudassar's departure and was not out on 4. Everyone was talking about the 48-year-old record Mudassar and I had equalled. Several smaller records had been smashed on the way. All the talk of records made me acutely aware that there were other landmarks and records within my grasp.

How I wanted to score a triple-century for Pakistan. Hanif Mohammed's immortal 337, scored in a Test at Bridgetown in 1957-58, remained Pakistan's only triple-hundred at the time. I had set my mind on being the next Pakistani to get to that batting landmark.

I was also looking beyond 300. I felt I had a fair shot at the king of all batting records, the highest individual innings in Test cricket. I dreamed of going past Sobers's 365 not out.

Off the field at the end of the second day, there was no talk of a declaration. Imran never brought it up overnight and gave me no specific instructions. By the time we were ready to start the third day, Imran still hadn't mentioned a declaration. I took this to mean that I was being given a chance to go for all possible records.

I resumed my batting on the third morning with aggressive intent. Soon, though, I realized that the wicket had developed variable bounce and conditions were not going to be as easy as they had been during the first two days. I was still connecting bat to ball fluently, but the Indians had come out with a rearranged defensive field scattered at the ropes, making it a real challenge to hit boundaries and score rapidly.

Of course, I took up the challenge. My plan was to add around 30 or 40 runs in the first hour of play, taking me up to about 275 by the drinks' break. I then hoped to secure a triple-hundred before lunch and get to the magical mark of 365 in the post-lunch session.

I realized that by batting well into the third day, we may not be leaving ourselves enough time to bowl the Indians out and push for a win, but with our team 2-0 up, the series was already good as won. The Indians had hardly any fight left in them and there was no real danger that they would make a comeback in the fifth or sixth Test. Their bowling had taken a good deal of punishing and could not be considered a threat; and their batsmen could hardly face Imran, who had been taking wickets throughout the series almost at will. So the outcome of this particular fourth Test in Hyderabad was not especially crucial. Now here I was being presented with the batting opportunity of a lifetime. I reasoned that Imran would not stand in the way of my shot at history.

How wrong I was! Imran declared our innings closed when drinks were called on the morning of the third day. It wasn't as if I had been slow to get going. After the first sixty minutes of play, I had added 42 to my overnight score and was batting on 280.

The declaration came as a complete surprise; I just couldn't believe it.

I had been very pleased at having got to 280 by the time drinks were brought on. As we were having drinks, I noticed Zaheer looking intently towards the pavilion. I turned around to look as well, and saw that Imran was waving us in. It was like a kick in the stomach. I remember just standing dumbfounded, not knowing what to do. Then I noticed that Zaheer was starting to walk back. Numb with shock and anger, I followed him in a daze.

As we headed off towards the pavilion, Sunil Gavaskar came up and started walking back with me. 'What's going on?' he asked.

'We've declared,' I said, barely able to get the words out.

Gavaskar was incredulous. He said he would never have declared had an Indian batsman been as close to 300 as I was. In fact, he thought no other captain in the world would have done what Imran did that day.

As I walked through the pavilion, the shock started to wear off and anger took over. I headed straight for the dressing room, but found it deserted. It was just as well. I was fuming, and would not have been pleasant company for anyone at that time. I later learnt that the dressing room had been emptied on purpose. No one wanted to be near me when I got back after being robbed of the opportunity of a lifetime.

Quite apart from his batting talents, Sunil Gavaskar is also an astute cricket scholar, and he was indeed correct that no other captain has done what Imran did that day.

In fact, in the annals of Test cricket, that particular decision by Imran in leaving me high and dry on 280 is unique.

Declaring the innings closed is a powerful tool for a batting captain. It allows the captain to increase the hopes of a result in the match. In effect, a declaration 'speeds up' time, as it were.

The timing of a declaration can often be a complex matter. Although the basic aim of a declaration is to allow enough time to be able to bowl the opposition out, declarations are often delayed to allow the achievement of a batting landmark that appears to be within striking distance. A captain will often delay a declaration just so that a batsman can get to his century or double-century, or so that the team can go past a natural numerical mark, like 600 or 700. Delaying a declaration in this manner is common in cricket at all levels.

Consider the following example. During Pakistan's second Test match against New Zealand at Christchurch in the 2000-01 series, when I was the Pakistan coach, we delayed declaring our innings closed to allow Saqlain Mushtaq to get to his maiden Test hundred. It would have made more cricketing sense for us to declare late on the fourth day and have a bowl at New Zealand in the day's dying moments. By that time we could have been 100 or so ahead on the first innings and would have had a crack at the New Zealand openers during the day's final tense minutes. But with Saqlain in the 90s, we decided to defer any declaration until after he had posted his century.

Saqlain didn't achieve that personal landmark until the next morning, early on the final day. By that time we had lost the opportunity to apply pressure to New Zealand's second innings, but we all felt it was worth sacrificing the match to satisfy Saqlain's burning ambition to complete a century in Test cricket.

A Test hundred isn't always a particularly momentous landmark, but it was for Saqlain, whose batting ambitions were famous in the team. Though a star off-spinner, Saqlain was by no means a frontline Test batsman and in fact was often sent in as nightwatchman. His previous highest Test score had been 79 (made during a world-record seventh wicket partnership with Wasim Akram). Ever since that fine performance, Saqlain had made no secret of his ambition to some day make a Test century. Both the captain Moin Khan and I knew this and, when the chance came, we gave him every opportunity to achieve his dream.

If a declaration can be delayed for a Test hundred, is it too much to ask for it to be delayed for a triple-hundred?

Test match records show it has never happened that a captain has declared abruptly without warning if one of his batsmen was within striking distance of a mega-score.

Except, of course, in my case.

By the end of the 2002 season, there had been ten instances in Test cricket of a batsman left not out on a score of 250 or greater because of a declaration. One of these is my own case of being abandoned by my captain on 280. In each of the remaining nine instances, it is clear that the batting captain waited to declare until after some important batting landmark had been achieved.

The one exception is New Zealander Brian Young's score of 267 versus Sri Lanka in 1996-97 which was associated with no particular milestone; but even in that situation, Young had been informed well in advance by his captain Stephen Fleming that a declaration would come at tea on the second day. I, of course, had received no such advance notification from my captain.

Gary Sobers's innings of 365, made in a Test against Pakistan in 1957-58, had also ended with a declaration, but obviously captain Denis Atkinson had waited to allow Hutton's longstanding record of 364 to be passed. Something similar had happened when Walter Hammond made 336 in a Test against New Zealand in 1932-33; English captain R.E.S. Wyatt had waited for Hammond to pass Donald Bradman's then record innings of 334 before declaring.

In a Test against Pakistan at Peshawar in 1998-99, captain Mark Taylor waited to equal the highest Test score by an Australian before declaring the Australian innings closed with his personal score at 334.

In a Test against New Zealand at Leeds in 1965, Captain Mike Smith waited for John Edrich to reach his triple-hundred before declaring the England innings. Edrich returned not out on 310.

In a Test against West Indies at Birmingham in 1957, English captain Peter May declared their innings closed with his personal score at 285 not out. There seems to have been no particular batting landmark to coincide with this declaration but May himself was captain and therefore obviously free to do as he pleased.

In a Test against New Zealand at Auckland in 1998-99, a South African declaration left Daryl Cullinan not out on 275. Captain Hansie Cronje had waited to allow Cullinan to pass Graeme Pollock's 274 and record the highest individual score in Tests for South Africa.

A similar thing had happened in Kingston in 1934-35 when a West Indian declaration left George Headley not out on 270. But by this point Headley had made the highest individual score by a West Indian in Tests at the time.

And finally, a South African declaration against New Zealand at Wellington in 1952-53 left Darryl McGlew on 255 not out. But again the declaration came after a batting milestone had been reached—in this case, South Africa amassing their highest innings total in Tests (524-8) at the time.

There remains in Test cricket, therefore, only one instance of a captain declaring without forewarning his batsman, and leaving him stranded within striking distance of a triple-century.

Imran has often been asked to explain the timing of this mean-spirited declaration. His answer has always been the same—that he doesn't believe in playing for records. Over the years, people have also asked me whether I agree with this and, if not, what I believe was the motive or motives behind Imran's decision.

I, too, am not ordinarily in favour of playing solely for the pursuit of records. But these were special circumstances, as I was nearing no ordinary record. It was the opportunity of a lifetime—and not just for me, but also for Pakistan. Had I been able to realize the full potential of my innings that day, it would have been an achievement not just for me but also for my captain and my country.

I had done so much for my captain, and had hoped he would also look out for me. I had trusted Imran to make concessions for me if and when the time came. When I came out on that third morning of the Hyderabad Test batting on 238, I had expected Imran to let me play on and get as big a score as I could. At the very least, he should have allowed me to get to 300. If nothing else, he could have given me a set timeframe in which to make the most of my opportunity. But he didn't. I remain greatly disappointed by Imran's decision to declare that January day in Hyderabad in 1983. He should not have done it.

There are no guarantees in cricket. Who knows, if Imran had allowed me to continue, I may have got out on the very next ball. I may or may not have established any new records, but since I remained not out, we will never know. This is why that 280 still rankles with Pakistani supporters. There will always be the permanent question about what could have been. Pakistani fans have not forgiven Imran for that action and I doubt if they ever will.

As for that fourth Test match itself, we won it easily. The Indians failed to put up any meaningful resistance and lost by an innings and 119 runs. It turned out in the end that there had been no shortage of time; when the last Indian wicket fell, there were still hours to spare.

God knows best the true motivations behind Imran's decision to declare prematurely. The action can be interpreted in a number of different ways. Were his motives genuine, aimed at ensuring a result in the match, or were they malicious, meant to deny me what could have been a spectacular batting triumph? There were rumours that Imran had been influenced in this decision by arguments put to him by certain individuals in his company while I was out in the middle inching towards a triple-hundred— that my batting achievements might overshadow his own bowling feats and his success as captain. I cannot say for certain if indeed these arguments influenced Imran, for I cannot read his mind. I just don't know.

All said and done, though, I think Imran's declaration actually ended up benefiting me. By denying me the king of batting records, Imran kindled in me a raw obsession to eventually get to 365. Ever since that day, whenever I reached 100, my mind went straight to the possibility of 300. This attitude has been responsible for all my long innings. It is thanks to Imran that I have the highest number of double-centuries in Test cricket after Bradman and Hammond. So, in a way, I am actually perversely grateful to Imran for that particular action of his. Without his stinging declaration, my subsequent batting record for Pakistan might not have been what it eventually became.

CHAPTER 8
Australian Rules Cricket

In Australia they play football by their own rules—footy, they call it, or Australian Rules Football. It sometimes seems that they play cricket with their own rules too. Australia of course is, and has been, one of the leading international teams, doing well both at home and on tour. At home they are really invincible: they become a different team, leaner, meaner—and with an attitude. It can be quite intimidating for visitors. Get the Australians in rhythm on their home turf, and they will simply give you hell. The fast Australian wickets force everyone to play positive cricket, and contests in Australia—though they may be one-sided—are never dull.

Pakistan has a poor record on tours to Australia. We've never won a series there—in fact, of the twenty-six Tests Pakistan played in Australia up until the 1999-2000 series, Pakistan had won only four compared to Australia's fifteen.

Not only are Australians much tougher opponents at home, Australian conditions don't particularly suit our players either. Technically, the most important thing about playing in Australia is the fast and bouncy nature of the tracks. It can be a very different experience from playing in countries like England or India. On the soft English wickets, for example, one has to worry about low bounce and vulnerability to LBW. Nothing of that sort in Australia, where the bounce is true and high and wickets are lost to speed and swing.

Facing Australia at home is not just a challenge for Pakistan. India and New Zealand have won even fewer Tests in Australia than Pakistan has, and South Africa has only won five Tests in

Australia. In modern times the only team that has managed to hold its own in Australia are the West Indies, which is perfectly understandable because Australian wickets seem to have been tailor-made for the West Indian fast-bowling battery of the 1980s.

Pakistan too has had an impressive fast bowling attack over the years but, except for the famous 1976-77 series when Imran cut loose, our quick bowlers have not performed up to expectations in Australia. A major reason is that Australian batsmen are well adjusted to their home conditions and are always very comfortable against fast and especially fast-medium bowling.

When I first toured Australia in 1976-77, I was struck by how at ease the Australian batsmen were against the kind of deliveries that would have had me all at sea. It was obvious they had complete command of their home conditions.

The domestic game in Australia is so well organized that the system ensures thorough exposure and acclimatization for all their frontline batsmen. They learn to read the line accurately and know exactly which balls to leave. I often saw them leave deliveries that I was sure were travelling at stump height, but which the Australian batsmen would leave alone—and they would inevitably sail above the bails because of the extra bounce.

Because of the experience of their home wickets, Australian batsmen also become very good at pulls and hooks, which are the shots to be played on quick and hard tracks. And when they cut they take advantage of the wicket's pace by playing uppish, well above what would be catching height for point or gully. These technical adjustments are difficult for visiting batsmen to master and they are an important part of the Australian home advantage.

Australian tours are an exciting experience. The cricket is tough and disciplined. I normally keep chatting away when I bat because I like to play mind games with the close-in fielders and bowler. It is my way of concentrating, and it is impossible for me to bat quietly. I've got to keep talking, preferably to others. In Australia, they figured this out very quickly and followed a strict code not to engage in any conversation with me while I was at the wicket. This was how they provoked me, by giving me the silent treatment, but I enjoyed it. I still kept talking, and would even sing or talk to the umpires. I relish being provoked in cricket. It makes me elevate my game and I respond by punishing with the bat.

To me international cricket is like a radio, and the various different countries and settings one can play in are like the different stations that the radio must be tuned to. My approach has been to tune my game according to the country I was going to be playing in. In Australia, more than in any other country, I felt I had to tune myself to the particular frequency of Australian cricket and adjust to the demands of playing in Australia.

When I first toured Australia, in 1976-77, it had been a completely novel experience for me and it had taken me quite by surprise. Soon after I had landed in Australia with the Pakistan team, some of the press asked me for interviews. I had come to Australia after a debut series against New Zealand in which I had scored 504 runs in five innings at an average of 126. Apparently my reputation had preceded me, and now the Australian press was keen to see how I would hold up against the likes of Lillee and Thomson.

From what I had already seen in the Australian papers, it seemed very common for players on both sides to give such interviews to the press, and I could see how the newspapers would use these interviews to generate excitement about the upcoming cricket contests. One of the reporters asked me to be photographed with a couple of models. I agreed, not making much of that either.

The next day my picture was prominently displayed in the papers, flanked by two beautiful Australian girls, under a headline that read 'MIANDAD SAYS HE IS READY TO FACE LILLEE AND THOMSON.' It was a little unsettling, to say the least, as I certainly did not remember saying what was being attributed to me. It would have been stupid for me to say something like that in any case, since I was just a kid on my first visit to Australia and had never faced anyone with the demonic skill of Dennis Lillee. And I suppose it must have been eye-catching publicity, but at the time I could not see what, if anything, those models had to do with cricket.

Soon after that headline appeared in the papers, I faced Dennis Lillee for the first time in my career. It happened in a four-day side match against Western Australia at Perth that took place shortly before the first Test. Dennis must not have appreciated what the newspapers were claiming I had said, because he gave me a very torrid welcome. The first four deliveries I received were all bouncers, each more menacing than the one before, and each helped on its way by the lightning-quick Perth wicket. Along with the bouncers came sledging—a torrent of verbal abuse comprising four-letter words and ancestral references. It was a very interesting initiation to Australia and international cricket at its most brutal and most competitive.

Sledging is an art form in Australian cricket and Dennis used it better than most, although all the Australians were really good at it. The goal, of course, was to disturb the batsman's concentration. The bowler and the close-in fielders considered it their duty, but you could expect it from any Australian on the field with whom you made eye contact. If you turned around and looked behind the wicket, often the slips and the wicketkeeper would let you have it too.

On my first tour there, I had been unfamiliar with the Australian accent and had a limited English vocabulary, so I had not been able to appreciate the finer points of sledging, but on later tours I was left in no doubt about the practice. I could never match the Australian verbal repertoire, but I did come up with a few responses of my own. One of my favourites was to point to the ball after I had played it into a gap and tell the fielder 'Go, fetch!' (I don't know about the Australians, but I really enjoyed that one.)

The important thing about sledging is that at the end of the day, no hard feelings should be carried off the field. In recent times with the implementation of the match referee system, a stern view is taken of sledging. I personally think this is too harsh. I have always enjoyed aggressive cricket, and sledging is one of the things that gives cricket an aggressive edge. It should be thought of as gamesmanship.

As I have already described (Chapter 4), I failed to adjust to Australian wickets on that first outing in 1976-77 and felt technically exposed. I did better with the bat on the next trip, in 1979-80, when I made 129 not out in the second Test at Perth. In 1981-82, I went to Australia for the third time, carrying on this occasion the added burden of captaincy (Chapter 5). On that trip I also had a more famous run-in with Dennis Lillee, not to mention the Australian media, though through little fault of mine (revisited in Chapter 19).

In the autumn of 1983, we were due to undertake another tour to Australia. Visits Down Under are always daunting for cricket teams, but this particular tour promised to be especially demanding. It was the first time we would be playing a five-Test series in Australia. The trip was also going to include the Australian season's signature one-day triangular competition. This season again, as in 1981-82, the tournament would involve the hosts, ourselves and the West Indies.

Since my last tour to Australia much had happened in Pakistan cricket. Imran had succeeded me as captain and a number of new players had been inducted. Most alarmingly, Imran had developed a stress fracture of the shin, which had made him unavailable as a bowler. Imran was by now amongst the best opening bowlers in the world and this development was a blow to our morale. The fracture ended up keeping Imran out of the first three Tests. And though he did return for the last two Tests as captain and batsman, it proved to be premature in the long run as the injury was further aggravated.

Australia had enjoyed a successful build-up to that series. The previous season they had hosted England for a five-Test series and regained the Ashes 2-1. Later they won their one-off inaugural Test against Sri Lanka. We were going to be facing a confident Australian side on a winning streak, on home turf.

Although we had completed a 3-0 series whitewash when Australia visited Pakistan early the previous season, Australia were still the clear favourites to win this five-Test home series. It was a measure of how well the Australians were suited to their home conditions that their losses in Pakistan in 1982-83 didn't really count.

With Imran ruled out as a bowler, our work was going to be cut out for us, with Australia's batting line-up including stars like Greg Chappell, Kim Hughes, Allan Border, Graham Yallop and Kepler Wessels. Lillee would open the bowling, along with Rodney Hogg, whom I had played before and who tended to make me uncomfortable.

We were defeated in that series 0-2, losing the first Test by an innings and the fifth and final one by ten wickets. With Imran unavailable and Sarfraz having retired, our bowling centred on three young medium-pacers, Tahir Naqqash, Rashid Khan and Azeem Hafeez. These were bowlers of some promise but they lacked experience and our bowling failed to make an impression.

Azeem Hafeez did manage two 5-wicket hauls but failed to deliver when most needed. Abdul Qadir also bowled well in that series, including a 5-wicket haul in the fourth Test, but could not penetrate at crucial times.

The series was not as one-sided as the result suggests, though, because our batting often managed to hold its own. We lacked the bowling to get Australia out twice, but our batting allowed us to draw three Tests. In the third Test at the Adelaide Oval, we made 624 as Mohsin Khan, Qasim Umar and I all posted centuries.

The Tests were all played in a friendly climate. When the cricket got dull, such as when a Test was petering out into a draw, we would let our hair down and indulge in horseplay. I remember when the drawn third Test was in its dying stages late on the final day, I bowled a couple of overs imitating the bowling actions of Dennis Lillee and Rodney Hogg. It was a big hit with the crowd.

The Benson and Hedges triangular series took place after the Tests. The triangular tournament is hugely popular and has become an indispensable part of the Australian season. It includes the hosts and two visiting teams, with each team playing the other two four times each, followed by a best-of-three final. That's a minimum of twelve matches in the league stage and up to three in the finals. It is a gruelling part of the Australian season and one in which Pakistan has usually failed to excel. We've won it only once, in 1996-97 (defeating West Indies in the finals), even though by 1999-2000 we had participated on seven different occasions.

In fact, most often we have ended up as the third team in the competition, sitting out the finals. Apart from the tournament win in 1996-97, we've got to the finals of the triangular on only two other occasions: once in 1989-90 when the third team was Sri Lanka, and then in 1999-2000, when the third team was India.

We've participated in two other limited-overs competitions in Australia in which we did well in the league stages, but failed eventually to finish the job.

In 1986-87, we participated in the four-nation America's Cup that also included the West Indies and England. This tournament was held as part of a sports festival marking Australia's defence of the America's Cup in yachting. The competition's official name was actually the Benson and Hedges Challenge, but because of the yachting association, everyone referred to this cricket part of the festival as the America's Cup as well.

In the America's Cup, we started out by comfortably defeating the West Indies, then defeating Australia in an absolute cliff-hanger by one wicket with one ball to spare in which Asif Mujtaba shone with 60 not out in tense conditions. Though we then lost our next league game, against England, our run rate was still good enough to get us in the final, where we met England again.

The final proved an anti-climax as England defeated us comfortably, but I won something in the match that I could keep forever. Australia is the most capitalist of the cricket-playing nations, and for several days in the build-up to the final, Australian television kept advertising a Longines gold watch that was to be the prize for the man-of-the-match in the final. It was a beautiful watch, and the TV cameras would catch it gleaming in the sun. Whenever I saw that watch on TV, I allowed myself to think about winning it.

While relaxing around Perth shortly before the final match, some of my teammates and I came upon a wishing well. Everyone wanted me to make a wish, and I wished for that Longines watch. I would not say I was obsessed over it, but I did think it would be nice to have.

England won the toss in that final match and put us in on a pacy Perth wicket. Our innings started poorly—and never recovered. We were reduced to 89-5, and then collapsed from 127-5 to 131-9. I was still at the other end when last man Saleem Jaffer walked in, and I made sure we batted our full fifty overs. The unbeaten last wicket stand put on 35, of which Saleem's share was 3. I contributed 77 not out to our total of 166. England's bowlers had split the wickets, with none really dominating. England then overtook our score easily, with ten overs to spare, but none of the English batsmen reached 50. When it came to deciding the man-of-the-match award, my innings stood out from the other performances. It was a bitter, embarrassing defeat, but I have to admit that that gold watch did ease the pain somewhat, at least for me.

Pakistan had also participated in another limited-overs tournament in Australia, the Benson and Hedges World Championship of Cricket held in 1984-85, in which I captained Pakistan. In that tournament we had done well in the league stages and also reached the final, only to falter at the last hurdle. This competition was organized to commemorate the 150th founding anniversary of the Australian State of Victoria and it featured all seven nations then playing Test cricket. We defeated Australia and England in the group games to reach the semi-final, in which Mudassar Nazar's 5 for 28 held the West Indies to a low score that we easily overtook. India had defeated New Zealand in the other semi-final, setting up an India-Pakistan decider at the Melbourne Cricket Ground (MCG). But we could not deliver and lost a one-sided game by eight wickets.

Some years later—in 1992 to be exact—there would be another MCG final of a limited-overs tournament, somewhat more important than the others, and this one we would finally win. But more about that later.

Even though we have tended not to do well in Australia, the tours have nevertheless been highly enjoyable. The quality of the cricket is very high, the facilities are excellent, and the crowds are always knowledgeable and involved. It all makes for a wonderful cricketing experience—even if one happens to be mostly on the receiving end.

At a personal level, Australians are excellent hosts and—except out on the pitch—they make visitors feel very welcome. A wonderful Australian cricket tradition (that was observed at least until the late 1980s) has been to visit the opposing team's dressing room at the end of the first day's play in a Test match. It is a warm gesture that puts everyone at ease and players from the two teams interact with each other in a relaxed and friendly atmosphere. The next day the visitors reciprocate by going to the Australian dressing room. It is one of those things that makes touring Australia extra special.

A similar famous tradition is the barbecue get-together. This is an evening of food and fun that takes place at least once during each four-day tour match. I understand this is a regular feature during the Sheffield Shield games in Australia's domestic cricket, but it also extends to first-class fixtures involving touring teams. The atmosphere is casual and everyone relaxes after a hard day's play.

I really enjoy being in Australia, especially the warmth of their friendship and the generosity of their hospitality. I made a very special friend in Australia, a wonderful man called Dr Jain. He was originally from India but had been settled in Melbourne for many years. He always threw a party whenever the Pakistan team happened to be in Melbourne, and he would insist on telling everyone that the party had been thrown by me—Javed Miandad. Through Dr Jain I also became close friends with Ian Chappell. Ian and I had known each other through cricket, of course, but Ian turned out to be a close friend of Dr Jain's as well and that made Ian and I close too.

The crowds are another big part of the Australian experience for touring cricket teams. Australians love their cricket and make it obvious, which is very enjoyable for the players out in the middle. Some sections of the crowd get ugly at times, but they also appreciate good cricket and can be generous with their praise.

I have always been one to play to the crowds, and the strengths and responsiveness of Australian crowds has been very important to me. I have felt a bond with the crowd from my earliest cricket-playing days. In Pakistan, I had learned to gauge the crowd's mood and to get them involved in my batting. The female sections of the crowd especially would shout messages and slogans to me, and I would acknowledge them every now and then by playing a shot in their direction or hitting a boundary when they demanded it. Invariably the girls would go berserk. It was an electric feeling.

I took my feel for crowds wherever I went on tour. After my home crowds in Pakistan, I found the Australian crowds the most responsive.

The best thing about Australian cricket crowds is that they are always there, they never fail to come to the games. Cricket matches in Australia attract some of the best crowd attendance anywhere, for Test matches as well as for limited-overs games. Except for the fourth and fifth days of Tests heading for a draw, thin crowds are rare. It is ultimately a credit to the Australian cricket system—including the cricket organization as well as projection and presentation of cricket in the media—that it is consistently able to maintain public interest at such a high level. The Australian capitalist economy also helps, with corporate outfits like the McDonald's restaurants and big-name departmental stores getting involved in projecting and publicizing visiting teams.

One comes across a good number of Pakistani fans in the Australian crowds, mostly in the large cities of Sydney and Melbourne. When I first toured Australia back in the mid-70s, one hardly came across any Pakistani immigrants. Over the years the number of Indian and Pakistani immigrants has increased steadily. On my later tours we invariably met a number of Pakistanis who had settled in Australia and had come to support the team that represented the country of their birth.

Another special feature about the crowds in Australia is the presence of families. A lot of young people come to watch the games, many accompanied by their parents, making cricket-watching a family experience that has been integrated into their culture. It is a very charming aspect of the cricket in Australia that one does not see in other parts of the cricketing world.

Another plus point is the weather, which stays fine for most of the cricket season. It is a far cry from the depressing wetness of an English summer or the searing heat of the subcontinental season. Of course it does get hot in Australia, but more often the cricket conditions are ideal, mostly sunny, a comfortable temperature, usually with a fair wind to assist the quicks.

In my assessment, the only really negative aspect to touring Australia is the high level of the hosts' cricketing skills and their ability to maximize their potential with their home advantage.

Cricketers have been known to complain about the long distances between Test centres in Australia, but I think that is a non-issue. The only really remote city is Perth. The flying time between the other centres—like Adelaide, Melbourne, Sydney and Brisbane—is actually quite modest, usually 60-90 minutes and never more than two hours. When you look at all the joys of touring Australia, that's really only a minor hassle.

CHAPTER 9
Sharjah

Who would have thought that a desert city in the Middle East would one day go on to host more One-Day Internationals than any other venue in the cricket world? Sharjah's emergence as a major cricketing centre has been fantastic for the game, especially for the game in Asia. It is the greatest expansion in cricket since the days of Empire.

Sharjah has a very special place in my heart. I've played some of my most enjoyable innings there. One of those innings—perhaps the best innings of my career, ending with what is perhaps the shot of my career—took on a life of its own, and created possibilities for me that I could never have imagined.

I had suffered a serious head injury in India towards the end of the 1983-84 season (described in Chapter 10). By the spring, I had sufficiently recovered to be able to spend the 1984 summer with Glamorgan. In the autumn of 1984, I headed back to Lahore to resume Test duty for Pakistan. The eventful innings at Sharjah was still two home seasons in the future.

A packed itinerary was planned for the 1984-85 season. The schedule listed six Test matches at home, followed by a three-Test tour to New Zealand, and then a limited-overs tournament in Australia that was to feature all the Test-playing teams.

The season began with what was meant to be a three-Test tour from India, but the rubber was cut short after the second Test because of the assassination of Indian Prime Minister Indira Gandhi. It was a lacklustre series in any case, and both completed Tests ended in soporific draws.

The only drama in that series came when news of the assassination broke. The second Test had ended on 29 October, and on 31 October 1984, we were in Sialkot playing India in a One-Day International. Indira Gandhi was shot in New Delhi shortly after 9 a.m. that day (8:30 a.m. Pakistan time) but we didn't learn of it until a few hours later. Meanwhile, Zaheer had won the toss for Pakistan and put India in, who had ended their 40-over innings with 210 for 3. Soon after the Indian innings ended, we were shown to our buses and quietly taken back to our hotels; *en route* we learnt of the assassination. The Indian team immediately departed and the remainder of the tour was cancelled.

Next up was a visit from New Zealand. This was New Zealand's first visit to Pakistan since the 1976-77 series in which I had made my Test debut. I enjoyed making runs against New Zealand and was anticipating a great batting opportunity.

It didn't disappoint. In the second Test at Hyderabad, I made 104 and 103 not out and became the second Pakistani (after Hanif Mohammed) to record a century in both innings of a Test match. I had deliberately sought that particular record and I felt a sense of achievement when it was finally under my belt. I was always conscious of batting records like this one, which had been accomplished by a very select group of batsmen.

I even dreamed of some day scoring two double-hundreds in the same Test—something that's been done only once in the whole of first-class cricket—but of course that never came to pass. I wanted to have a rich and full batting career, one in which I would touch all the high-notes by the time I was finally ready to quit. I wanted a career that could eventually be held up against the greatest batting names in cricket and not found wanting. It was a very conscious desire, and it remained alive throughout my playing years.

We comfortably won that home series against New Zealand 2-0, recording victories at Lahore and Hyderabad. This was immediately followed by Pakistan's tour to New Zealand for a return three-Test rubber. New Zealand were very eager for that series because they badly wanted to tackle us on their home soil. Of our previous eight series contests with New Zealand prior to the visit in January 1985, New Zealand had lost all but one (their only victory being a series win in Pakistan in 1969-70).

In Pakistan, New Zealand were captained by Jeremy Coney and Pakistan had been led by Zaheer Abbas. Now both captains were changed for the return series as Geoff Howarth took over for the hosts and I took over the Pakistan captaincy from Zaheer. Imran, of course, was still ruled out with his stress-fractured shin. I had made myself available to the PCB to be captain as and when needed, and I had no hesitation in accepting the job when asked. It was going to be my first return to the captaincy after being removed by the players' revolt in 1981-82.

I knew New Zealand would amount to very different proposition on their home turf, but I still expected us to win. The first Test ended in a tame draw. In the second Test, our batting failed to hold up and we were defeated by an innings. This set up an anxious third Test in Dunedin, with Pakistan desperate to equalize and New Zealand sensing a long-overdue series win against Pakistan.

In fact, we nearly won that third Test. It was a relatively low-scoring match, with neither team crossing 300. Eventually, New Zealand were set a target of 278 to win. Wasim Akram had made his Test debut in that series and was playing in his second Test at Dunedin. To complement his five wickets in the first innings, he took 5 for 72 in the second innings as we reduced New Zealand to 228 for 8, still 50 short of victory. We needed just one more wicket to win because Lance Cairns had retired hurt with a knock on the head and wasn't going to bat again. But we failed to get that final wicket and lost the series 0-2. It was a very frustrating and disappointing loss. We had been so close, yet so far.

From New Zealand we travelled to Australia to take part in the Benson and Hedges World Championship of Cricket, a high-profile limited-overs tournament featuring all the Test nations. Imran was back in the side for this trip, but I continued as captain. We did well, eventually losing in the final, as discussed in the preceding chapter.

After that tournament, my obligations with Pakistan ended for the season. In the spring of 1985 I was back at Sophia Gardens and enjoyed another full season with Glamorgan (described in the next chapter, along with the rest of my Glamorgan seasons).

The next home season began in Pakistan in October 1985. Things would start with a three-Test series against Sri Lanka, followed by a short trip to Sharjah to play in the Rothman's Three Nations Trophy, and then a visit to Pakistan by the West Indies to play five One-Day Internationals. Then we would pay the return visit to Sri Lanka in early 1986 to play another three Tests.

To end the 1985-86 season, we were due to return to Sharjah. In April 1986, Sharjah would host the Austral-Asia Cup, a limited-overs tournament that was going to feature ourselves, India, Sri Lanka, Australia and New Zealand, i.e., all the teams then playing Test cricket except for England and the West Indies.

A spectacular fate awaited us in that Austral-Asia competition, but of course we had no forehand knowledge of it. I was just excited at the prospect of such an extensive one-day tournament in Sharjah, the Desert City that was fast becoming a regular stop on the international cricket calendar.

At the beginning of that 1985-86 season the Austral-Asia Cup was still some months away and there was the immediate matter of dealing with the Sri Lankan visitors.

I was retained as captain for the home series against Sri Lanka. Imran was in the side, too, playing under me. This situation must have revived the ghost of the players' revolt against my leadership in 1981-82, because the captaincy became an issue yet again.

In fact, this would be the last time I captained a side that included Imran. I had the choice of continuing as captain following that series, but decided against it. I did so because Imran didn't give me his full cooperation in that series, and it was a great disappointment for me.

As captain, I would tell Imran to bowl a certain way, ask him to pitch one short or to mix in a slower one, but instead he said he was not able to control the ball or was afraid of getting hit about. I thought this was laughable because in 1985-86 he was at the peak of his craft as a fast bowler and had acquired impeccable control over the ball.

The captain sets the strategy and his bowler complies—that's the cricket ethic I know and that is followed around the world. It doesn't matter who the bowler is and what his own plans might be; the captain's strategy supersedes everything. Imran didn't observe this discipline when he played under me in that 1985-86 Sri Lanka series.

After that experience, I decided never to captain Pakistan if Imran was also playing. What would be the point if I could not rely on my leading bowler to fall in with my plans.

Whenever I have played for Pakistan, I have always tried to excel, regardless who the captain was. As I did for other Pakistan captains, so I gave my best for Imran as well. I was hurt that Imran didn't return the gesture, but ultimately I figured that that was his problem, not mine.

It was not easy to give up the captaincy again as I knew I didn't lack the ability, which made it all the harder to step down voluntarily. What made it even harder was that I was under pressure from the Pakistan Cricket Board to continue. Indeed the Board went to great lengths to try and retain me as captain, offering me various inducements, such as free passage on tour for my wife and family and other concessions. I had felt powerless when Imran would not follow my instructions, and I had no mind to relive the experience, so I declined the Board's request.

As in the 1981-82 captaincy crisis, concern for team unity remained uppermost in my mind. Imran had had a taste of the captaincy and was obviously loath to participate as merely another player now. The Board may have wanted me to remain as captain, but Imran was now an important man and if both of us wanted our way there was going to be an inevitable divisive power struggle. So as before, I gave up the captaincy after the Sri Lankan series and fell in line behind Imran.

Captaincy conflicts aside, the cricket turned out to be enjoyable. Sri Lanka had brought along a new batting star, the talented P. Aravinda de Silva, who entertained everyone with his brashness and confidence. He made 122 in the first Test at Faisalabad and 105 in the third Test at Karachi. Aravinda had a keen eye, electric reflexes, and hooked like a demon. In one of the One-Day Internationals, he took Imran on and hit him for two arresting sixes. In another game, he hooked the very first ball of the Sri Lankan innings for six. We thought Aravinda would go on to become Sri Lanka's most successful batsman, and today his name sits right on top of Sri Lanka's batting elite.

I had a good series with the bat. In the drawn first Test at Faisalabad's Iqbal Stadium, on the predictable batting track that Faisalabad had become famous for, I managed to get 203 not out. Qasim Omar partnered me and also got a double-century, as we piled on 397 for the third wicket. I got 40 and 63 in the second and third Tests, both of which we won.

While batting in the third Test at Karachi, I got a thumb injury in my left hand. Initially I thought it was nothing, and kept on playing, but even after I had been dismissed and had returned to the dressing room, the thumb still burned. When it was still sore the next day, some of my doctor friends insisted I get it checked, and an X-ray confirmed that it had been fractured.

The injury happened on 8 November. On 15 November, we were due to play the West Indies in the opening match of the Rothman's Three Nations Trophy in Sharjah (not to be confused with the Austral-Asia Cup, which Sharjah was hosting the following April). The medical advice for me was not to play but Imran, who was now captain, would have none of it and insisted I accompany the team to Sharjah. He made a huge fuss about how I was indispensable to our batting. I, too, was conscious of my batting responsibilities and relented.

We lost the opening game of that short tournament in Sharjah to the West Indies and then met India, the third team in that competition, who then happened to be the reigning world champions. The Indians were really enjoying themselves in limited-overs cricket in those days. Since winning the World

Cup in the summer of 1983, they had played seven One-Day Internationals against us and won all but one of them.

Twice before we had faced India at Sharjah, and lost both times. The last time we played against them, in March 1985, we had failed to chase 125, collapsing for just 87. We were definitely the underdogs going into that Rothman's Trophy match. My thumb was still painful, but in that final match I still managed an unbeaten 37 in our total score of 203-4 (from 45 overs), which India failed to make. It was a rare limited-overs defeat for India in those days.

Back in Pakistan, I played in all five One-Day Internationals against the West Indies. This obviously was not the way to heal my thumb, but I was reluctant to use injury as an excuse not to play. So I convinced myself it was a minor injury and kept on playing. I made an adjustment in my batting grip so that I wouldn't let my left thumb touch the handle. I also fashioned a home-made cast for my thumb, and wore it both while batting and fielding. I ended up putting a lot of bottom hand into my shots. Even so, I still kept getting the occasional knock on my broken thumb, and whenever that happened, I wanted to scream with pain.

All these physical adjustments made for very awkward batting. But I still made 22, 41, 2, 67 not out, and 28 in the five games. The series was tied 2-2, but in the final game in Karachi our batting collapsed in front of Malcolm Marshall, Michael Holding and Courtney Walsh, and Vivian Richards's team took the series. We had been pitted against some quality West Indian bowling and I still find it hard to believe that I pulled off all those runs with a fractured left thumb and what basically amounted to a one-hand grip. I should have paid more attention to my injury, but I felt the thumb would probably heal given enough time, and in any case I felt far more passionate about stabilizing the Pakistan middle-order.

When that limited-overs series against the West Indies ended, there was nothing left to distract me from my painful thumb and I could take it no longer. The day after the final game, I went to see Dr Mohammed Ali Shah, a renowned orthopaedic surgeon who runs a famous clinic in Karachi. Dr Shah injected my thumb with a local anaesthetic and drilled a nail into it. I was uncomfortable after the anaesthetic wore off, but Dr Shah assured me this was a new technique to manage the kind of fracture I had, and gave me some painkillers to help with the discomfort.

After a couple of weeks I went to see Dr Shah again. He asked his assistant for a pair of pliers, with which he abruptly pulled out the nail from my thumb. After that it stopped hurting and a follow-up X-ray showed the fracture line had disappeared. Luckily there was no cricket for the next several weeks, and it gave my thumb a chance to finally heal.

We were slowly inching towards the Austral-Asia Cup in Sharjah. In February 1986, we went to Sri Lanka for the return series, playing three Tests. The rubber was drawn 1-1, though we should have won it easily. The umpiring in that series was particularly disappointing. At one point things got so bad we nearly packed our bags and came home. In the second Test at Colombo, I was personally targeted by a section of the crowd and decided to walk into the crowd to deal with a spectator who was pelting me with stones (an incident described later in Chapter 19).

After the Test series, we stayed on in Sri Lanka for the limited-overs Asia Cup featuring ourselves, the hosts and Bangladesh, in which we lost to Sri Lanka in the final match. I top-scored in our innings with 67, but was very disappointed because the effort wasn't good enough to win. The Sri Lankan fans were overjoyed, and I believe they celebrated their team's win with a public holiday. After playing that final game against Sri Lanka, we departed for Sharjah.

Over the years, a great thing has happened in Sharjah with the development of a cricket oasis. It is like a cricketer's dream. What Sharjah has done for cricket, and especially for Asian cricket, cannot be praised enough.

Many individuals have contributed to the rise of Sharjah as a cricket centre, but credit ultimately goes to one man, Abdur Rahman Bukhatir. I first got to know him in 1976, when he was studying in Pakistan. Bukhatir's mother is a Pakistani, but his father's family has deep roots in the United Arab Emirates. Bukhatir has gone on to become a well-known figure in Sharjah and one of the region's leading entrepreneurs. He has combined his love for cricket, his management acumen, and the considerable resources of his business empire, to create a cricketing extravaganza in Sharjah.

Bukhatir was introduced to cricket in Pakistan, where he fell in love with the game and its players. He especially became a passionate admirer of Hanif Mohammed and Asif Iqbal. Bukhatir later carried his love for cricket further by forming the Cricketers Benefit Fund Series, the organizational set-up that brings international cricket to Sharjah. There was a noble motive behind this, as he wanted to provide monetary benefits to players who had served the game well and were now retired.

Sharjah sits at the tip of the Arabian Peninsula, and is one of seven emirates forming the United Arab Emirates, a union that also includes major international destinations like Dubai and Abu Dhabi.

Large Indian and Pakistani expatriate populations have come to Sharjah because of the regional oil boom. These expatriates are an important part of Sharjah's cricket story. By the late 1970s, Bukhatir had set up an elaborate club league in Sharjah in which Indians and Pakistanis participated. The Sharjah club teams even made tours of some of the Test-playing countries. A vigorous cricket culture developed.

In 1981, Bukhatir organized an exhibition limited-overs match in Sharjah between teams from India and Pakistan. It wasn't recognized as a One-Day International, but all the top players from both countries participated. I led one of the teams, which were called the Miandad XI and the Gavaskar XI. We played on a synthetic pitch in Sharjah Stadium in front of a large crowd of Indians and Pakistanis. It was an instant hit and one felt that a phenomenon had been born.

Many good things began to flow from cricket in Sharjah. World-class cricket was exported to a completely new destination, probably the most remarkable geographic expansion of the game in modern times. The Cricketers Benefit Fund Series started paying out large sums to noted ex-cricketers from all countries. And being a neutral venue, Indian and Pakistani fans were able to sit alongside each other and enjoy the game in the right spirit, without the traditional hostility surrounding India-Pakistan clashes.

The most important reason for Sharjah's success is the first-rate management team that Bukhatir assembled around him. Pakistan's cricket genius Asif Iqbal has been his leading technical advisor. After Bukhatir, I credit Asif and a Pakistani businessman named Qasim Noorani, with the success of cricket in Sharjah. Other notable names behind Sharjah cricket are the Pakistanis Ali Anwar, Raza Abbas, Falak Naz, and Saeed Choudhry, and also Sheikh Faysal of Sharjah.

Some people trivialize the cricket in Sharjah as just another profit-making business venture. There is no doubt that international cricket in Sharjah generates tremendous revenues, but before anyone begrudges Bukhatir and the others this bounty, one should reflect that in the beginning Bukhatir financed this project from his own pocket. It could not have been easy. Teams had to be given large guarantee sums when there was no guarantee that there would be any gate money or advertising revenue. In the early years there would be just a handful of matches in a whole year, but the international facilities at Sharjah Stadium had to be maintained year-round no matter what. Hats off to Bukhatir for believing in himself and in the cause of cricket. He has done a great service to the game.

Ultimately the best thing about cricket in Sharjah is how enjoyable it is. The spectators have a great time, but I think the cricketers have an even better time. The facilities are second to none, both for playing as well as for practicing. The dressing rooms are plush with everything a player could want. It is neutral territory, which takes away any home advantage factor and puts all teams on an equal footing.

Beyond the cricket, Sharjah and the surrounding regions are fine places to visit. The shopping and the accommodations are world-class; a major cosmopolitan centre like Dubai is just a short drive away; and the leisure scene offers everything, from golf and tennis to scuba diving and water sports. And it is also such a central location, in terms of international access: Sharjah is a comfortable two-to-three hour flight from the major cities of the Indian subcontinent, and it is no more than six hours flying time from London in the West and Pacific rim cities like Singapore and Hong Kong in the East. So Sharjah has many advantages that make it a highly attractive cricket destination.

However, I think the real reason behind Sharjah's spectacular success is yet another factor altogether. Sharjah's early years as a cricket centre coincided with a period of great transition in international cricket. Commercialism brought money into the game at the same time as the limited-overs version became very popular. Sharjah was in an ideal position to benefit from these developments, and it did so very effectively.

In fact, I would say that Sharjah has itself contributed to the rise in popularity of One-Day International cricket, having staged some fantastic encounters and demonstrated that this form of cricket is also great entertainment.

Sharjah has allowed the players to flourish from the rise in cricket commercialism. The monies paid out as benefits to ex-cricketers from the Cricketers Benefit Fund Series now total millions of dollars. The amounts for tournament prize money have also been raised. Sharjah was the first venue to start offering serious prize money in cricket, up to one hundred thousand US dollars or more. The largesse made it possible for even a team finishing third to go home with something substantial, like fifteen to twenty thousand dollars.

With all these attributes, it is hardly surprising that cricket tournaments in Sharjah have become very glamorous events. Celebrities flock to these games; the regular attendance of many Indian Bollywood mega stars has put Sharjah cricket matches in the centre not just of the international cricket itinerary but also a must on society calendars.

Consequently, the Austral-Asia Cup in 1985-86 became a much anticipated and well-attended event. The competition began on 10 April 1986. The organizers were honouring me as one of the beneficiaries of the tournament, along with Wazir

Mohammed from Pakistan (Hanif's elder brother), and Dilip Vengsarkar and Vijay Hazare from India.

We played our first match against Australia in which I didn't get to bat as we won comfortably by eight wickets. We then met New Zealand in the semi-final, in which again I didn't bat. It was a one-sided game, with New Zealand dismissed for 64 thanks to analyses of 10-4-9-4 from Abdul Qadir, and we won by ten wickets. India meanwhile had first defeated New Zealand and then Sri Lanka in the semi-final, so the final was to be an India-Pakistan clash set for 18 April.

I ended up playing an innings in that final match that proved to be an historic watershed in my career. Perhaps it was an answer to my prayers. My cricket has always been guided by my faith, and from my earliest days as a batsman, I would always ask Allah to help me one day accomplish something wonderful in cricket.

We humans are vain creatures; we all want to be remembered for something special we have done in our lives. My innings in that Austral-Asia Cup final in Sharjah in 1986 is for me that single most important achievement in my professional career. It is something I hope I will always be remembered for. That innings transformed the way I was seen and respected as a cricketer and a batsman, and it ultimately transformed the way I saw myself.

I have always had a great sense of destiny. Looking back at the events leading up to that final match, and the way the match eventually played out, a set of circumstances were created where I could make a difference. I feel it was all destined, like it was part of a story, something magical, which had to go a certain way, my way.

Pakistan were not regarded as a frontline limited-overs team back then. By contrast, India were world champions, having slain the giant West Indies in the World Cup of 1983. Since then they had won other major tournaments, including the Benson and Hedges World Championship in 1984-85. Pakistan had never won any limited-overs tournaments up to that point in its cricket history. We didn't know it then, but this Austral-Asia Cup in Sharjah was going to be the first of many.

I have already alluded to the head-to-head record of Pakistan versus India prior to that match—it wasn't inspiring. In fact, India and Pakistan had met in sixteen One-Day Internationals prior to that Sharjah final, of which India had won eight and Pakistan seven (one ended without a result—the Sialkot match that had been abandoned when Indira Gandhi was assassinated). Leading up to that Austral-Asia Cup, India had an overwhelming edge, having won six of the last eight contests with Pakistan.

The final was awaited with great anticipation, as 18 April 1986 was a Friday, the weekly holiday in Sharjah. When we arrived at the stadium there was already a large crowd, and it soon filled to its capacity of twenty thousand plus. It was a society occasion as much as a cricket one, with the big movie stars and celebrities from India and Pakistan in attendance. There was a nervous hum in the crowd. An India versus Pakistan final meant it was war.

My own individual gains aside, as a team we learnt a great deal from that match. We realized that you can never write-off a limited-overs game, whatever the odds and whatever the advantage one side may have built up in the match. As they say in American sport, 'it ain't over till it's over'. We learnt how to win One-Day Internationals, and how to keep our nerve in the final stages of a tournament. Since that first tournament victory in the Austral-Asia Cup, Pakistan has gone on to win not just one or two but numerous other One-Day International tournaments.

The Indian team started the day brimming with confidence. They were expecting to win easily. The Indian fans seemed even more certain of an impending victory—many had come in decorated cars, bringing fruit baskets, sweetmeats and garlands, anticipating a celebration. Right away they must have been pleased with their preparations, because India got off to a tear-away start. At one point we feared they might get to 300. But

Imran and Wasim Akram managed to keep them quiet in the final overs and they only managed 245.

We were facing a target of 246. At 4.92 per over, it was a reasonably tough task. We lost Mudassar at 9, Ramiz at 39, Mohsin Khan at 61, and Saleem Malik at 110. The regular loss of wickets slowed us down and by the time Saleem Malik departed, the asking rate had risen to 7 an over.

I had walked in with the Pakistan score at 39 for 2. At that point I thought we had a decent chance, but when another couple of wickets fell and the asking rate rose, my hopes diminished. I had no idea of what was to come; I just kept playing.

After Saleem Malik left, I had a partnership with Abdul Qadir, and it took us to 181. The tempo picked up. Then I put on another 28 runs with Imran. When Imran left, the asking rate had risen to 8 an over. I thought then that we had no serious chance of victory. I just wanted to salvage some honour for Pakistan. I had no plan, other than to bat out the full fifty overs in the hope that we would at least lose with some dignity.

As the final overs approached, we needed 51 from the last 30 deliveries. India still had the upper hand, as they had had from the beginning of the match. The crowd seemed to be holding its breath. Nothing was being taken for granted and one could feel the tension all around the ground. At the start of the 48th over, for the first time I felt that we were in with a real chance. We were 215 for 6, needing another 31 from 18 balls, and the hard-hitting Manzoor Elahi was partnering me. Chetan Sharma had two overs left to bowl and Kapil Dev had one.

The rest is drama. Here is how the final three overs were played out:

47.1   Sharma to Elahi: OUT, caught by Shastri off a skier. Wasim Akram in but the batsmen had crossed. 31 still needed.
47.2   Sharma to Miandad: Six runs over long-on (I move to 96).
47.3   Sharma to Miandad: Two runs (I refuse the third).
47.4   Sharma to Miandad: One run, pull to mid-wicket.
47.5   Sharma to Akram: One run, leg-bye.

47.6   Sharma to Miandad: No-ball; two runs, square-cut towards
        backward point (Miandad's century).
47.6   Sharma to Miandad: One run, push to mid-on; I retain
        strike. Another 18 still needed.

48.1   Kapil to Miandad: One run, sweep towards backward
        square-leg.
48.2   Kapil to Akram: Two runs, lofted shot to mid-on.
48.3   Kapil to Akram: One run, played to mid-wicket.
48.4   Kapil to Miandad: Two runs, tap-and-run; Kapil shied at
        batting end, conceding an overthrow.
48.5   Kapil to Miandad: One run; I swung at a yorker but made
        poor contact.
48.6   Kapil to Akram: No run, a swing and a miss. 11 needed
        from the last over.

49.1   Sharma to Miandad: One run, slog to long-on (Akram run
        out going for a second run, Zulqarnain in, batsmen had
        crossed).
49.2   Sharma to Miandad: Four runs to the mid-on boundary.
49.3   Sharma to Miandad: One run, pulled from off-stump
        towards backward square-leg, certain boundary saved by a
        diving Roger Binny.
49.4   Sharma to Zulqarnain: OUT, bowled for nought. Last man
        Tauseef Ahmed in.
49.5   Sharma to Tauseef: One run, tap to short cover, desperate
        scramble, shy at the non-striker's end misses. Four needed
        from the last ball.
49.6   Sharma to Miandad: Six runs, Pakistan win by 1 wicket.

I have played that final over in my mind again and again. At
the end of the 49th over the score was 235 for 7. Eleven more to
get from the last six deliveries. Sharma in to bowl, Akram at the
other end. My plan: get two boundaries right away and then a
couple of runs here or there, and we'd be home with one or two
balls to spare. I definitely didn't want to leave it to the last
delivery.

The first ball of the over I played down the ground and was hoping for two. But Akram was run out going for the second run. In fact, he sacrificed his wicket. We had crossed, so I still retained strike.

The second ball I sent to mid-on for four.

Then the third delivery, which frustrated me. There was an unprotected stretch on the long-leg boundary. I had made up my mind to hit the next ball in that region. I was certain it would be a boundary, as long as I connected.

The ball pitched slightly short of a length around the line of off-stump. I made good contact and hit a slog-sweep towards long-leg. It was a premeditated stroke. The moment I hit it, I thought the boundary was mine. But Roger Binny leapt out from backward square-leg and threw himself at the speeding ball. It was a brilliant save—and I couldn't believe it. Worse, we ended up running a single, which exposed the newcomer number ten Zulqarnain.

Zulqarnain walked up to me and asked 'Javed bhai, what should I do?'

I told him to hit out. I figured if he did that, with some luck we might get a boundary. Even if he was caught, there was a good chance we'll end up crossing and I would regain the strike.

'You've got to go for a big hit,' I told him. He did try for a big one, but missed it and was bowled for nought—241 for 9.

So, I thought to myself, it has come down to this last desperate situation. The last man is due to come in, there are two balls to go, we need another five to win, and I'm at the wrong end!

Tauseef Ahmed, our number eleven, now walked in. He came up to me and asked what he should do. I had to be at the other end for the last ball, otherwise we would have no real chance. I told Tauseef he absolutely had to get us a single. I gave him a straightforward plan of action: just touch the ball and run.

Someone must have been watching over us. The next delivery, Tauseef managed to touch the ball all right, but he ended up finding one of the most outstanding fielders in Indian cricket

history, Mohammed Azharuddin, who swooped in from cover
to pick up the ball.

Then a bizarre thing happened. Azhar's throw at the non-
striker's end missed its mark. Had Azhar hit, Tauseef would
have been out by yards, and India would have won. But there
was a desperate scramble, Tauseef was home, and I had regained
the strike. It was an uncharacteristic miss from Azhar, who
wasn't even side-on but had a straight shot, coming in from
short cover. The wishes and prayers of the entire Pakistani nation
must have come to our rescue then, because I can't explain it
any other way.

Now for the final delivery. The Indians were together,
excitedly talking strategy. The whole contest had been reduced
to getting four from the last ball. I came up with my own
strategy. I was certain Sharma was going to attempt a yorker
and aim for my legs. So I decided to stand well forward of the
batting crease. My plan was to lean back, make room for myself,
and give it everything I had.

It was going to be a slog. I was not out on 110 from 113
deliveries and was seeing the ball extremely well. I had
confidence that if the ball came on to the bat, it would reach the
boundary. I surveyed the field again. I knew exactly where
every fielder was, but still I took another look around, counting
off the fielders one by one. Nothing was going to be left to
chance. I took my time, calmed my nerves, settled into my
stance, and said a prayer.

Poor Chetan Sharma. They say he did try for a yorker, but
the ball slipped out of his hand. Or perhaps it was the fact that I
was standing well forward of the batting crease that threw him
off his length. Whatever the mysterious origins of that last
delivery, it ended up being the perfect ball for me and for
Pakistan—a full-toss at the right height, slightly towards leg, all
I had to do was take a swing and it sailed out of the ground.

After that, it was pandemonium. We had won, Pakistan had
won, Tauseef had won, I had won. What a match! It is of one of
the best memories of my life.

People say that Austral-Asia Cup final made Sharjah famous. It certainly made everyone—especially the Indians—sit up and take notice of the Pakistan cricket team and what it was capable of. People say that that match is one of the great high-points in Pakistan's cricketing history, that it has become part of our cricket folklore. This humbles me.

There is also a sad side to this story. The match was, quite literally, a heart-stopper. It was decided on the last ball, by a one-wicket margin. You can't get any closer than that. There were reports that some people had died watching that game. They were heart patients, and they could not take the excitement. It really saddened me to hear that news. I felt responsible for these people's deaths, and it sickened me. It is something that made me not want to play this kind of innings again.

I heard later that in Karachi my mother had found the tension unbearable and had stopped watching the match as the final overs approached. In Islamabad, the Federal Cabinet was in session, but the meeting was interrupted to follow the game. The whole nation it seemed had tuned in.

It was the classic situation where victory was snatched from the jaws of defeat. India had dominated the game from the very start of the match. They had batted first and their batsmen had thrashed our bowlers. Then they had taken quick early wickets and slowed us down. Starting at 9:30 a.m., India had held the advantage for all but the last five minutes of the match. We needed four runs from the last ball. Up until the final delivery, India's dominance remained supreme. Pakistan moved ahead only with the final ball of the match, and it was enough for victory.

With that victory, the tide turned in the history of Pakistan-India limited-overs cricket. As noted above, prior to that game Pakistan and India had played sixteen One-Day Internationals, Pakistan winning 7 to India's 8. From that match onwards all the way up to the 2001-02 season, the two countries have played another sixty-nine One-Day Internationals, with Pakistan taking 45 to India's 21. Even more interesting, in all the years since, Pakistan have hardly lost to India at Sharjah again.

Whenever I watch that match on video, it never fails to move me. I love the commentary that Iftikhar Ahmed did for Pakistan Television. Then too on TV, one of my peers made a comment during that match that instantly stuck in my mind. New Zealander John Wright was in the commentary box at one point and he refused to concede victory to India. 'As long as Javed is there, anything can happen,' Wright said. It is one of the best compliments I've received in all my batting years.

When I returned to the dressing room after my innings, the whole team was there. Everyone had tears in their eyes, including Imran. Two of the youngsters, Mohsin Kamal and Zulqarnain, were openly bawling. The atmosphere was enough to make anyone speechless, and I was.

When I hit that six off the last ball, there was chaos in the stadium. The Indians were crestfallen. But there was no stopping the Pakistanis, they were jubilant. Outside the stadium, many people had gathered around our bus, and as it started to head back towards our hotel, a huge motorcade of honking cars and waving and screaming fans followed us the whole way. It was just electric. I was wracked to the bone and should have been dead with fatigue, but I felt none of it.

I thought I had played a fine innings and achieved a great victory for Pakistan, but nothing more. In the coming hours and days my idea of what I had really done would undergo a radical change.

After I got back to the hotel, I felt like being alone for a while and ran myself a soothing hot bath. A little later, I heard someone knock on the outside door to the room. My wife answered it and I heard Abdur Rahman Bukhatir's voice, asking for me.

'Where is Javed?' Bukhatir asked hurriedly.

My wife told him I was having a bath.

'You don't know what a great thing he has done!' Bukhatir kept saying. He sounded intensely excited and happy.

I came out and embraced Bukhatir, who is like a brother to me. I tried to calm him down. So we had won a match, what was the big deal?

But Bukhatir's joy was on another plane altogether. He couldn't understand why I was being so matter-of-fact about the victory. His elation was infectious, and it made me dizzy with joy too. That was the first time I realized that I may have pulled off more than just a limited-overs win.

It has been years, but people still have not forgotten that match. That six off the last ball has come to define me; it has become part of my personality. Wherever I go, not only in Pakistan, and in Sharjah, but even in India that innings is mentioned. Rivalry with Pakistan aside, at the end of the day Indians are among the best cricket connoisseurs and know how to appreciate a performance.

In the wake of that victory, events took on a life of their own and things started happening that no one could have predicted.

Later in the evening after the match, all the teams attended the tournament banquet. Everyone was talking about my innings and what happened on the last ball. Even a number of Indians came up and congratulated me.

I received a lot of gifts. They covered a wide spectrum, ranging from small items of personal use all the way up to a luxury Mercedes automobile. I was overwhelmed by dinner invitations, and did my best to honour as many of them as I could.

There has been a lot of speculation about the material gains I made as a result of that performance in Sharjah. Many people said I had become a millionaire overnight. I did of course enjoy a great windfall, but certainly not to the extent made out by the press. Someone wrote that my sixer had proved the most valuable shot in cricket. I don't know about that but it didn't fetch a million by any means.

I think because of all the visible gift-giving, people started to feel that I was very materialistic, but it is not true. Had I been after money, I would have exploited the situation for all its commercial potential, but that's not in my nature. I was grateful and accepted whatever people felt moved to give me, and thanked Allah for His blessing.

Back in Pakistan, there was an outpouring of affection from everyone. I received a call of congratulations from President Ziaul Haq, and there were a number of high-profile dinners given in my honour. It was all quite overwhelming.

I never lost sight that all the good fortune coming my way was ultimately Allah's benevolence. Soon after returning to Pakistan, it was Ramadan, the holiest month in the Islamic calendar. A month of fasting and prayer, Ramadan is a very special time of the year for Muslims. It is the month in which the Holy Quran was revealed to Prophet Muhammad (PBUH). I resolved to offer my thanks in Ramadan by travelling to Makkah in Saudi Arabia and performing Umrah, an observance of prayer and supplication at Islam's greatest place of worship, the Holy Kaa'ba.

My elder brother Bashir already had plans to travel for Umrah, and I wanted to join him. But I ran into visa problems. Numerous travel agencies were approached, but none of them was able to get me visa clearance from the Saudi Arabian embassy. I even sought the help of two Pakistani government ministers whom I had come to know in the heady days following the Sharjah match, but they too, were unsuccessful.

I had set my mind on going for Umrah, and the visa troubles came as a big disappointment. Then a strange thing happened. At one of the celebratory parties, I met a man called Muzaffar Usmani, who heads a non-governmental organization devoted to children's welfare. This gentleman came up to me and told me he had had a dream in which I was performing Umrah. I told him I was, in fact, desperate to do so, but had been unable to get past the visa formalities. With deep conviction in his voice, he told me not to worry and said he would arrange for the visa.

I was sceptical. I found it hard to believe a stranger could succeed where I had tried desperately and failed. I had exhausted my own options and, with little to lose, I handed over my passport. Early the next morning, I received a telephone call to say that the visa had come through. I was simply overjoyed. By lunchtime, I had the stamped passport in my hand and by late afternoon, I was on a plane to Saudi Arabia.

I had asked to be allowed to give thanks at the Kaa'ba, the House of Allah, and Allah had heard me. The whole affair left me with intense feelings of gratitude and humility.

I landed in Saudi Arabia to find everyone there in the grip of Sharjah fever as well. I had come to pray and worship, but the cricket buzz swirled all around me. My brother Hanif Miandad was living in Jeddah at that time and through him I met scores of cricket fans—Pakistanis, Indians, Arabs and others—who couldn't get that six out of their minds.

I performed my Umrah, and it brought a great sense of relief and contentment. It was the first Umrah of my life, but since then I have performed one every year.

Finally, I also want to bring up something without which my Sharjah story would not be complete. Not everyone in Pakistan was happy with my Sharjah performance. Javed Burki, Pakistan's former Test captain and a cousin of Imran Khan and Majid Khan, appeared on Pakistan Television and commented that I hadn't paced my innings properly and that it had been a technically flawed performance.

Burki's comments were widely noticed because he appeared as the lone dissenting voice. It seemed that out of 130 million Pakistanis, he was the only one to find something in my innings to criticize.

Over the years, many people have asked me how I felt about those comments from Javed Burki. What can I say? I respect Burki's right to his opinion, and I accept it. Burki spoke his mind, and assessed things as he saw them. He's played cricket at the highest levels of the game, which qualifies him as an expert. He has also led Pakistan, and while his record suggests that he was probably Pakistan's worst captain, that doesn't change the fact that he holds the Pakistan colours just as I do, which to me counts for something.

I did what I had to do. I was doing my duty for my country. I was also fulfilling a contractual obligation because, after all, I was an employed professional being paid to do the job. I suppose

Burki said whatever he felt he had to, but ultimately, Pakistan's flag fluttered proudly that day, and to me that's what really matters.

After that innings in Sharjah, I became acutely aware of the public's future expectations of my batting. It is something that stayed with me for the remainder of my playing career. But it has never been a burden. Far from putting me under pressure, the public's expectations have given me a great deal of confidence. The fans trusted me; as long as I was batting, I knew they held out hope for a win. I could feel their trust, and it both humbled and inspired me. Gaining the fans' trust is not easy. It comes from being consistent and dependable, and from beating the odds and giving the fans the gift of victory that at some point may have appeared very unlikely. You can't afford to disappoint the fans otherwise the trust is gone. Later in life, when I became the Pakistan coach, I would tell my players to bat so that others may have confidence in you. If you can inspire confidence in others, imagine how much you can inspire yourself.

CHAPTER 10

Prince of Wales

T he Austral-Asia Cup in Sharjah had been my last commitment for Pakistan in the 1985-86 season. As the 1986 summer approached, I began thinking about returning to play for Glamorgan, as I was on contract with the club through 1987.

Reporting back to Glamorgan was no longer straightforward for me. I had just played the innings of my life at Sharjah, and there was a lot going on with me in the wake of that performance. After hitting that six, it was harder to get back to the grind of county cricket.

As the time for my return approached, I struggled with a complex mix of emotions and sentiments. I had a long and successful association with Glamorgan, but lately things had not been the same. The management had changed, and in both 1984 and 1985, I had been made to sit out many of the matches. Although my contract was coming up for renewal in 1987, the club wouldn't tell me one way or the other about my future after that.

The nature of English domestic cricket had also changed for the worse. In the first-class fixtures of the county championship, new restrictions had been introduced that limited each innings to a maximum 100 overs. This effectively made these matches limited-overs games, with the result being decided by an inevitable run chase, often set up by a contrivance of declarations. These new rules were breeding attitudes more suitable for the John Player League rather than the county championship. I simply rejected it as a form of first-class cricket.

I had come to Glamorgan with great hopes in 1980. It had never been one of the leading cricket counties, but Ossie Wheatley, the club chairman, and Bill Edwards, one of the grand elders of Glamorgan cricket, had charmed me. Even though things were never the same after the management changed, I never regretted my decision to go to Glamorgan. I had enjoyed a tremendous run with the club, breaking several records, and playing many pleasurable innings.

Through my cricket, I had formed a special relationship with the people of Glamorgan. I had connected with the crowds who came to see me bat. They had nicknamed me 'Prince of Wales' and for them I played with all my heart.

If the cricket had lost some of its fun for me after the first few seasons, life off the field still sustained me. The love and respect I received from the people of Glamorgan will remain a deeply cherished memory all my life—it is a unique bond.

The Glamorgan area is not in England but in Wales, to the west of England. Life there has its own special character. The cricket headquarters are at Sophia Gardens in Cardiff, but a lot of the cricket is also played in Swansea, in a lovely ground that has a view of the seaside. Whenever I hear anything about Glamorgan or Wales, it immediately gets my attention. I feel like my own country is being mentioned.

I spent five summers in Wales and had a house in Swansea. My family would join me for the season and we have some great memories. I made many friends.

I was recognized everywhere I went. Once I was speeding and a traffic policeman stopped me to give me a ticket. When he saw who it was, he just said a few nice things about my batting and let me go with a warning. Those little things from my Welsh summers have stayed with me; it is a very special feeling.

It was customary for Pakistan's well-known cricketers to spend summers in English county cricket. In Pakistan it is impossible to play cricket in the unbearable summer heat, and— at least back in the 1960s and 70s—the English domestic season offered a cricket education unequalled anywhere in the world.

I had played my first season of English county cricket in 1976, when I signed with Sussex. This was even before I started playing Tests for Pakistan. As I have described in the early part of the book, I had caught the eye of the Sussex and England captain Tony Greig and my Pakistan teammate Sadiq Mohammed had helped negotiate a contract for me.

The Sussex side also included two other overseas players, Imran Khan and Kepler Wessels. Limitations regarding overseas players meant that none of us could consider ourselves automatic selections. It forced me to look elsewhere.

Ossie Wheatley and Bill Edwards from Glamorgan aggressively pursued me when I was considering offers after being released from Sussex in 1979. Glamorgan hadn't been doing well in the county championship and signing with them certainly wasn't a natural choice for me. I finally joined because Ossie and Bill went out of their way for me, and I developed a special relationship with them.

I like starting things with a bang. In my first match for Glamorgan, against Essex at Swansea on 30 April 1980, I made 140 not out in quick time and followed it up with 67 in the second innings. I felt at home right away. In that debut season for Glamorgan, I played in thirty-eight matches and averaged 48.26.

The following year—1981—proved to be a bumper season. I made 2,829 runs from 43 matches at 61.50, including nine 100s. The number of centuries broke a Glamorgan record that had stood for thirty years.

Some of the innings I played in 1981, I would rank among the best efforts of my career. In June, I made 137 not out and 106 in the same match against Somerset at Swansea, against an attack that included Ian Botham and Joel Garner at their peak. The following month I made 200 not out in the return game against Somerset at Taunton.

Late in August, we played a match against Essex at Colchester. Eventually, we were set 325 to win in 323 minutes, on a crumbling wicket that had started to turn square. Essex had two experienced spinners in Ray East and David Acfield, and

Acfield had already taken 6 for 64 in our first innings. I am sure they thought we had no chance. The target was a tall order to begin with, and when we were reduced to 44 for 4, everyone seemed to feel the match had been all but decided.

I was captain of Pakistan by then and considered myself a reasonably experienced batsman. Having learned to bat in a land of spinners, I thought I knew a thing or two about playing spin. In the first innings of that Colchester match, I had already top-scored with 81, and was feeling in good touch. I thought we were facing an achievable target.

A sports journalist later wrote that the wicket had deteriorated so much that the balls were coming off its surface like fat flying off from a frying pan. It was an accurate description, but in fact the pitch was playing even worse than that. Not only was it taking spin, it was also quick. Once the ball pitched, it could end up doing virtually anything—it might keep low, it might skid, and it could turn square in either direction. The ball ended up jumping around and spinning like a top. But when you're in rhythm, you're in rhythm. I was using my feet and finding the gaps, and the runs kept flowing. I started to correctly anticipate speed and turn off the surface, and it allowed me to take liberties with the bowling.

I love to talk when I'm batting—it helps to settle my nerves. I started ragging the bowlers and I could tell that it was wearing them down. After a while I could sense they had started to panic.

It was very important to exploit the field arrangement. As my innings developed, I soon discovered a predictable pattern in the field placements that I could take advantage of. The field started coming in for the last two balls of the over to keep me from taking a single and retaining the strike; with the field all close in, I was free to lift for boundaries over their heads, which I kept doing over after over.

At 227, with just under a hundred runs to go, our seventh wicket fell, and I decided then to keep the strike as much as I could. For the next eight overs straight, I managed to play every single ball bowled. When the new man Robin Hobbs finally got to face his first ball, he got out, caught off Acfield. By then we had reached 270.

The ninth wicket fell at 291, still 34 short. Time was also running out, but I still thought we could do it. With the last man Daniels, I put on another 20 and got to my double-century. We were so close to our target, I could smell victory. Then Daniels fell to a ridiculous LBW decision. I was stranded on 200 not out in a total of 311. We lost the match by 13 runs, but I can tell you that we didn't deserve to lose.

That Colchester innings was never well known in Pakistan, but it attracted a great deal of attention in England. A number of cricketers, including my Essex opponent and English batting hero Graham Gooch, later said it was the best example of batting they had ever seen. It was the most generous compliment one cricketer can give another, and I was deeply honoured by it.

The other compliment I received that season was an inclusion in Wisden's list of Five Cricketers of the Year. To be honest, though, that didn't mean as much to me as the words of praise from fellow cricketers and from the Glamorgan fans.

I was offered an extended contract by Glamorgan, which I accepted. My initial contract, signed in 1980, had been for three years. After the 1981 season, the club management offered me a five-year contract to run through 1987.

I was back at Glamorgan in 1982 and 1983, but could not participate fully in either season. In 1982, I had to split the season between county cricket and Test cricket, as Pakistan toured England for three Tests in July and August. In 1983, I missed the June games on account of the Third Prudential World Cup.

When I returned in 1984, it was clear to me that things at Glamorgan had changed. In fact, the changes had come in 1982, when there had been a shake-up in the Glamorgan management. I hadn't spent enough time with the county in the preceding two seasons to really feel the difference.

It was no secret that the club was in poor financial health. The cricket fortunes weren't helping matters either; despite my best efforts in 1981, Glamorgan had still finished thirteenth in the championship table.

It was enough to precipitate a change in the club's organization, and late in the 1982 season Gwyn Craven replaced Ossie Wheatley as chairman, and a new man called Philip Carling took over as the club secretary.

I never warmed to some of the new management. They knew next to nothing about cricket but posed as experts, and I couldn't stomach the deception. I have never shied away from speaking my mind, and I had no reservations in telling the new officials what I thought of them and their limited grasp of cricket affairs.

I was especially irritated by Carling, whom I thought unnecessarily officious. He had come to Glamorgan after heading the management at Nottinghamshire, and I suppose he fancied himself something of an administrator. In my opinion, he wasn't fit to manage a high school team.

I had a very uncomplicated interpretation of my job at Glamorgan. The club management was paying me to do a job, and I went out and did it. As far as I was concerned, there was nothing more to it than that. I had little patience for niceties, and I was certainly no yes-man.

What really irked me was that an administrator like Phil Carling thought he could tell an internationally experienced batsman like myself how to go about my job in county cricket. The new Glamorgan management believed they could win matches with their bowlers, but they were wrong. New regulations had effectively reduced county games in England to highly contrived limited-overs matches, but I suppose this subtle point was lost on the officials. They didn't understand that under the new regulations where innings were limited by overs, batsmen would serve them better. Even a casual cricket fan knows, Test cricket is won by bowlers, but limited-overs cricket—in any form—is won by batsmen.

There was also the question of overseas players. There was a feeling in English cricket that the overseas players in county teams had somehow brought about the decline in England's cricket fortunes through the late 70s and early 80s.

It was a myopic assessment, when in truth overseas cricketers had been good for English cricket. I was surprised that the administrators and cricket policy-makers couldn't see this.

When I joined Glamorgan in 1980, the regulations allowed for two overseas players in a county side. The limited number of spots made it very competitive for foreigners to play county cricket, and the jobs invariably went to the most accomplished players. This was a boon for English cricket. Alongside the two top-quality overseas players, the county would maintain anywhere from 25 to 35 local English players, the great majority being non-Test players. This was an extremely valuable opportunity for the less accomplished English cricketers to gain experience from practicing and playing with their world-class overseas teammates.

Look at the list of overseas players in county cricket from any season around the late 70s or early 80s. It reads like a Who's Who of international cricket. In 1981, this list included New Zealand's Glen Turner, John Wright and Richard Hadlee; South Africa's Ken McEwan, Garth le Roux and Clive Rice; Pakistan's Imran Khan, Asif Iqbal, Sarfraz Nawaz, Zaheer Abbas and Sadiq Mohammed; West Indians Gordon Greenidge, Malcolm Marshall, Clive Lloyd, Michael Holding, Alvin Kallicharran, Viv Richards and Joel Garner; Australia's Jeff Thomson; and India's Kapil Dev and Dilip Doshi.

This was an absolute godsend for English county cricket—a squad of cricketing legends right in your own backyard to show you all aspects of the game.

But in 1983, England and Wales's Test and County Cricket Board (TCCB) somehow managed to conclude that the number of permitted overseas players in county cricket should be reduced to one per team. Their intention was supposedly to improve the quality of English cricket, but it still doesn't make sense to me.

There was a time when as many as four overseas players could appear in a county team, and those were the years when English cricket truly flourished. Now as the overseas presence in county cricket was declining, so too was English cricket. It was argued that the overseas players ended up learning a great deal from county cricket, but the English players were in fact learning far more from exposure to the overseas players. I still can't understand how the TCCB failed to see this.

So with the new management at Sophia Gardens, the 100 overs-per-innings restriction in county cricket, and the negative sentiments towards overseas players, my honeymoon with Glamorgan had come to an end.

I remained on contract and still reported back in 1984 and 1985, but it had all become a bit of a chore.

There was also speculation that I had some differences with the Glamorgan captain during those years, Rodney Ontong. This, however, is untrue. I never had any issues with any of the captains I played under at Glamorgan.

Pakistan had no commitments in the summer of 1984 and I went to Swansea that year expecting another full summer with Glamorgan. But as the season got underway, I found myself repeatedly overlooked for selection and sat out match after match.

It was quite disheartening. I thought perhaps my recent head injury, sustained in Calcutta in early 1984 (described in Chapter 11), had put some doubts in the management's minds whether I was able to play. I felt fit, however, and made this clear to the committee, but I still ended up sitting out the matches, which I was unhappy about.

From what I could tell, many of the Glamorgan fans too were unhappy about my repeated exclusions from the playing eleven. The supporters came through for me and there was noticeable dissent when I was made to sit out matches in 1984 and 1985. At one point, the blundering club management was convinced the overseas spot should go to a fast bowler, but I ended up attracting great support in the club's cricket committee and retained the position.

I had played for Glamorgan with sincerity and hard work, and tried to display my craft of batting as best I could. Eventually, I approached the club chairman Gwyn Craven for an explanation of why I was being left so often from the playing

XI. He was not able to come up with a sensible answer, so I brought up the possibility of my leaving the club. I had certainly enjoyed my seasons with Glamorgan, but it was no longer the club that I had been drawn to. It forced me to rethink my status with them.

When I did eventually get selected for the Glamorgan team in the 1984 season, I played to prove a point. In my fourth game of the season, against Leicestershire at Swansea, I made 212 not out and enjoyed a great reception from the fans. Later in the season I made 171 against Hampshire at Cardiff.

I came back in 1985 hoping for a better welcome from the club, but was again overlooked for a number of games. When I did get to play, I scored freely, which made it difficult for me to understand why I was being repeatedly left out. That season, I made sixteen 50s and four 100s from 45 innings, including a top score of 200 not out against the visiting Australians at Neath.

Events during both the 1984 and 1985 summers had raised questions in my mind about my future with the Glamorgan side. So in 1985, I again approached the management to ask about my role in Glamorgan County Cricket Club. I didn't get a straight answer. I was just told that I was on contract through 1987, and the management expected me to fulfil it. I got evasive answers as to what would happen when my contract came up for renewal.

To me, the conclusion was clear—the club had no interest in re-hiring me after my contract expired the following year, which really meant that I had no future with Glamorgan.

To be honest, it was something I already suspected. I had enjoyed a tremendous run at Glamorgan ever since joining in 1980, but it had started to go sour in 1984. Things came to a head in 1985, when I confronted the management about my future with the club, which had nothing to do with my batting skills, but rather with the management's misconceptions about what it took to win county games.

With all these changes in Glamorgan and the county cricket system, I really felt I had very little to go back for in 1986. Early that season, I telephoned Phil Carling from Pakistan and asked him to release me. I realized the request meant I was compromising my contract, but my concession to Glamorgan was to forego the money the club would have paid me. I told Carling I would instead just ask for a small settlement.

Quite apart from the change in management and attitude at Sophia Gardens, I now had new obligations to attend to in my life. The Pakistan team had found a new confidence after Sharjah and seemed ready to escape the affliction of underachievement. As one of the two senior players in the side, I wanted to devote myself completely to Pakistani cricket.

I never played for Glamorgan again after the Sharjah innings in the Austral-Asia Cup. I resigned from the club in 1986 after reaching a settlement. I then collected my thoughts, and began dreaming of a wonderful future for Pakistan cricket.

CHAPTER 11

Wars with India

They say the Ashes contests between England and Australia is *the* great cricket rivalry. That's all very well, but what do you say about a cricket rivalry that's based on a history of real war between two nations and where the blood spilt is still fresh?

It is all about history.

Before 1947, Pakistan and India used to be one country under British rule. As independence approached, the Muslims of British India were concerned about being a minority in the Hindu-dominated country. A separatist movement began that led to the creation of Pakistan.

Colonial India had already been admitted to full ICC membership in 1926. Up till independence in 1947, they had played ten Tests, all against England. After independence, India retained its full ICC membership and the newly created nation of Pakistan applied for Test status.

We received Test status in 1952. Our first-ever series was a five-Test tour to India, in 1952-53. This was a good five years before I was born. They say it was an intensely contested series—India taking it 2-1.

One can see why Pakistan-India matches generate so much tense excitement. The two countries have been uneasy neighbours from the very beginning. When British India was partitioned into Pakistan and India, there was widespread communal rioting and bloodshed. Since then the two countries have continued to dispute territory, and have fought three bitter wars. It is a sad history of genuine enmity that has kept alive a climate of mistrust.

It is regrettable that politics has spilled over into sports. This puts the Pakistan-India cricket rivalry on a completely different plane from the Ashes. Each time there has been war or the threat of war, cricketing ties have been suspended. In the public mind on both sides of the border, national self-esteem is at stake each time the two countries meet on a cricket field.

One of the great things about Pakistan-India cricket has been that despite the political uneasiness, relations between the players both on and off the field have always been excellent. More than anybody else, it is the players who have come to loath the mixing of politics and sports.

Pakistan and India have still managed to play a good deal over the years, and it's produced some outstanding cricket. India is by far the larger country, but Pakistan has a clear edge over India in head-to-head statistics. Until the 2001-02 season, the two countries had met in forty-seven Tests, of which Pakistan had won 9 to India's 5. Four of Pakistan's Test victories over India have come in India, but India has yet to win a Test in Pakistan. There have also been eighty-five One-Day Internationals, with Pakistan taking 52 to India's 29 (four no-results).

I have been involved in twenty-eight Tests with India. These include fifteen Tests played in Pakistan and thirteen Tests in India, the latter played over the course of three tours. I have already discussed my home encounters with India in 1978-79 (Chapter 4) and 1982-83 (Chapter 7). This chapter is devoted to touring India.

My first tour to India was in 1979-80 under Asif Iqbal when we played six Tests, and lost 0-2. I next toured India in 1983-84 under Zaheer Abbas for a three-Test series, which was drawn 0-0. My third and final tour to India as a player was the five-Test series in 1986-87. (I was also with the Pakistan side that toured India in 1998-99; by that time I was the national coach.)

It was in November 1979 that I made my first trip to India. The itinerary called for six Tests. We all knew it was going to be a tough tour because India have always been formidable opponents at home. I am sure they were also eager to take revenge for the 0-2 loss suffered in Pakistan the previous season.

My career then was just 21-Tests-old, but I fancied my chances against India. I was batting at a solid average of 70.42 and had already made six 100s. I had even acquired some touring experience, having played in Australia, England, New Zealand and the West Indies. I felt things were going well and I wanted to keep up the momentum and take the fight to India on their home soil.

Events leading up to that series were not auspicious for us. Political scheming about the captaincy marred the preparations. I thought Mushtaq Mohammed should have captained us on that tour. I know he had wanted to. He had certainly been a very successful captain, leading us to Test match victories in Australia, New Zealand and the West Indies. But a group of players had been working against him, and he was marginalized.

Our major cricket commitment prior to that Indian tour had been the 1979 Prudential World Cup in England. The plot to remove Mushtaq had its origins in the build-up to that tournament. By that time Mushtaq had already been one of our most successful captains, and he remained a dependable no. 5 or 6 batsman and a skilful leg break and googly bowler. But a feeling was created that his fitness could not match up to the agility required in One-Day International cricket. Mushtaq himself also became convinced of this, and gave up the captaincy of our World Cup team to Asif Iqbal.

Mushtaq made it clear, however, that he would like to return to lead the Test side following the 1979 summer. When it came time to choose the captain for the 1979-80 tour to India, the argument was put forward that if a man was not fit for one-day cricket, he could hardly be considered fit for five-day cricket. This was enough to unseat Mushtaq. It was unfair to him, and because he was the most deserving captain, it was also unfair to the team.

Mushtaq still wouldn't give up, and offered to go along simply as a regular player, but he wasn't included. I know he had badly wanted to represent Pakistan in India, and received the news of his non-selection with tears in his eyes.

The plot against Mushtaq was played out by a handful of players who each fancied himself as the next captain of Pakistan. In the event, the honour went to Asif Iqbal. (When the team returned from India, it was I who would take over the captaincy from Asif, but leading up to that Indian tour my candidacy was nowhere in sight.)

Another important player who should have made that trip to India was Sarfraz Nawaz. He was a difficult man to get along with, but he was an experienced bowler who had learned to make the most of unhelpful conditions. He could have made a huge difference on that tour.

The tour itself proved disastrous. Our batting failed miserably and we lost 0-2. Wasim Hasan Raja and I were the only batsmen to manage any kind of success. I made scores of 76, 30 not out, 34, 0 (run out), 16, 64, 8, 45, 52, 50 and 46, and at 42.50 had the second-best batting average for Pakistan. Raja topped the averages from our side at 56.25, including two scores in the nineties. None of us managed to reach three figures. The celebrated Pakistan batsmen of that time—Zaheer, Majid, and Asif—were all big failures.

This tour was particularly bad in terms of umpiring. I received some very unfair LBW decisions. The justification offered for my frequent LBWs was that I shuffle in front of the wicket. I find this laughable because I have always shuffled, but it was only on that particular tour that I was judged LBW so frequently. When I shuffle, I know exactly where my pads are in relation to the wicket. In my career overall, 20 per cent of my Test dismissals have been LBWs; but on that tour the proportion jumped to 60 per cent. It is impossible to bat with any confidence when any ball on the pads can get you out. Towards the end of that series, I had to train myself not to let the ball touch my legs. I stopped wearing pads during nets!

My first visit to India had left a bad taste in the mouth. Everyone came back from that tour very demoralized. Even now when I think back to that tour, a sense of gloom colours my recollections. Everything about that tour was a strain, on the field, and off the field as well.

The result of that series triggered major changes in Pakistan cricket, including the replacement of the PCB chief and my appointment to the captaincy, as discussed in Chapter 5.

The next time we toured India was in the early part of the 1983-84 season. The tour proved an anti-climax after the eventful 1979-80 tour and the exciting home series in Pakistan in 1982-83. In 1983-84, we played three Tests and two One-Day Internationals. It was a dull series with all three Tests drawn.

Sunil Gavaskar had been the Indian captain when we had toured in 1979-80, but Kapil Dev had now replaced him. Although Gavaskar was still in the team, India were nevertheless missing some key players, notably Gundappa Vishwanath, Ravi Shastri and Dilip Vengsarkar.

Pakistan were missing Imran, who was unavailable because of his stress-fractured shin, and the team was led by Zaheer Abbas. It remained a relatively low-profile series.

I remember getting out for 99 in the first Test, at Bangalore— the only such instance in my career. It was a simple case of wanting to play my shots at all times. Even though I was batting on 99, I still felt like smashing a square-drive off a good-length ball from Madan Lal. Unfortunately it found the hands of Kris Srikkanth who took a good low catch.

During that innings of 99 I had some memorable exchanges with Dilip Doshi, India's tireless left-arm spinner. I was playing quite freely and Dilip had been forced to set a defensive limited-overs style field. Almost everyone was at the boundary ropes. Every now and then, I would deliberately play a lofted stroke towards silly point or short cover, and each time I did that I would tell Dilip he could have had me caught had he kept a fielder there. Dilip knew I was toying with him, and I could see it was getting to him.

A little later in the innings, I asked Dilip what the number of his hotel room was. Both teams were staying at the same hotel, very near the stadium. Dilip tried to ignore me but I could see the question perplexed him. Each time he would come in to bowl, I would ask him the same thing. Finally he got exasperated and complained to Sunil Gavaskar, who was fielding not far off. With great irritation, he asked Sunil 'Why does Javed keep asking me for my hotel room number?'

Sunil just shrugged his shoulders and looked at me. I decided to put Dilip out of his misery. 'You've put all your fielders so far away, why don't you place one of them in your hotel room.' Dilip wasn't amused, and Sunil just looked at me and gave a knowing smile.

I enjoyed doing this to Dilip because I knew it would get him worked up, but it was just light-hearted stuff as Dilip and I were good friends and there were never any hard feelings in our exchanges.

Immediately after that first Test ended on 19 September, I got a serious bout of the flu and all my energies were sapped. The next Test was due to start in Jullunder five days later on 24 September, but I was laid up in bed and doubted I would be able to play. Our captain Zaheer, however, insisted that I play. It was an extraordinary demand considering I barely had the energy to get out of bed, but Zaheer persisted and I relented.

I don't know how I got through that match. I did manage 66 in my only innings, but it was a superhuman effort. The rest of the time I spent lying in the dressing room, drugged on pills, feeling chilly and running a temperature up to 102-103 degrees. At one point during the game, I asked one of the local doctors to give me an injection of multivitamins; he must have missed his mark, because the needle hit bone and produced such excruciating pain, which hardly helped matters.

I really missed not being in good shape during that match. Jullunder is an historic city in the Indian part of Punjab, not too far from the border with Pakistan. New to international cricket, Jullunder's Burlton Park had attracted good crowds for the second Test. Visa restrictions had been relaxed, and many people had crossed the border from Pakistan to watch the cricket in Jullunder. I hated not being able to enjoy the entire atmosphere.

We then moved on to Nagpur for the third Test. This game too left me with a negative feeling, though for quite a different reason. In my only innings in that game, I had played myself in nicely and felt well set for a large score when I was out at 60 to a shocking LBW decision.

India had been held to only 245 in their first innings. We were at one point down to 83-3 in our reply, but Zaheer and I had come together for the fourth wicket and were on course to post a large first innings lead. With my personal score at 60, I went to cut a delivery from the Indian left-arm spinner Adwai Bhat. The ball had pitched outside the off-stump and it hit me on the pad well outside the line as I played my cut. The umpire adjudged me LBW, which was just atrocious. I find it hard to imagine this was just human error on the umpire's part. It certainly marred my enjoyment of that Test match, and coloured my whole series experience.

Quite apart from the umpiring errors and the uninspiring cricket, our team's reception by the Indian public during that tour remains a great memory. Crowds remained impressive throughout, and showed a willingness to appreciate good cricket from both sides. Off the field, the level of hospitality and courtesy was unbelievable, and we were made to feel at home wherever we went.

That 1983-84 tour ended in early October 1983. I then travelled to Australia for a five-Test series (discussed in Chapter 8), that took us to early January 1984. I then had several weeks off from duty for Pakistan. During this time, I made another trip to India—to Calcutta, in February 1984. It was an unofficial trip, as I was going to be playing in an individual capacity in a double-wicket cricket festival.

Once again during that visit, Indian hospitality and kindness touched me deeply, and I experienced first-hand the affection and warmth that the Indian and Pakistani peoples have for each other.

Central to the following story is the figure of Jagmohan Dalmiya. In 1984, Dalmiya's tenures as head of the ICC and of the Indian Cricket Board were still in the future, but he was still a major businessman and a highly influential figure in the West Bengal cricket administration.

In the double-wicket competition I was partnered with Sarfraz Nawaz. At one point we found ourselves playing against an Australian pair that included Dennis Lillee.

Ever since the 1981-82 trip to Australia when Lillee tried to kick me (an incident discussed in Chapter 19), there had been an edge to our interaction.

This time around, Lillee bowled some loose ones, which I had soon hit for three consecutive fours. Then Lillee came back with a nasty bouncer. I went to hook it but I had played too early, and the ball hit me in the back of the head. Regrettably, I wasn't wearing a helmet. Although I had started the innings wearing one, I had later dispensed with it out of sheer bravado.

Immediately, I felt dizzy and nauseous, and lost my balance. I tried to get up, but my head was spinning furiously and I fell flat again and started vomiting. I was groggy and disoriented, but remember that everyone had crowded around me. I could see concern on their faces; they became very worried when I began vomiting. I vaguely remember being lifted onto a stretcher and into an ambulance. After that, I passed out. It was a terrible blow, without doubt the worst injury of my sporting career. I feel that after that injury, I have been granted a second chance on life.

I was taken to a Calcutta hospital where I remained unconscious for three days. I was later told that the doctors had been measuring my progress in hours, as my condition remained critical for the first couple of days.

When I regained consciousness, I realized that I had been left alone in Calcutta. Imran and Sarfraz had been with me in the double-wicket tournament, which had ended a day after my injury. They had since flown back to Pakistan.

Jagmohan Dalmiya was the head of the double-wicket tournament's organizing committee. He and his associates felt personally responsible for my injury and made every effort to make me feel comfortable, but I still felt lonely and was desperate to have my family around me. Telecommunications were not as good then as they are now, and I felt even more isolated and alone. Once I did manage to have a brief telephone conversation with my wife who was in Lahore, but I must have been in a daze because I don't remember what I said. I do remember thinking that I might be talking to her for the last time. Such was the state of my mind.

But Allah was kind and I recovered. I underwent a brain scan, which came out clear. I was confined completely to my bed as each time I tried to move my head, I got a terrible headache and was incredibly dizzy.

I badly wanted to be home in Pakistan but the doctors were not prepared to release me. Dalmiya looked after me and was a great comfort during that time, and he became my family in Calcutta. His warmth and companionship in those difficult days is something I will never forget.

It was proving very hard to arrange a flight back to Pakistan. I kept insisting that I had to return as soon as possible. Eventually a flight was arranged, but only up to New Delhi. The medical team had decided that I needed to be accompanied by a doctor *en route*, and since the doctor could not fly with me to Pakistan, the best they could arrange was to take me as close to the Pakistani border as possible.

Having thanked the doctors and nurses who had looked after me so well in Calcutta, I said a warm good-bye to Jagmohan Dalmiya, and took off for New Delhi.

In the Indian capital, I received some good news from a friend who had come to meet me. He said a chartered Pakistan International Airlines (PIA) Fokker plane might be available to take me back to Lahore. The Station Manager of the PIA office in New Delhi was Pervez Sajjad, a left-arm spinner who had played for Pakistan in the 1960s and whom I knew well. Pervez talked to the plane's captain who, recognizing my medical condition, offered me a complimentary flight home. Sarfraz Nawaz was also in New Delhi and accompanied me back to Pakistan. I was still finding it difficult to walk and had to be taken to the plane in a wheelchair.

In Lahore, I had a joyous reunion with my wife and family. I made a gradual recovery, started walking, and slowly resumed my activities. I flew to Karachi to consult the late Dr O.V.

Jooma, Pakistan's renowned neurosurgeon, who reassured me that I had received good care in India and was now on the road to recovery.

Many friends sent their love and best wishes and I was deeply touched by the outpouring of affection and concern. Abdur Rahman Bukhatir, father of cricket at Sharjah, called and offered to send me to the United States at his expense; his generosity overwhelmed me. I also got a call from Air Marshal Viqar Azeem, then head of PIA, who said I was a national asset and the country's airline would fly me free of charge anywhere in the world to get me the best medical care. I was still reeling from my terrible head injury, but all this love and concern comforted me greatly.

Dr Jooma had given me 4-5 months to make a natural full recovery. He said there was no medicine to speed things up but the brain injury was not permanent and would gradually heal itself. He had put me on a drug that was a symptomatic treatment for the dizziness that continued to plague me.

Around this time I met Dr Rafiq Jan, a Pakistani physician settled in New York who was visiting Pakistan. Dr Jan offered to take me to the United States and arrange for my medical evaluation at one of New York's leading medical centres. It a generous offer and I accepted.

The opinion of the American doctors was t   Dr Jooma's: I was lucky to have survived and re   st a matter of time.

In New York, Dr Jan was a well-know   being the official doctor for PIA, and a leading   akistani community. He looked after me very   main ever grateful for his care and hospitality   come great friends.

Because of this injury, I ended   istan's home series against England in March   first Test I had missed in seven years of playi   , and it is the only series I ever missed because

I have already discussed the years 1984 through 1986 in the chapter on Sharjah (Chapter 9). The chronology now brings us to the 1986-87 season.

Our first engagement that season was a three-Test home series against the West Indies, to which I will return in a subsequent chapter. After that were two limited-overs tournaments—the Champions Trophy in Sharjah featuring ourselves, India, Sri Lanka and the West Indies, which the West Indies took, and the America's Cup Benson and Hedges Challenge in Australia in which we lost in the finals (discussed in Chapter 8).

A major engagement awaited us on our return from Australia. In February 1987, we were due to take on India for a five-Test series on Indian soil. It would prove to be the beginning of a new era in Pakistan cricket.

By the mid-80s, a new cricket generation had emerged in Pakistan. From the team of the 1970s into which I had made my Test debut, only Imran and I survived. Zaheer, Mushtaq, Majid, Sadiq, Asif, Bari, Intikhab, Sarfraz—the stalwarts I had admired and looked to f   d dance—were all gone.

As on   o most experienced members of the side, I   nsibility. I know Imran felt it, too. We   e that historically had never played to its full p   an had produced some breathtakingly talented cri   but we had little real success as a team to s   ty years after getting Test status, we h   victories abroad, both against New Z

Imra   nding fast bowler and a serious ba   learned how to handle a bat well e   nst any bowling side. There were   ld not score overseas; I was determ

I saw in Imr   uld try and take the Pakistan side to a   nt.

It wasn't a consc   as if one day Imran and I sat down and said   hat we're going to do.' It is no secret that the two of us didn't always see eye to eye on many things. But I think in this we understood each other very well, that we wanted to take the team up a notch. The time had come for Pakistan to move up and take her place among the elite teams of the world. That meant winning overseas, and we thought we could do it for our country. I wanted that by the time we were through, people would fear Pakistan. It wasn't something that needed to be said; it was something that needed to be done.

It was a young team that we took to India in 1986-87. I was the only ex-captain in the side. People expected me to be resentful of Imran's captaincy, but I wasn't. Credit goes to him for holding the side together. He had unshakeable principles, which earned him respect.

I wanted to see Pakistan succeed. I continued to think up strategies on and off the field. My mind was always on cricket and the ideas flowed effortlessly. It had little to do with whether I was captain or not—this was simply my nature. I had been dispensing cricket advice throughout my career, right from my very first Test innings when I was telling my senior batting partner Asif Iqbal what to do and how to do it. When I was captain, I was free to implement my own ideas. I was no longer captain, but I would share my ideas with Imran and he would implement them. Sometimes he wouldn't give in right away but, almost always, he eventually did. That was good enough for me.

We wanted so badly to win in India, but we were facing a star-studded team on its home turf. We were going to have to contend with specialist players like Gavaskar, Srikkanth, Amarnath, Vengsarkar, Azharuddin, and Maninder Singh, not to mention accomplished all-rounders like Ravi Shastri, Kapil Dev and Roger Binny.

The one weak spot in the Indian team was their discomfort against fast bowling. With the notable exception of Gavaskar, this was an area they had traditionally struggled with. We were well equipped to exploit this weakness. The Indians had no one who could match the fast bowling skills of Imran Khan and Wasim Akram.

India, in fact, remains the only established Test side that has
yet to produce a genuine world-class fast bowler. All the other
established teams—England, Australia, South Africa, West
Indies, New Zealand, Pakistan—have each produced elite
pacemen. If I were an Indian fan, this deficiency would disturb
me deeply, especially when right across the border Pakistan has
fired off in quick succession the likes of Wasim Akram, Waqar
Younis, Imran Khan and Shoaib Akhtar.

It is the absence of a genuine fast bowler that keeps India
from winning overseas—and until they start winning overseas,
they cannot be considered a frontline Test side. They can be an
outstanding team in limited-overs cricket, which is ultimately a
batsman's game. But they are chronic under-achievers at the
Test level, where you have to take twenty wickets to win a
match.

India needs to make fast pitches if it wants to encourage the
development of fast bowlers in the country. Indian strategy of
wicket preparation remains singularly defensive, because the
authorities don't want to risk losing. So they prepare wickets to
suit their own strengths. But it is an absurdly short-sighted
approach because it doesn't address the team's traditional
weakness—the lack of genuine pace—which keeps India from
winning abroad.

Even within Pakistan, the positive effect of supportive
conditions for producing fast bowlers is obvious. Our best fast
bowlers have come from Punjab, with its grassy grounds,
seaming wickets and cool winter weather. Karachi, in contrast,
has been a nursery for our top batsmen and not for quick
bowlers. Conditions in Karachi do not suit quick bowlers and so
the city has traditionally lagged behind in this department.

My advice to the Indian Cricket Board would be to prepare
fast pitches that encourage seam bowlers. Right now it is just
the fear of losing that keeps India from adopting this strategy.
But one can't worry about that when making long-range policy.
You may initially lose a few matches on seaming wickets, but

before long an indigenous crop of fast bowlers will emerge and turn the tide.

The cricket-following public expects and demands victory all the time, but it is ridiculous to make this the goal of national cricket policy. No team can keep winning all the time, and if that's all you're after, you'll always be miserable. It is good to be defeated every now and then. One learns little or nothing from victory, but one can learn a lot from defeat. The Indian cricket administration has yet to embrace this philosophy—and that's why a billion people have yet to produce a genuine fast bowler.

As expected, we found slow wickets throughout the tour on that 1986-87 trip. The first four Tests were dull draws. There was some excitement during the third Test at Jaipur, as President Ziaul Haq flew in from Pakistan to watch the day's play. He had been invited by the Rajasthan Cricket Association and used the visit to score some diplomatic points off Rajiv Gandhi, the Indian Prime Minister.

An on-field incident from that Jaipur Test has stuck in my mind. There had been crowd trouble, and some of the Pakistan players had been subjected to verbal abuse. We were also disappointed with some of the umpiring decisions; the two teams were on edge with each other and the atmosphere was tense. At one point, I was fielding close in and was airing my feelings to the batsman, who happened to be Mohinder Amarnath.

When Mohinder survived what I thought was yet another very legitimate appeal, I reached boiling point. I used an expletive to describe India and Mohinder heard it. Calmly, he walked up to me.

'Look, Javed,' Mohinder said, 'call me anything you want but don't say a word against my country.'

That affected me deeply. I have always regarded my own country as being above everything except Allah. I was embarrassed that I hadn't respected Mohinder's right to feel the same way about his country. I immediately apologized to him. That exchange reminded me what was at stake in our contest. It was far beyond anything personal. It was about one's country, and what one could do for it.

For the fourth Test at Ahmedabad, I suggested we call in as reinforcement someone who could bat reliably at no. 6 or 7 and could also bowl spin. We settled on the name of Ijaz Faqih, who was flown in from Pakistan. He had played two Tests for Pakistan in 1980-81 and was a respected all-rounder in Pakistan's domestic cricket. Ijaz ended up being Man-of-the-Match at Ahmedabad, making a hundred and even taking a wicket with his first ball, but it wasn't enough.

During that series we had also called upon Younis Ahmed. A left-handed Pakistani batsman who had spent his career with Surrey, Younis had played two Tests for Pakistan in 1969-70 and was then banned by the Pakistan Cricket Board for touring South Africa during the apartheid years. The ban was relaxed in 1986 and Younis became available for selection. He made 14 in the third Test at Jaipur and 40 and 34 not out in the fourth Test at Ahmedabad. During the Ahmedabad Test he complained of back trouble and was told to rest but instead went to a discotheque. Imran was incensed and Younis never played another Test for Pakistan. Imran's word was nothing less than the law in Pakistani cricket in those days.

I had to sit out the Ahmedabad Test because of back trouble but recovered in time for the final match. After four drawn Tests, we headed to Bangalore for the potential decider. As we approached Bangalore, our team morale was very high. We felt we had it in us to beat India at home.

We knew there was bound to be a spinning track at Bangalore. From the team that played the fourth Test, Imran wanted to drop Ijaz Faqih who had taken only one wicket at Ahmedabad. His place went to off-spinner Tauseef Ahmed. I was fit and took the place of Younis Ahmed, who was *persona non grata* after his discotheque escapade. Imran also wanted left-arm medium pacer Saleem Jaffer in the side, which left room for only one other spinner.

The choice was between Abdul Qadir or Iqbal Qasim.

Imran never had much faith in Qasim's orthodox left-arm spin. He used to think Qasim wasn't really a threatening bowler. In contrast, Imran's confidence in Qadir's wrist spin was complete.

Abdul Qadir had come with us to India but took only three wickets in the first two Tests and was dropped for the third Test at Jaipur. He came back for the Ahmedabad Test but took only one wicket.

By the time of the second Test, Imran had been openly talking about the need for a left-arm finger spinner. He kept asking us to pick the right man who could be called in from Pakistan. Iqbal Qasim's name was mentioned to him a number of times but he wouldn't accept it. He kept looking for some other name but there was none.

I finally confronted Imran. 'You make all this talk about country,' I told him, 'why don't you do what's best for the country now? Iqbal Qasim is what the country needs right now.'

I urged Imran to look beyond his biases and face facts. We needed a left-arm spinner on this tour and Iqbal Qasim was the best man available to fill the spot. Imran knew that Qasim was a close personal friend of mine but he eventually realized that my support for him in this situation had little to do with friendship.

So Qasim was flown in. Initially, he did nothing dramatic. He played in the third Test at Jaipur but ended up taking only two wickets. He also played at Ahmedabad but took just one wicket there.

When it came time to select someone to complement Tauseef's off-spin in the fifth Test at Bangalore, Imran was still leaning heavily in Qadir's favour.

I have nothing against Abdul Qadir. He has been my teammate at Habib Bank in Pakistan's domestic cricket and I have the highest regard for his bowling skills. But I had read that Bangalore wicket and I knew Qasim would wreak havoc on it. It was the kind of strip that would assist finger-spin much more than wrist spin.

Right up to the morning of the Test, Imran was in two minds whether to play Qadir or Qasim. Eventually I prevailed on him to include Qasim in the team, but our exchange wasn't pretty. We ended up getting involved in a heated argument and I had to invoke Allah and Pakistan before Imran finally gave in. It was no secret that I had forced Qasim's selection through, and this upset my friend Abdul Qadir, but I was simply doing what I thought was best for Pakistan.

It was going to be an important toss, and Imran's luck held up. We had no hesitation in batting first. No team would have chosen to bat last on that strip.

In the first innings, Maninder Singh spun us out for 116 and took 7 for 27. When India batted, Tauseef and Qasim found their mark and we restricted India to a first innings lead of only 29. Tauseef (5-54) and Qasim (5-48) took all the wickets between them. We were desperate to do better in the second innings and wanted to set India a tough target.

Pakistani teams have never been good chasers, but we usually do well at setting targets. This time we managed to set India 221 to win. Iqbal Qasim contributed 26 with the bat in a fighting nightwatchman's knock late on the second day. Imran made 39, and Saleem Yousuf, our big-hearted wicketkeeper, topscored with 41 not out. Saleem Yousuf's innings was crucial. His glovework was average but he was a tenacious fighter and played several inspired innings for Pakistan, including this one.

The wicket was by now turning square and 221 was never going to be an easy task. India lost wickets steadily. One man, however, remained solid at one end and slowly but surely they kept edging towards their target. Sunil Gavaskar batted like a champion that day. He pulled out all the stops and played Qasim and Tauseef with incredible skill and concentration.

That knock from Gavaskar is one of the finest Test batting performances I've seen from anyone. He was using his feet beautifully and negotiating turn in both directions with equal command. The height of his mastery was when he stepped out to play a well-timed on-drive off Qasim. Qasim was moving the ball away from Gavaskar at sharp angles, yet Gavaskar was playing against the turn and timing those on-drives perfectly. For any other batsman, playing an on-drive on that wicket to a ball spinning away from the outside edge would have been suicide; for Gavaskar, it meant getting boundaries. It showed the great depth and range of his skill.

Eventually Gavaskar fell, too. He was caught in the slips off Qasim for a riveting 96. Once Gavaskar was out, we knew the match was ours. The final margin of victory was 16 runs. Qasim and Tauseef took 4 wickets each in India's second innings. They had clearly come through for Pakistan. I thought Qasim deserved to be Man-of-the-Match but the judges opted for Gavaskar. That was a fair choice too, but perhaps Qasim and Gavaskar could have shared the award.

Victory at Bangalore brought a tremendous sense of achievement. We now felt ready to take on the world. Our schedule for the next twelve months included a forthcoming tour of England, followed by the World Cup in the Indo-Pak subcontinent, then a home series against England and finally a visit to the West Indies. We were eyeing victory at every step. It felt like the start of a golden era.

The momentum of that Test win carried us to a 5-1 victory in the six-match One-Day International series. In fact it should have been 6-0, but for some lack of concentration from Abdul Qadir. In the third One-day International, Qadir attempted a needless second run off the final delivery and was run out with the scores tied. India won having lost 6 wickets to our 7. Had Qadir stayed put after taking the first run and levelling the scores, we would have won the game on account of having a better score after the first twenty-five overs.

At the time I didn't think this would be my last playing trip to India, but it was. I also didn't think we would see an interruption in play between the two countries, but sadly we have.

We are neighbouring countries that share a cultural heritage and a deep love for cricket, so Pakistan and India should be meeting each other for a major series at least once every other season. Unfortunately, Indian authorities have decided to mix sports with politics, which is a very short-sighted strategy from which no one benefits. It certainly does not advance India's cause in any way. I am amazed that the people behind this

Indian policy of refusing to play cricket with Pakistan cannot see this. The huge cricket-following public in India and Pakistan are the ultimate losers.

Sporting relations have the potential to bring nations and peoples together. Far from shunning sports encounters, Indian authorities should be looking towards sports to advance India-Pakistan relations. It may seem old-fashioned, but I think there is a great deal of merit to reviving the old idea of the 'goodwill' tour, a sporting exchange aimed at thawing icy international relations.

When sports and politics are allowed to mix, you get the kind of ridiculous situation in which we found ourselves during the 1998-99 tour to India, when I was the Pakistan coach (Chapter 20). Throughout that tour, local extremists targeted us and we were constantly under threat for absolutely no reason other than that we were Pakistanis.

It is a very sad development. On previous tours we felt relaxed and welcome in India; we mixed freely with the Indian fans and the fans seemed at ease with us. One could go out and enjoy the sights of India. Now we were hardly allowed to venture beyond our bus or hotel, assuming we're allowed inside India at all.

Indian authorities need to realize that winning or losing is part of sportsmanship. A nation's self-esteem cannot be held hostage to its sporting fortunes. If it is, then that doesn't say much for the nation. If the Indian powers that be are at all sincere, then they should jump at the opportunity offered by sporting relations as a means of improving ties with Pakistan.

In fact, I strongly feel that cricket tours between India and Pakistan can be a forum for a much larger exchange of culture and ideas between the two countries. One could even get celebrities from other walks of life involved on both sides of the border. Imagine performances and exchanges between Bollywood and Lollywood on the sidelines of a Pakistan-India cricket tour—the possibilities are enormous.

And while there may be political and security reasons for maintaining visa regulations between Pakistan and India, concessions should be made during cricket tours. This is an ideal mechanism for facilitating interaction between the two peoples and is bound to lead to friendship and understanding.

Border tensions and the threat of war have soured Pakistan-India relations from the very beginning, when the two countries gained independence from British rule in 1947. Fifty years on, one would ordinarily have expected the animosity to die or at least to have abated. Attempts to exploit and rekindle it at this stage of the region's geopolitical evolution are really unforgivable.

Cricketers, like other men and women in sports, are short on time. Their active playing careers are limited and their peak really lasts for only a handful of years. It is criminal to sacrifice sports opportunities in favour of some misconceived political gain.

Ultimately, the greatest beneficiaries of an active cricket exchange between Pakistan and India are the two countries themselves, for the more we play each other the more our cricket will improve. Clearly, both sides stand to gain. To take but one example, India has failed to produce a genuine paceman while just across the border Pakistan has virtually rolled them out on an assembly line. It is the sort of disparity that tours of Under-19 and Under-17 teams, as well as exchanges between Indian and Pakistani cricket academies, could conceivably eliminate.

One has to stop seeing a cricket match as a proxy war and a cricket loss as a political failure. It is easily done when one understands that sports and politics cannot be allowed to mix. As the two cultures are so nearly identical, it would be a terrible shame if this straightforward goal could not be achieved.

If sporting relations flourish, benefits will accrue to other areas of cooperation, such as business, industry, education, arts and science and—who knows—perhaps ultimately even politics.

The peoples of India and Pakistan ultimately want peace more than anything else. We each have but one life to live, and we'd all much rather live it in peace and harmony than in hatred and hostility. This simple logic should be enough for both countries to recognize each other's sincerity. I have a strong belief that sense will ultimately prevail.

CHAPTER 12

England with a Difference

There is something special about playing England, because you really have to do well against England, in England, to get the stamp of accomplishment in world cricket. Through the 1990s, England ceased to be the dominant team it once was, but the importance of playing England has remained unchanged. The quality of English cricket, in fact, has little to do with England's special status as cricket's mother country. England will always be a very special cricketing nation because it is from this country that cricket began. Nothing can ever change that.

I have spent a lot of time playing cricket in England. This includes touring with Pakistan for four Test series and for three World Cups, as well as several seasons spent with Sussex and Glamorgan. But my very first trip to England came even before I had played my first Test. In the summer of 1974, I was seventeen years old and the vice-captain of a Pakistan Under-19 team that played matches against Second XIs from some of the major English counties. The following year I was back to make my One-Day International debut in the 1975 Prudential World Cup. In 1976, I signed a contract with Sussex and thereafter spent every summer in England until 1987, either playing county cricket, or representing Pakistan. In 1992, after going four summers without English cricket, I returned to England as the Pakistan captain for a five-Test series.

This chapter is about my tours to England with the Pakistan team. My first Test series in England was in 1978; it was a miserable tour that I would rather forget. (I've described it in

Chapter 4.) By the time we toured again, in 1982, Pakistan was a different side, and in my subsequent tours, in 1987 and 1992, it was different yet again.

It is worth going over some background history because the cricketing relationship between Pakistan and England is very interesting.

It begins in 1951-52, when Pakistan was not yet a Test side. In fact, Pakistan owes its entry into the Test-playing club to a victory over England that season. In November 1951, England visited Pakistan to evaluate our bid for full ICC membership. The first match in Lahore was drawn, but in the second match at Karachi, Pakistan successfully chased 285 in the fourth innings to win by five wickets. It made getting Test status a mere formality.

Our performances in England have mirrored Pakistan's fortunes in world cricket. Pakistan managed to win a Test on its first tour to England, in 1954. This is the famous Oval victory in which seam bowler Fazal Mahmood took 12 for 99. This was a promising time for Pakistan and there were some other memorable victories in those inaugural Test years.

In the 1960s, Pakistan toured England twice. This was an unhappy cricketing decade for Pakistan and it showed in the performances. The five-Test series in 1962 was lost 0-4 under the captaincy of Javed Burki and the three-Test series in 1967 was lost 0-2 under the captaincy of Hanif Mohammed.

Pakistan then had two solid tours to England in 1971 and 1974. By then we had become a strong batting side. The bowling still lacked teeth though, and we didn't have the talent to bowl the opposition out twice, so all the six Tests covering those two series were drawn. In 1978—my first Test series in England—we were depleted by the loss of star players to Kerry Packer's World Series Cricket, and lost the three-Test series 0-2.

In 1982, we returned to England in many ways a new side, having beaten India and Australia in Pakistan, and won Tests against New Zealand and Australia overseas.

The bowling had improved with Imran's development into a frontline fast bowler. He was now bowling ferocious in-dippers and off-cutters at 95 mph. That three-Test series against England in 1982 also happened to be Imran's first as captain. He had taken over after I had had to step aside following the drama of the players' revolt. I didn't mind touring under Imran, whom I had recommended to the Pakistan Cricket Board as my successor. I thought it would be the next best thing to my own captaincy.

Bob Willis led England in that series, though David Gower captained in the second Test while Willis was unfit.

Having just handed over the captaincy, I naturally closely scrutinized Imran's actions as captain. I would go over his decisions and wonder what I would have done in the same situation. I thought Imran did fine on the field, but he did a thing or two off the field that perhaps I would have handled differently.

One of these situations was Imran's strange attitude towards our senior batsman Majid Khan. Majid had been a great servant to Pakistan cricket over the years and had also acquired a rich experience of English conditions during his seasons with Glamorgan.

Majid was one of the Pakistan teammates I respected the most. He was the kind of person who said what he meant and meant what he said. He and I had very different personalities but I grew to like him a lot. One of my habits during batting was to keep giving tips to my batting partner—how I was finding the bowling, where and whom to hit, what to do and what not to do, stuff like that. Everyone put up with it, although I can see how it might be annoying to have such a batting partner. Majid didn't like this and once said as much to me in his blunt no-nonsense style.

'Please spare me your batting advice when I'm out in the middle with you,' Majid said to me once early in my career. I appreciated his frankness, and thereafter kept myself in check whenever he was at the other end.

I feel Imran treated Majid unfairly during that 1982 England series. He ignored Majid for the first two Tests and when Majid was finally included in the third Test, it was probably too late to make amends. Imran's action was hard to understand because Majid was also his cousin. Perhaps Majid had hoped Imran would seek him out for advice.

I would certainly have given Majid a chance at the beginning of that series. Admittedly, he hadn't done well in the limited-overs games or the side matches that preceded the first Test, but he had some highly valuable experience, and I would certainly have played him in the opening Test.

Once Majid was sidelined, it caused a good deal of tension, which affected team morale. It got to the point where Majid wouldn't join the team for practice sessions. While the rest of us worked away in the nets, Majid would be seen in some corner of the ground, sitting around in street clothes, showing no indication that he was part of our outfit. Imran certainly failed to handle that situation with Majid properly.

Nevertheless, we went on to enjoy some high quality cricket in that series. We lost it 1-2, but we could well have won it as the contest was closely fought.

In the first Test at Edgbaston we were set 313 in the fourth innings but had a disastrous start and never recovered. In the second Test at Lord's, Mohsin Khan made a fine 200 and we made England follow on. This time our fourth innings target was just 76, which we achieved without losing a wicket. It was our first Test victory in England in twenty-eight years. I was proud to have hit the winning runs.

We moved on to Headingley for the decider. We managed to get a modest first innings lead but couldn't build on it and set England only 219 in the fourth innings. They barely managed to get there, eventually winning by the slim margin of 3 wickets. I made 54 and 52 in that game and enjoyed playing my shots, but I was too impetuous and still regret that I couldn't consolidate either innings into a bigger score.

It also needs to be said that the umpiring in that series was below par. Much is made of the impeccable standards of English umpiring, and while I will say that the umpiring in England is the best I've come across anywhere on tour, they are no saints either. In places like the West Indies, the umpiring would sometimes be so openly biased that there was no doubt about the umpires' true intent. The difference in England is that the interference would be intelligent and subtle so that the possibility of human error could never be completely ruled out.

In that 1982 series, the English umpires invariably ruled against us at crucial moments. For a series that remained in the balance until the final session of the final Test, this sort of partiality proved decisive.

We came back to tour England in 1987 to play five Tests against a team led by Mike Gatting. Ian Botham and David Gower were also in that side, as were Neil Foster, Phil Edmonds, Philip DeFreitas and John Emburey.

Compared to 1982, Pakistan were a vastly different team— perhaps not so much in skill, but certainly in self-belief and temperament.

It was an incredibly important tour for us. Keeping a reputation is often harder than making one. We were buoyant after ending the 1986-87 season with victory in a Test series in India. We now had that reputation to keep. We wanted to be regarded as the best team in the world. We had just posted our first-ever series win in India, and we were now determined to do the same in England. We had to be consistent, as there's very little value in being good only in flashes.

I was also under pressure to come good with the bat. I hadn't scored a century in a while. My last hundred had been nearly two years earlier, when I had made 203 not out against Sri Lanka at Faisalabad in October 1985. Since that knock and up to the beginning of the 1987 England tour I had played another nineteen innings spread over twelve Tests. These included five 50s and a top score of 94 (run out), but my batting average for this period was only 35.78. I desperately needed to shake off the lean patch.

I knew the upcoming five Tests presented an excellent opportunity to make a big score in England and put to rest once and for all the criticism that I couldn't score outside Pakistan. Once you've got a big one in England, everyone concedes you could get a big score anywhere.

Pakistan dominated that tour right from the beginning, starting with the county games. Our batting outclassed the best bowling attacks the counties could put together. All our batsmen clicked and began making hundreds. Only the very top of the order was getting batting practice because the batsmen were hardly getting out. We starting promoting our middle-order batsmen to open so everyone could get some good knocks in before the Tests.

I was a little late joining the touring party because I had to stay back in Lahore for the birth of my second son, Jahangir. I found my touch right away. In a side match against Sussex at Hove, I made 211 and enjoyed it thoroughly. We played three One-Day Internationals for the Texaco Trophy before the end of May and I continued to be in good touch. In the first match at the Oval I made 113 in our total of 232, though we still lost. Two days later we met for the second match at Trent Bridge and I made 71 not out in a game that we won by 6 wickets. The third match went down to the wire—we lost by one wicket with three balls to spare. I had made 68.

The first two Tests were rain-affected draws. In the first Test I made 21 in our only innings. The second Test was so badly washed out that Pakistan never got to bat.

We went to Leeds for the third Test where England decided to bat in conditions known for seam and swing. Imran Khan, Wasim Akram and Mohsin Kamal took 3 wickets apiece as England managed only 136. I knew it would be tough batting on that pitch, but Saleem Malik made 99 and Ijaz Ahmed and Wasim Akram also made sizeable scores and we got to 353. I was unfortunate to get out for a duck. Then Imran cleaned up the English innings with 7 for 40 and they couldn't make us bat again. It was a convincing innings victory and we hoped to turn it out into a series win.

With two Tests to go, I was still looking for a big score. We came across a good pitch in the fourth Test at Edgbaston; I made 75 in the first innings but only 4 in the second. Mudassar Nazar and Mike Gatting got hundreds in that drawn game.

We returned to London to play the fifth Test at the Oval. Imran won the toss and we started batting in sunny conditions on an easy wicket. I came in at 45 for 2 and never felt troubled.

I remember that innings as one of my most pleasurable. I got my hundred and ended the first day not out on 131. I came out the next day feeling in total command and set my mind towards a big score. Imran's abrupt declaration leaving me 280 not out against India back in 1982-83 (Chapter 7) had left me with an obsession to one day overtake Sobers's 365. At 131 that target was far away, but I was still very conscious of it.

I got to 200 and then 250 with no trouble at all. With my score at 260, I played an over from Graham Dilley during which Dilley injured himself and decided to finish his over off a short run. My concentration finally lapsed and I handed him a low return catch, which he eagerly took. We ended up walking back to the pavilion together.

It wasn't 365, but a score of 260 was nevertheless very, very satisfying. Most important, it was made in England and was a great boost to my international standing as a Test batsman. Sir Gary Sobers mentions in his autobiography that he was following this innings of mine and feared for his record. That's a fantastic tribute from one of the game's geniuses.

With Imran and Saleem Malik also contributing centuries, we posted Pakistan's highest innings total ever, 708 all out. There was no way we were going to lose after that. England followed on but managed to pull out a draw, and we had pocketed our first ever series win in England.

We eagerly lapped up the praises in the press and media. It seemed that what we had set out to do after the Austral-Asia Cup victory in the previous year—to push Pakistan into the top cadre of cricket teams—was finally going to be realized. The English newspapers were calling us the best cricket team in the world. We had felt that way ourselves for a while, but it was nice to have others acknowledge it too.

As on our previous tours to England, we found large Pakistani contingents in the Test match crowds, especially in the matches at Leeds, Birmingham and Manchester. Pakistani crowds in

England are not always a positive thing for us because they can be very unforgiving if we don't do well. At Headingley, though, they ignited our spirits and their support lifted us to victory in the series.

Imran led the team well. He commanded authority but a major reason for his success was that he was a good listener. I continued to enjoy a good understanding with him regarding strategy and on-field decisions. I frequently saw situations in the game where a strategic move on our part could make a difference, such as if a batsman revealed a particular weakness or developed a predictable pattern of strokes. As I have said, I like to share these insights, and Imran was always receptive.

There was no shortage of other distractions from the cricket. Pakistan had asked that David Constant not umpire in the series because we felt we had suffered enough on previous tours to leave no doubt as to his bias. Our hosts didn't agree with us on this issue.

Throughout that tour, the English tabloid press seemed to be on the lookout waiting for us to make some gaffe that could be used against us. In the third Test at Headingley, Saleem Yousuf claimed a catch at the wicket that he had collected on the half volley. The English media whipped it up and made it into a bigger issue than it really was.

You really have to watch what you say with the press in England, because they're extremely good with words. Whatever they report, it will be accurate according to the facts, but it will be written in such a way that one starts to wonder about hidden meanings. The English public have a huge appetite for sensationalism and the tabloid press is only too eager to cater to this demand.

During that 1987 tour, we had an outspoken and confident manager in Hasib Ahsan, a former Pakistan Test off-spinner. Hasib had a subtle understanding of cricket, and an even subtler one of controversies. He did an excellent job projecting our interests while minimizing our distractions so we could focus on the cricket. In any case, once we had won the series, the controversies became meaningless.

If the cricket is going well, there is nothing like touring England. Everything about the tour is well organized and hassle-free, and the cricketing facilities are second to none.

The most interesting thing about touring England is adjusting to the English conditions, which are unique in the cricket world. The conditions are tremendously enjoyable if you're in form but they are also unforgiving and can make you struggle. It is hard to bounce back if you've hit a lean patch. By far the trickiest thing is the weather. It is unpredictable, and can be very wet and cold, especially before the end of May. Dodgy, the English call it.

I have often wondered why it took me so long to play a big Test innings in England and I think it was probably a question of adjusting to English conditions. The 1987 tour was my first five-Test series in England and it gave me enough time to finally acclimatize to the conditions by the time of the last match.

English grounds offer great variety, far more than in any other country. At some places one finds excellent pitches that retain true bounce for five days. But you also come across spinning tracks where the ball turns square, as well as seaming tracks where the ball bites into the surface and can do anything if the seam is up.

My favourite English ground is Edgbaston, in Birmingham. It is a reliable batting track and if the sun is out the pleasure of batting there is unmatched anywhere. I've enjoyed a number of innings at that ground during county matches.

I also really enjoy Headingley, in Leeds. A demanding pitch, it is the opposite of Edgbaston and truly tests your wits as you can't take any liberties there. You have to be extra watchful because if you let your guard down at any time, you're gone. You could be batting seemingly well set at 80 or 90 but if you decide to take any chances, that's the end of it for you. It is a classic seaming track, and as there is also often cloud cover, you end up having to negotiate a lethal mix of seam and swing.

I am also very partial to Old Trafford, in Manchester, but mainly because of the huge Pakistani support one invariably finds there. Pakistan hasn't been able to play much cricket at

Old Trafford because we've always encountered terrible weather there.

Finally of course you have Lord's, cricket's headquarters, which has all the trappings and atmosphere of an exclusive gentleman's club. There is so much tradition and decorum there that the pitch and the cricket are almost irrelevant. Yet there are some quirks to the ground that add to its unique character. The pitch slopes slightly towards the pavilion, and you are batting virtually downhill from the bowler at that end. Another famous oddity is a very short boundary on one side, where a leg flick (or lofted cover drive from the opposite end) can sometimes end up fetching you an easy six.

Pakistani participation in the crowds has always been an exciting part of the English tours for me. As I have already said, this doesn't always work in our favour because sometimes these same sections can be our harshest critics, but when they're with you, there's nothing like it.

There has been some criticism of the Pakistanis settled in Britain still supporting Pakistan in the cricket rather than England, their adopted country. The English would like them to support England, their new adopted home. That's the feeling one gets from the English broadcast media and newspapers. I can see the English point of view because England has been good to these immigrants and given them much better opportunities than Pakistan could ever offer them. But if their hearts are still with Pakistan, there really is nothing one can do about it.

Some observers have said that this issue is related to Pakistani or Asian discontent in Britain. One cannot deny the discontent—many of the Pakistani immigrants don't feel treated as equals—but I don't think they support the Pakistan cricket team as some kind of a response to racism. I think it is simply a question of love and nostalgia for your first home because clearly the Pakistani population in Britain continues to have strong emotional ties with Pakistan. There is an English saying that you can take the boy out of England but you can't take England

out of the boy. I suppose this could apply just as well to a boy
from any country, including Pakistan.

I returned to England with the Pakistan team in 1992. This
was the last time I would be there doing Test duty for Pakistan.
By this time Pakistan had become World Champions, Imran
had retired, I was the most senior player in the side and was
captain, and I had a phenomenally talented team at my
command.

I can say without hesitation that that 1992 trip to England
proved to be the most enjoyable cricket tour I've ever
undertaken.

I was a reluctant captain for that series. Imran had been
captain for our 1992 World Cup campaign, as he had been for
the last several years leading up to it, but a number of players
had started grumbling about his leadership, especially after what
they perceived as his high-handedness. Certainly his self-
absorbed World Cup victory speech (described in Chapter 16)
hadn't helped matters.

Imran felt that I was somehow involved in sowing these seeds
of discontent. This was untrue and I was hurt by the suggestion
as I have never been a political person and do not plan ever to
be one either. I like to make my intentions clear and to do
things openly. Lobbying and political grouping is simply not
the way I do business, and I certainly never did anything to gain
the Pakistan captaincy.

As the 1992 World Cup was coming to an end, our team had
become sharply divided off the field, Imran versus the rest. So a
leadership crisis had been precipitated within the team. It was in
these circumstances that I took over the captaincy.

I knew it was going to be a challenging series. We had just
been responsible for England's third loss in a World Cup final
and they were out for revenge. With Imran gone and team unity
uncertain, our chances for that series didn't look very good. I
took over the leadership and it proved to be an exceptional tour.

The series included some of the best cricket I have ever
played and I know other players on both sides have felt the
same. What made the tour particularly memorable was that a

great feeling of camaraderie was present in our camp, and it was probably one of the most congenial and cohesive Pakistan sides ever.

As captain, I ensured that a relaxed atmosphere prevailed. Everybody put their heart and soul into the cricket and we won that series 2-1. We also did well in the side games and received cash awards for winning against many of the county teams.

In fact, the series would have been won 3-0 but for Graham Gooch being saved from a run out by an appalling umpiring decision in the third Test. TV replays showed it to be quite a gaffe.

Being freshly crowned world champions who were playing good cricket, we also enjoyed tremendous respect from a highly involved and knowledgeable English audience. The Pakistani expatriate community in Britain had been fired up by Pakistan's World Cup win and came in large numbers to cheer us on. In fact in the side matches, they often outnumbered the English, and we loved every minute of it. The team management on that tour, led by Khalid Mahmood, was also wonderful. It was as close to flawless as a cricket tour could be.

The one thing that kept that tour from being completely perfect was, of course, the matter of ball-tampering. Wasim and Waqar were making the ball talk all over England and the English were finding it hard to stomach it as a legitimate skill. Their way of dealing with it was to accuse the Pakistani duo of ball-tampering.

I remember a situation in that series when the captain and manager from both teams appeared together for a joint press conference. The England manager Mickey Stewart made a statement saying that he knew very well what the Pakistani bowlers were up to but he wasn't going to say what it was. It was the classic English ploy when you say something without really saying it.

Mickey's coyness got the reporters all excited and they all turned to me asking what it was that the Pakistani bowlers were really up to. I said that I had no idea, but if Mickey Stewart knew then by all means lets hear it because I too would like to know what it is that my bowlers are doing!

That's how it goes in England. You have to watch very closely what you say, because what you say is going to be very closely watched by others, and there could well be a completely new spin put on your words.

CHAPTER 13

Heartache in Lahore

After the inaugural World Cup held in 1975, this competition became recognized as one of the major events in world cricket. It has been held approximately every four years since, and has now come to dominate every cricket-playing country's ambitions and preparations.

The first three World Cups—1975, 1979 and 1983—were all held in England. I played in all three. In 1975, I made my One-Day International debut in a World Cup match against West Indies, which I have narrated earlier in Chapter 2. I scored 24 (run out) and took 1 for 46 from twelve overs, but it wasn't a debut experience I would wish on anyone. Deryck Murray and Andy Roberts put on 64 for the last wicket to win in the final over of that game and we ended up losing a match that we had all but won.

In 1979, we made it to the semi-finals but came up against a great West Indian side on the warpath. Pretty much the same thing happened in 1983. We had different expectations from the World Cup to be held in 1987.

The graph of Pakistan's cricket fortunes had been steadily going up and up ever since the Austral-Asia Cup victory in Sharjah in April 1986. Since then we had tied a series with West Indies and beaten both India and England on their home turf. The momentum was now set for only one thing—victory in the World Cup. We were being openly considered hot favourites to win the tournament.

There was something very special about the 1987 World Cup. For the first time the competition was to be staged outside

England and, most exciting for us, it was coming to Pakistan and India.

The populations of both countries were in the grip of World Cup frenzy. As the tournament approached, every Indian and Pakistani became a cricket expert and fan. India were defending their title, and Pakistan were desperate to attain it. Both teams would be playing with a home advantage. The stage seemed set for an epic final clash between the traditional rivals.

It was also a relaxed time in India-Pakistan relations. The mutual and successful staging of the 1987 World Cup was a fine example of what Pakistani and Indian cooperation could achieve.

It was a superbly organized event, with the sponsors making large amounts of money available, and everything about that tournament went off without a hitch.

That 1987 World Cup in India and Pakistan also had a lasting impact in a way that isn't always appreciated. It transformed the way the World Cup competition itself was perceived. The previous three World Cups had certainly been major events, but after 1987, the cricket World Cup became an extremely serious, do-or-die tournament with the highest stakes. In the process, limited-overs international cricket came into its own. The 1987 World Cup tournament is really a watershed in the evolution of international limited-overs cricket.

Eight teams participated in the 1987 World Cup. They included all the seven teams then playing Test cricket, plus Zimbabwe, who were not yet full ICC members. South Africa was still under the apartheid ban and didn't participate. The teams were organized into two groups, A and B. Pakistan were placed in Group B, with West Indies, England and Sri Lanka. According to the tournament rules, each team would play its group mates twice in the league stage, with the top two teams from each group advancing to the semi-finals.

The tournament was inaugurated on 8 October 1987, with a match between Pakistan and Sri Lanka at Niaz Stadium in Hyderabad, Pakistan. We batted first and made 267 for 6 from fifty overs, of which I was able to contribute 103 off 100 balls.

It happened to be my ninth consecutive score of 50 or more in One-Day Internationals. Sri Lanka fell short by 15 runs, and our World Cup campaign was off to a promising start.

We proceeded to blaze our way through to the top of our group. In the next match we beat England by eighteen runs and then beat West Indies by one wicket in a cliff-hanger. In the second round of matches, we disposed off England by seven wickets and Sri Lanka by 113 runs, and stood at the top of our group. We did lose our final group match, to West Indies by twenty-eight runs, but that defeat had no bearing on the group standings.

India, meanwhile, had reached the top of Group A with a similar run of victories. The final group standings looked like this:

GROUP A

TEAM	PLAYED	WON	LOST	RUN-RATE	POINTS
India	6	5	1	5.41	20
Australia	6	5	1	5.19	20
New Zealand	6	2	4	4.91	8
Zimbabwe	6	0	6	3.76	0

GROUP B

TEAM	PLAYED	WON	LOST	RUN-RATE	POINTS
Pakistan	6	5	1	5.01	20
England	6	4	2	5.12	16
West Indies	6	3	3	5.16	12
Sri Lanka	6	0	6	4.04	0

By topping their respective groups, India and Pakistan had managed to avoid each other in the semi-finals. Instead, Pakistan would take on Australia and India would take on England. Up to this stage, the anticipated final clash between Pakistan and India at Calcutta's Eden Gardens seemed written in the stars.

We were upbeat and bursting with confidence, but we eyed our semi-final encounter with Australia cautiously. Australia had achieved some emphatic victories in the group games and appeared to be peaking at the right time.

On 4 November, we met Australia at Gaddafi Stadium in Lahore, in the first of the two semi-finals. Imran lost the toss and Australia, led by Allan Border, decided to bat first. They played with their heads down and managed to get a couple of good partnerships right up front. Their first wicket put on 73 and the second added another 82.

Then the first of two unfortunate events happened that determined the outcome of the game. Our wicketkeeper Saleem Yousuf took a ball in the mouth and had to leave the field. I was the natural substitute, having previously kept wickets in Tests, and took over from Saleem. I ended up performing wicketkeeping duties for the better part of the innings, nearly thirty overs. I gave it my best effort, conceding no byes and even managing a stumping and a close run out. The extra exertion took a lot out of me, and I would pay the price when I later came out to bat.

The other tragic development was that we were misinformed about the number of overs we could bowl. It so happened that our over rate was a little slow. Word was sent from our dressing room that since we were running behind on time, we wouldn't be allowed to bowl the full fifty overs—and therefore we should try and make sure our frontline bowlers rapidly completed their quotas.

So Imran made certain that our four top bowlers—Wasim Akram, Abdul Qadir, Tauseef Ahmed and himself—bowled out their full quotas by the 49th over; then we found out we still had to bowl the 50th over anyway.

Someone in our management had obviously got it all horribly wrong and created this incredibly stupid misunderstanding. I am also amazed that we didn't check with the umpires about the completion of overs. But I suppose being saddled with a substitute wicketkeeper and having to deal with a batting side on a roll, we were already pushed to the ropes. Once we received word of this 'problem', we just wanted to find a way out of the mess and it didn't cross our minds to check with the umpires whether there really was a problem. We never bothered to find out who had sent out that message, either. After we had lost it seemed irrelevant.

So the responsibility for bowling the 50th over fell to Saleem Jaffer, who had been played as the 'fifth' bowler. Many people have questioned Imran's decision to leave that last over to him. They are right, because it was an inexplicable decision in cricketing terms. Incredible as it seems, the only reason Jaffer was called upon is because he was the only option left.

Saleem Jaffer played fourteen Tests and thirty-nine One-Day Internationals for Pakistan in the 1980s. He was a lanky left-armer who could generate some lively medium pace, but he was inexperienced.

Jaffer's five overs earlier in the innings had conceded 39 runs. Now Steve Waugh took him apart in that 50th over and plundered it for 18 runs. In the space of the last six deliveries, the Australian total jumped from 249 to 267. From being a potentially achievable target, the task suddenly seemed impossible. It was a great psychological edge for Australia and it demoralized us completely.

During the lunch interval we tried to reassure ourselves that 268 was still an achievable score. The strategy was straightforward—make a steady start and hold on to your wickets.

It sometimes happens that one dramatic error in a match will trigger a series of misfortunes. That semi-final match against Australia proved to be such a situation. Our innings could not have got off to a worse start. Ramiz Raja was run out for 1 off the third ball of the innings. Mansoor Akhtar went for 9 and Saleem Malik went for 25, and we found ourselves reeling at 38 for 3. The heart had been ripped out of our batting before we had even crossed 40. It was now down to Imran and myself.

Imran and I eliminated risks for a while and tried to steady the innings. Gradually we put together a partnership. From 38 for 3 we took the score to 150, leaving another 118 to get at around 7 runs an over. A couple of big hitters were still to come and we thought if we could stay together for another 50 runs, we could pull off a win. Then Imran tried to sweep Allan Border and the ball went past him into wicketkeeper Greg Dyer's gloves. Border appealed and Dickie Bird gave Imran out, caught behind.

There has been some controversy whether Bird made an umpiring error on that decision. I don't think he did. In deciding on catches by close-in fielders or the wicketkeeper, a lot depends on hearing the right kind of noise. In these situations the human ear is far more reliable than the human eye. There was certainly a noise as the ball rushed past Imran's bat, and the ball had been nowhere near his pads or clothing. Perhaps the noise came from his bat brushing the ground—one can never be sure. If an umpiring mistake was made, though, I think it was an honest one.

With Imran's departure, all the pressure was on me. It was an extremely tough situation as we needed at least one boundary an over, but we couldn't take chances and hit freely either. I tried desperately to make runs but was overwhelmed with fatigue and could hardly lift my bat; those thirty overs of keeping wickets were now taking their toll.

We needed exceptional batting performances from both ends at that stage because in that exhausted condition I simply could not have done it on my own.

The lower order batsmen who followed tried hard to score. Wasim Akram came in and hit a couple of sixes, and Saleem Yousuf hit a couple of fours in his 21, but none of them could settle down. It was too much to expect of them, as the situation demanded that they come in and start hitting out right away. They just couldn't afford the luxury of trying to play themselves in.

Eventually, I had to take a chance and ended up being bowled by Bruce Reid for 70.

The final margin of defeat was 18 runs, exactly the same amount that Steve Waugh had taken off Saleem Jaffer in that fiftieth over.

That semi-final defeat in the 1987 World Cup was an intense disappointment. On paper the cricket team had lost, but it seemed that indeed the whole nation had been defeated. All around the stadium, people had tears in their eyes. It seemed our national self-esteem had been staked on the outcome of that semi-final at Lahore. Defeats like these do happen in limited-overs cricket, but there was no way to explain that to our huge national public with all the hysteria built up around our World Cup campaign. The entire Pakistani nation was inconsolable.

While luck clearly deserted us at every step in that match, you also have to hand it to Australia. It was their day. They batted beautifully and put us under pressure right from the start, capitalizing on every opportunity they got.

In the wake of that loss, people looked for explanations to help them come to terms with their heartache.

One of the theories that went around was that the Pakistan players had taken money to throw the match. This had no basis in reality but it was a convenient explanation for many people and it found some credence with the public.

The accusation came in a press statement given by Sarfraz Nawaz. It wasn't really surprising coming from him. Although Sarfraz has been a fine bowler for Pakistan, on a personal level he's always been a little strange and unpredictable.

Imran publicly denied the charges and said there had been no question of match fixing; Australia had simply been the better team that day.

Sarfraz wouldn't back off. In fact, he decided to be more specific, and went on to name me as one of the players who had been bought off.

On top of everything else, this was just too much, so I hired a lawyer and took Sarfraz to court in Lahore.

In the new set of allegations, Sarfraz also implicated my friend and Sharjah cricket visionary Abdur Rahman Bukhatir. Bukhatir had been in India and Pakistan following the World Cup and had been in Lahore for the semi-final. He was close to many people in Pakistani cricket circles and there was nothing unusual about this.

I suspect Sarfraz was motivated by his personal difficulties with Bukhatir. He had never got on with Bukhatir, who had certainly never understood Sarfraz. I think this friction probably motivated Sarfraz to concoct his far-fetched idea of a Bukhatir-Miandad match-throwing collusion.

Bukhatir, too, hired a lawyer and sued Sarfraz for libel.

For my defense, my lawyer Mr Ali Sibtain prepared a simple case documenting my performances in that semi-final match. He began by observing that I had topscored in Pakistan's innings with 70. He then pointed out that I had served as substitute wicketkeeper for 30 overs after our main wicketkeeper had been injured—something that would have been impossible for anyone to predict. He noted, moreover, that I had kept the wickets quite well, conceding no byes and even getting in a stumping and a run out. Mr Sibtain argued these were not the actions of a man trying to lose the match.

Had Javed really wanted to lose, my lawyer told the court, why would he have made the highest score and would he not have conceded at least some byes when he unexpectedly had the chance to keep wickets?

Another compelling point against Sarfraz was Saleem Jaffer's final over. I could not possibly have influenced Jaffer to give away those 18 runs, the eventual margin of defeat.

Sarfraz's charges were so fanciful and he had such a reputation for being whimsical, that many people advised me to simply ignore him and the whole affair would die down. I had to take the matter to court because I was incensed and deeply hurt. I had played for my country with unquestioned honesty and sincerity and had worked hard so that people could count on me to be a match-winner for Pakistan. I wasn't just a player for Pakistan; I was a committed Pakistani fan, too. I had been as deeply disappointed by that semi-final defeat as any other Pakistani and I didn't deserve to hear from anyone that I had thrown the match for money. What I had actually tried to do for Pakistan in that match was obvious, and the idea that I had really somehow been working against my own team was outrageous.

My lawyer's arguments were so watertight, I am sure Sarfraz and his lawyers soon realized he was going to lose.

As the case neared a decision, Saleem Asghar Mian, an influential and high-ranking officer in Pakistan's Income Tax department, approached me and asked me to let Sarfraz off.

Saleem was a friend of mine, but as he was also close to Sarfraz, he was offering to mediate.

Soon afterwards, Sarfraz's wife, Rani, also approached me. Rani was a major film actress in Pakistan and she put on quite a show. She asked me to forgive Sarfraz and to withdraw the case. With tears streaming down her cheeks, she said Sarfraz had made a mistake but he didn't know any better. She made him sound like an errant juvenile.

I wanted an apology from Sarfraz but Rani urged me not to place this condition as it wouldn't resolve the matter. Rani's pleas eventually had an effect. My lawyer was against withdrawing the case because he was certain we were going to win, but Sarfraz had some influential friends who kept getting the court to postpone the date of the hearing. It was starting to look as if things would degenerate into a stalemate. After a while my anger abated and I let the whole thing go.

The court hearings for Bukhatir's case against Sarfraz also suffered the same fate. Bukhatir then sued Sarfraz for damages in Dubai, but I understand the case has never been heard there either. It keeps Sarfraz from turning up in Dubai or Sharjah though, where he would probably get slapped with a court subpoena on his arrival.

Australia went on to win the 1987 World Cup even though we had been the favourites. England were the other finalists, having beaten India in the second semi-final at Bombay. The much-anticipated Pakistan-India final at Calcutta's Eden Gardens never came to pass. It is one of the vagaries (or one of the charms, depending on how you look at it) of limited-overs tournaments that many different outcomes are always possible. Being favourites doesn't mean much in the cricket World Cup.

Everybody agreed that Pakistan and India did a fine job hosting that fourth World Cup. The facilities, the travel arrangements, the crowds—it was all outstanding. England had hosted the first three World Cups and the English press had been reluctant to admit that Pakistan and India could do as good a job. As it turned out, Pakistan and India ended up doing it even better. The tournament proved a phenomenal success; not even the harshest critics could deny that.

Imran was disheartened after our failed World Cup bid and announced his retirement from international cricket. He said he was going to devote himself to building a cancer hospital in Lahore in memory of his late mother, who had succumbed to cancer.

After the World Cup ended, England stayed back in Pakistan to play three Tests. With Imran retired, I took over the captaincy. We were all tired and dispirited, and found it hard to get motivated. That series, in any case, is really remembered only for the infamous argument between Mike Gatting and the late Umpire Shakoor Rana, which I discuss later in Chapter 19.

Winning the World Cup in 1987 had been an important part of our vision for where we wanted to take Pakistan. One's playing years don't last forever, and I knew that a golden opportunity had been lost in Lahore. We were still a first-rate team, one of the best in the world; losing a limited-overs game didn't change that. But it still meant a lot to me to win the World Cup, and I know it also meant a great deal to Imran.

I wondered if we would be around to fight for it another day.

My father, the late
Miandad Noor Mohammed.
Miandad Collection

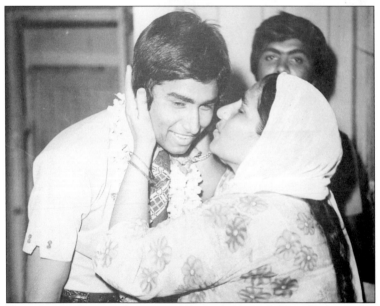

My mother sending me off on a tour of England with the Pakistan Under-19 side in 1974. *Miandad Collection*

My father (*seated 2nd from left, 2nd row*) as sports minister in Palanpur, a princely state that is now part of India. Others in the picture are the Nawab of Palanpur (*seated centre, 2nd row*) and his staff. *Miandad Collection*

My father with other KCA members on the occasion of a Test match at Karachi (early 1960s). From L to R: A.K. Majeed, Dalpat Sonavaria, Essa Jaffer, Lala, Amir Elahi, Adam Ali Alvi, Miandad Noor Mohammed and Usman Bhagat. *Miandad Collection*

With my father (L) and Mr A.R. Mahmood (R), the two big influences on my career (1969).
Miandad Collection

Being honoured by KCA for selection into the Pakistan Under-19 squad headed for England in 1974.
Miandad Collection

One-day International debut against West Indies, the first World Cup, June 1975. (Fielder is Bernard Julien, wicketkeeper is Derryck Murray.)
Miandad Collection

Cricketers from Pakistan and India mixing during the opening ceremony of the 1975 World Cup. Shafiq Papa (L) and I are crouching in the front. Others, standing left to right: Sadiq Mohammed, Abid Ali; Wasim Raja, Bishen Singh Bedi, Naseer Malik, Anshuman Gaekwad, Kersan Ghavri, Madan Lal, Gundappa Vishwanath, Eknath Solkar, Sunil Gavaskar, and Zaheer Abbas. (Sarfraz Nawaz is also seen, partly obscured behind Abid Ali).

Photo courtesy
M. Athar Chaudhry

The team into which I made my Test debut (1976-77). Seated L to R: Saleem Altaf, Majid Khan, Asif Iqbal, Mushtaq Mohammed (captain), Intikhab Alam, Wasim Bari, and Zaheer Abbas. Standing L to R: Sadiq Mohammed, Sikander Bakht, Taslim Arif, Wasim Raja, Mudassar Nazar, Asif Masood, Sarfraz Nawaz, Haroon Rasheed, Imran Khan, myself, and Iqbal Qasim. *Miandad Collection*

The Sussex team under the captaincy of Tony Greig (1978). Seated L to R: Peter Graves, Tony Greig (captain), John Snow, and Roger Knight. Standing L to R: Arnold Long, Paul Parker, J. Spencer, C.P. Phillipson, Michael Buss, J.R.T. Barclay, C.E. Waller, and myself. *Photo courtesy Bill Smith*

Returning to the pavilion after making my first Test double-hundred—206 against
New Zealand at Karachi in 1976-77.
Miandad Collection

Mr A.R. Wadiwalla—founder of the Habib Bank cricket team—
flanked by Mohsin Hasan Khan (L) and myself, 1975-76 season.
Miandad Collection

In Australia on my first Test tour with Pakistan, with Ian Chappell (L) and Richie
Benaud (1976-77). *Miandad Collection*

Bowling leg-breaks: I have just had Alan Turner caught by Sarfraz in the first Test against Australia at Adelaide, 1976-77.
Miandad Collection

With Sir Garfield Sobers. (Pakistan's tour of West Indies, 1976-77). *Miandad Collection*

With Asif Iqbal, on our arrival in Australia for the 1976-77 tour. *Miandad Collection*

Captain of Pakistan, 3rd Test against West Indies at Karachi, 1980-81. Seated L to R: Imran Khan, Zaheer Abbas, Wasim Bari, myself, Majid Khan, Sadiq Mohammed, and Wasim Raja. Standing L to R: Rashid Khan, Shafiq Papa, Ejaz Faqih, Mohammad Nazir, Iqbal Qasim, and Rizwan-uz-Zaman. *Photo courtesy Messrs. Foto King*

With my friend Jimmy Irani (L) and his son Ronnie, 1976. I spent a lot of time at the Iranis' residence and would bowl in their backyard to Ronnie, who has gone on to play for England. *Miandad Collection*

At a society affair that also attracted film stars from India and Pakistan (1979). Standing with me, from L to R: Manoj Kumar and Dev Anand (Indian film stars), Mrs Manoj Kumar, Zeba and Mohammad Ali (Pakistani film stars). *Miandad Collection*

With Dennis Lillee during Pakistan's 1981-82 tour of Australia. We made up not long after my well-publicized run-in with him (Chapter 19), and I consider him a friend. *Miandad Collection*

Imitating Dennis Lillee's bowling action during the third Test at Adelaide in 1983-84. It was a big hit with the crowd. *Miandad Collection*

Another controversial incident—the run out of Rodney Hogg (Chapter 19) in the first Test at Melbourne, 1978-79. Wasim Bari looks on. *Photo courtesy Iqbal Munir*

On my way to a century in each innings, second against New Zealand at Hyderabad, 1984-85. The wicketkeeper is Ian Smith and the fielder is Jeff Crowe. *Photo courtesy Zafar Ahmed*

Glamorgan days—returning to the pavilion after making 200 not out against the visiting Australians at Neath. (1985). *Photo courtesy Nickolas O'Neil*

Being congratulated by Zaheer Abbas after reaching my hundred, third Test against Australia at Adelaide, 1983-84. *Miandad Collection*

Captains of the seven teams participating in the Benson and Hedges World Championship of Cricket hosted by Australia, February-March 1985. From L to R: David Gower (England), Javed Miandad (Pakistan), Clive Lloyd (West Indies), Allan Border (Australia), Sunil Gavaskar (India), Geoff Howarth (New Zealand), and Duleep Mendis (Sri Lanka). *Photo courtesy Iqbal Munir*

One of my most pleasurable innings—260 against England at the Oval in 1987.
Photos courtesy Iqbal Munir

With my dear friend Abdur Rahman Bukhatir, the man responsible for the Sharjah cricket miracle. *Miandad Collection*

The winning six at Sharjah, Austral-Asia Cup final against India, April 1986. Tauseef Ahmed is the other batsman. *Photo courtesy Iqbal Munir*

With my wife, Tahira (1985). *Photo courtesy Iqbal Munir*

With my sons, Jahangir (L) and Junaid, (1997). *Photo courtesy Iqbal Munir*

Meeting President Ziaul Haq in Islamabad, after victory at Sharjah over India in the 1986 Austral-Asia Cup.
Miandad Collection

Glamorgan days—this one with the Duke of Edinburgh, an astute cricket fan.
Also seen are Jeff Holmes (to my right) and Rodney Ontong.
Miandad Collection

Imran and I, 1987.
Miandad Collection

Exercising my back—a chronic problem that recurred off and on.
Photo courtesy Iqbal Munir

Past point—my favourite shot.
Photo courtesy Iqbal Munir

Awards ceremony at the Oval after Pakistan's 2-1 series victory in England in 1992. Also seen are Pakistan cricket officials Lt. Gen. Zahid Ali Akbar (in the doorway), Khalid Mahmood (in sports jacket, to my right) and my son Junaid.
Miandad Collection

As coach during the awards ceremony at a Cable and Wireless limited-overs match (West Indies, May 2000). Moin Khan is to my right and Shoaib Akhtar has his arm slung over my shoulder. The crew-cuts reflect the jovial mood of the trip. *Miandad Collection*

With the Indian prime minister Atal Bihari Vajpayee during Pakistan's famous 1998-99 tour of India. *Photo courtesy Kamal Sharma*

Urging Imran not to lose heart after losing our Round Robin match against South Africa following a rain interruption (1992 World Cup).
Photo courtesy Iqbal Munir

With Imran, moments after semi-final victory over New Zealand, World Cup 1992. Also seen are the two heroes of that tournament—Wasim Akram (to Imran's left) and Inzamamul Haq (to Wasim's left). *Photo courtesy Iqbal Munir*

Dressing room scene after winning in the 1992 World Cup. L to R: Imran Khan, Iqbal Sikander, Asif Iqbal, myself, Zahid Fazal, Aamir Sohail, and Inzamamul Haq. *Photo courtesy Iqbal Munir*

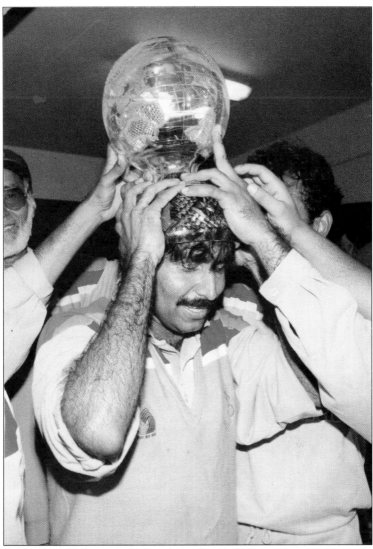

Celebrating with the Waterford crystal trophy, World Cup 1992.
Photo courtesy Iqbal Munir

Victory lap in front of a sell-out Melbourne crowd, 1992 World Cup final. *Photo courtesy Iqbal Munir*

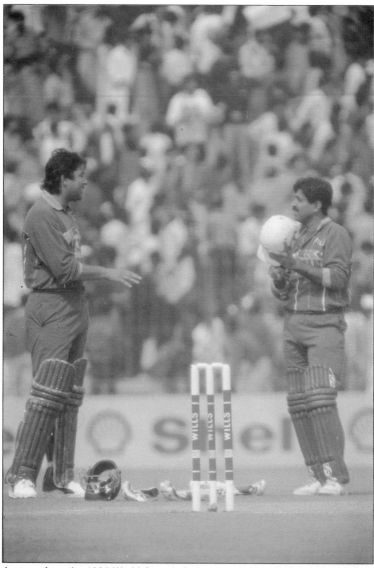

A scene from the 1996 World Cup, during a partnership with Inzamamul Haq.
Photo courtesy Iqbal Munir

Farewell to my hometown—my last international match at Karachi (versus England, World Cup 1996). *Photo courtesy Iqbal Munir*

Tit for Tat with the West Indies

This chapter is about supremacy in world cricket. In the mid-1980s, Pakistan and the West Indies vied with each other for the number one ranking in cricket. The West Indies thought they were the best, we thought otherwise. To sort it out, the two teams locked horns in a six-Test battle spread over two seasons—first in Pakistan, then in the West Indies.

The first part of the contest was in the 1986-87 home season in Pakistan when the West Indies visited for three Tests and five One-Day Internationals. The second part of the contest would come late in the 1987-88 season, when Pakistan paid a return visit for three Tests and five One-Day Internationals in the West Indies.

The West Indies were very formidable opponents. The team that came to Pakistan in November 1986 included names that were already legends, like Viv Richards, Malcolm Marshall, Gordon Greenidge and Desmond Haynes. Middle-order batsman Richie Richardson and wicketkeeper-batsman Peter Dujon were also there, both possessing exceptional ability. One of the visitors was a young Courtney Walsh, then in the early phase of his career, but with all the determination that would eventually get him a record 500 Test wickets.

An important feature of the series was the introduction of neutral umpires at both ends. In the second and third Tests of that series, two experienced Test umpires from India officiated, Umpires P.D. Reporter and V.K. Ramaswamy. This was a unilateral move on our part. The rationale was straightforward—we were tired of visitors to Pakistan complaining about the Pakistani umpiring and blaming this for their defeats.

We had been campaigning for neutral umpires (umpires are always meant to be 'neutral'—what I really mean is third country umpires) for a long time prior to that series. Many visiting teams had been defeated in Pakistan, but the world still remained reluctant to acknowledge that it was because of our superior cricket. Rather than accept defeat gracefully, it was much easier to blame the umpiring, and that's what everyone did.

In Pakistan, we felt our umpires were neither better nor worse than many of the umpires we came across around the world, including England and Australia. We had lost patience with all the complaints about umpiring in Pakistan. If we were going to defeat the West Indies, we wanted to do so without giving them a convenient excuse to fall back on.

The West Indies were the undisputed kings of world cricket in those days. They had reached the top under the leadership of Clive Lloyd in the 1970s, and their domination continued during the reign of Vivian Richards in the 1980s. In the years preceding that 1986-87 series in Pakistan, they had been on the rampage, marching from one conquest to the next. Of the thirty Tests they played prior to visiting Pakistan that season, they had won twenty-one and lost just one. The victories had included two 5-0 'blackwashes' against England, and series wins abroad in England, India and Australia. It was a phenomenal run of successes.

Our record had been nothing like the West Indian one, but still we fancied our chances against them. After the Austral-Asia Cup victory in Sharjah in the spring of 1986 we were mentally a new team. We had a new confidence, and we felt that the graph of Pakistan's cricketing fortunes was on the rise. We thought we might challenge the West Indies as the best team in world cricket, and we anticipated the West Indian visit in 1986-87 as an opportunity to test our hopes and capabilities.

That series was the first order of business for us in the 1986-87 season, coming before our trip to India. It ended up being an exciting series with some fantastic cricket played by both sides.

The final result was 1-1, which was accurate enough because the two sides were very evenly matched.

I thought the neutral umpires served an extremely important role. We no longer felt guilty nor felt the need to explain anything if the umpiring decisions appeared to favour us. Nor did we feel victimized by the umpires if they made a decision we didn't like; we just put up with it as part of the game. It was easy to do because there was no reason to doubt the umpires' impartiality. I think the third country umpires are a major reason that such a keenly fought series between two aggressive teams remained free of controversy. The value of third country umpires has finally been recognized throughout the cricket world, but we started it all, back in 1986-87.

One of the remarkable things about that home series against the West Indies is that none of the players reached triple figures, which was very unusual for a series played in Pakistan. The highest individual score for the West Indies was 88 not out, made by Haynes in the third Test, and for Pakistan the highest individual score was mine, 76 (run out), also made in the third Test. The average score for a completed innings in that series was only 173, which confirms the high quality of bowling in both teams.

The other interesting thing was that at some point during that series both the West Indies and Pakistan were dismissed for under 100.

We were bowled out for 77 in the second innings of the second Test, which we lost by an innings. It remains our lowest score in Pakistan.

The West Indians suffered even greater embarrassment. In the first Test, we set West Indies a fourth innings target of 240 to win the match. We were playing in Faisalabad, known to be a batting track, but on this occasion a turning wicket had been prepared. We thought 240 was a fighting target, but before we knew it the West Indians were bundled out for 53, a figure that remained their lowest Test score for many years. Abdul Qadir was in his element and returned figures of 9.3-1-16-6 in that innings.

I also remember that first Test for a personal duel that was played out between Imran Khan and Malcolm Marshall. We had batted first and Imran had made the highest score in our innings with a determined 61. During this innings, Marshall had bounced him a few times and the two had exchanged some hot words. When Imran returned to the dressing room he was fuming, and he told our bowlers to have a go at Marshall when he came out to bat. Sure enough, when it was his turn, Marshall received some torrid short-pitched stuff from Wasim Akram and edged one to Saleem Yousuf after making only 5.

However, the most memorable thing about that Test remains Qadir's bowling. He made the most of the spinning track and brought the mighty West Indies to their knees.

The second Test was played at Lahore and turned out to be another low-scoring game. West Indies won by an innings even though they scored only 218 in their only outing.

In the third Test, honours were shared. West Indies made 240, we made 239. Then West Indies made 211 and set us 213 to win late on the fourth day. It was a tough task, and we were already 16 for 2 when the fourth day ended. Early the next morning, I was bowled by a Marshall beauty for only 4. There was still a lot of fight left in our team, and we managed to hang on for a draw. The match ended with our innings at 125 for 7, terminated before time because of bad light. Thankfully, it was neutral third country umpires who had offered us the light, and nobody questioned the decision.

The five limited-overs games had been played prior to the Test series. West Indies dominated all but the last match and took the series 4-1. I have some interesting memories from one of those games—the second One-Day International of the series, played in the Punjab town of Gujranwala. Imran wasn't playing in that match and I was captain.

I won the toss and invited the West Indies to bat, restricting them to 196-7 from 50 overs. In response, we had slipped to 75-6. Then our plucky wicketkeeper Saleem Yousuf came to join me for the seventh wicket. I was feeling very comfortable at the

crease and, with Saleem stabilizing the other end, we started
approaching the target.

But the West Indians had bowled an extremely slow over-
rate, and as dusk approached, there were 8 or 9 overs still to go.
Gujranwala was not a frontline stadium and didn't have artificial
lights. Once the sun dips, light goes very quickly in our part of
the world, and pretty soon darkness had fallen. From nearby
mosques the call for *maghrib* prayers echoed, signalling sunset.
Outside the ground, one could see the lights coming on in the
shops and on the streets. The light was so bad one could not
follow the cricket on television, but still I kept making my
shots.

The West Indians were firing all guns with their fast-bowling
battery, but I had found a rhythm and was timing the ball without
difficulty. It came to the point that the West Indian fielders
were complaining they couldn't see the balls I was smashing
their way, and they were afraid of being unsighted and getting
hurt in a misfield. Since I was seeing the ball fine and edging
my team to victory, I had little sympathy with the fielders'
complaints. I thought if anyone should be worried about the
light, it should be the batsman, and if the light was fine by me,
well then everyone should just get on with the game.

The Laws certainly allow stoppage of play if bad light poses
a risk to any player. But it is really the batsmen's opinion about
the light that matters. As far as I know there is no precedent for
an international game having been stopped because the fielders
complained about the light.

For a while the West Indians persisted. It was so dark I am
sure they felt I would be getting out any minute. Frankly, I
think they were quite baffled. Finally, Viv lodged a formal
protest with the umpires. He was actually quite persuasive as he
said—referring to me—that the batsman was seeing the ball
from 22 yards but the poor fielders had to spot it from as far
away as 75 yards.

I knew exactly what Viv was talking about for I had been
targeting the third man and fine leg fielders and could tell from
their body language that they were completely unsighted. I knew

they couldn't tell if the ball was lofted or not, or if it was even coming towards them at all.

Viv's arguments forced the two umpires to confer, and they decided to abandon the match in the interest of the fielders' safety. West Indies won on a faster scoring rate.

When the match was stopped, we still needed another 42 to win from 37 balls. I was batting on 74 and timing cover drives blindly but felt in total control. I am confident I could have won that game for Pakistan had we continued.

I regretted conceding that game, but we were in a difficult spot being the host country and having our own umpires officiating at the game (the Indian umpires only stood in the Tests). The West Indians were our guests after all. Pakistani culture lays great importance on going out of your way for your guests, so we gave in.

That series ended in late November 1986, and the return series in the West Indies would not start until March 1988.

During this time Pakistan, as I have already recounted in the preceding pages, won their first Test series in India and in England. We were favourites for the 1987 World Cup but lost in the semi-finals to Australia, the eventual champions. And after that we beat England 1-0 in a 3-Test home series that is better known for the Gatting-Rana affair.

West Indies in this interval drew a three-Test series 1-1 in New Zealand and then drew a four-Test series 1-1 in India. They were out of sorts in the 1987 World Cup and failed to make the semi-finals.

Pakistan had made two previous tours to West Indies, in 1957-58 and in 1976-77. We managed to win a Test match on both trips, but lost the series on each occasion. In 1957-58, we lost 1-2 a five-Test rubber that was rich in records. Hanif Mohammed made 337 and Gary Sobers made his record 365 not out in different Tests during that series. In 1976-77, too we lost by the same tally a five-Test rubber. This was my first tour to West Indies, although I played in only the first Test after which I was dropped for being out of form.

The 1987-88 series against Pakistan was going to be the first home series for West Indies in two years as they didn't host any teams the previous season in 1986-87. I have already mentioned the amazing record that had created their tremendous reputation. West Indies hadn't lost a single Test series in eight years, not since they had lost a three-Test series 0-1 in New Zealand in 1979-80. And they hadn't lost at home for an incredible fifteen years. One had to go as far back as 1972-73 to find a home loss for West Indies, when they lost a three-Test series 0-2 to Ian Chappell's Australians.

We were now going to be engaging West Indies on their home turf with home umpires—a set of circumstances that made them, for all intents and purposes, invincible.

It was going to be a great challenge for Pakistan, and I knew it was going to be an even greater challenge for me. I had been able to make runs almost everywhere in the world now, but the ultimate test of my cricket mettle awaited in the form of the West Indian bowling attack on its own hunting grounds.

My team would fight the battle for world supremacy but I had chalked out for this series a personal battle of my own. I was going to be batting against the West Indies, but in my personal battle I was really going to be batting against my own expectations and the standards that I had set for myself.

I told myself I would deliver here in the West Indies if I was truly good enough. These were the stakes, pure and simple.

I had painstakingly built a reputation as a match-winner for Pakistan, and if that reputation was worth anything, I had to come good now in the West Indies. If I failed Pakistan now, all my previous achievements would mean little. If I really was the batsman I thought I had become, I would deliver for Pakistan and bring home my team victorious.

I can say without hesitation that that series in West Indies in 1987-88 represents absolutely the toughest cricket I have ever played in my life. It was real tit-for-tat, in your face, no holds barred cricket. The competition was brutal, with no mercy expected and none shown. In fact, the real contest was mental. The West Indian bowlers were on a roll and I played mind games with them to try and bait them into bowling a loose one. If they bounced me, I taunted them for more: 'Come on, show me what you've got'. It was the most closely fought series I've ever played in. We played our hearts out, but in the end, some controversial umpiring kept us from winning the series.

After that series, I finally came to terms with my insecurities about scoring overseas. The comments from my detractors finally ceased, apart from one or two cynics whom I would never win over. All the incessant carping about my batting that used to so rile me, stopped meaning anything to me now.

Imran, whose opinion mattered, had always been reluctant to hand it to me as a batsman. But after West Indies in 1987-88, he did. I thought his respect was long overdue, but if it took my batting in that series to finally convince him, that was fine by me. It wasn't something he said; he didn't have to. You can always tell when you've finally won someone's respect.

We came to West Indies with only one thing in mind— victory. We held nothing back and played the best cricket we possibly could. The question is, did we win? The scoresheets show we didn't, but I would argue that we did, at least in spirit. The reason our victory doesn't show up in the record books is that a number of crucial umpiring decisions went against us. We had invited neutral umpires to officiate when West Indies visited Pakistan in 1986-87, but on our visit to West Indies in 1987-88 our hosts didn't return the gesture. The Tests were officiated by West Indian umpires, and it remains an open question how 'neutral' they really were. The television replays are clear-cut and leave little room for doubt about what really happened.

That clash attracted the entire cricket world's attention. As I have said above, the West Indies had not lost a series in eight years and not lost a series at home in fifteen. People were saying if anyone could beat them at home, it would be this Pakistan team. The West Indians themselves admitted as much. We had always troubled them, and they said Pakistan was the only team with the potential not just to beat them, but to beat them at home.

The two teams had astonishing talents, but they were also evenly matched. Both teams played the same brand of cricket—aggressive, attacking, with no room for mercy. Both had bowlers who could rip it through and weren't shy to bounce, and both had batsmen who could hook like naturals. Both sides had a wicketkeeper who would throw himself everywhere and bat his heart out when needed, and both sides included young, agile fielders. And if the West Indies had a captain who led from the front, so did we.

Imran had announced his retirement from cricket after the 1987 World Cup fiasco, but he was now back to assume the captaincy for the tour to West Indies. I had long ago come to terms with having to vacate the captaincy whenever Imran was available, and had no difficulties in stepping aside. His retirement had been premature and emotionally motivated, and I think he also realized that his campaign for a cancer hospital in Lahore would be better served if he continued in international cricket. West Indies in 1987-88 was a crucial tour and we were all glad to have him back.

The tour started with the five One-Day Internationals. This part of the series was somewhat one-sided as we lost all five matches. I, nevertheless, had a reasonable time with the bat, and posted scores of 47, 24, 17, 59 and 100 not out. (The last innings happened to be the first limited-overs century by a Pakistani against West Indies.)

We didn't let defeat in the One-Day International series affect our approach towards the Tests. We knew we didn't have a limited-overs side to challenge West Indies on their home grounds, but it would be different in the Tests.

We moved to Georgetown, Guyana, for the first Test, which began on 2 April 1988. West Indies won the toss and batted, and by the end of the day Imran had taken 7 for 80 and removed them for 292.

Now I had my part to play. A good first innings lead was essential. Everyone was relying on me to be the anchor around whom our innings would be built. The situation had put great pressure on me, but I had put even greater pressure on myself. As I walked out to bat with the score at 57 for 2, I knew I just had to deliver—alternatives didn't exist.

The West Indian bowling artillery included the lethal pair of Walsh and Ambrose, who would eventually become the highest and second-highest wicket-takers in West Indian history. Patrick Patterson and Winston Benjamin provided the supporting fire.

Right away, I was greeted by some highly accurate short-pitched stuff. The balls would zip past my head and the bowlers would square their shoulders and glare down the track at me. It was hostile body language that left nothing to the imagination.

It was just the stimulus I needed to raise my game. I started taunting the bowlers. I pointed at my chest to Ambrose: 'Try and hit me and I'll show you,' I told him when he dug another one near his feet.

The bowlers made me fight for every run. It was a brutal combat, as they tried to knock me down and push me out of the way, but the harder they tried, the tighter I held on.

As my innings progressed, everyone's verbal language got more colourful as well. The bowlers began to go wild. Winston Benjamin bowled an over in which he delivered six bouncers at me straight, each with a healthy dose of expletives. Shoaib Mohammad was at the non-striker's end when Winston unleashed this torrent. Shoaib came down the wicket to tell me that Winston was deliberately no-balling himself, releasing the ball some yards past the bowling crease, trying desperately to bowl as threatening a delivery as he possibly could. Bouncers from 22 yards were bad enough, but I had to endure them from 18 yards. West Indies bowled no less than 38 no-balls in that innings and ended up conceding as many as 71 extras, which created a new world record.

I ended the second day not out on 96. Early the third morning I got my 100, and made 114 before being bowled by Patterson. Saleem Yousuf made an inspired 62 and Shoaib Mohammed, who had come in at no. 3, contributed a solid 46, as we made 435 and went 143 runs past the West Indian first innings. It was a punishing lead, and the West Indies were barely able to make us bat again. We won by 9 wickets. It was the first time in ten years that the West Indies had lost a Test at home.

That 114 at Georgetown is very dear to my heart. My memories of it are dominated by the hostile circumstances under which I made that century. It was easily the hardest hundred I have ever made. Everything about that innings was a fight, each run had been snatched with a struggle. The bowling, the attitude, the stakes, the responsibility—it had all been very tough going, but it was the kind of atmosphere I have always thrived in.

We then went to Queen's Park Oval in Port-of-Spain, Trinidad, for the second Test. It was another intense Test match—a draw, but only just. Going into the final session of the final day, either team could've won.

Imran put the West Indies in and he and Qadir took 4 wickets apiece to wrap up the West Indian innings at 174. We were anxious to get a good first innings lead, but by the end of the day we had been reduced to 50 for 5, and our eventual lead was only 20. In the West Indian second innings, Viv Richards and Jeffrey Dujon made centuries to then set us a fourth innings target of 372 with a day-and-a-half to spare.

It was an extremely tall order to get in the fourth innings, which is by far the toughest time to bat in a Test match. Had we achieved that target, it would've been the third-highest total ever to win a Test match.

What made the target especially difficult was that Malcolm Marshall was now back. He had had to sit out the Georgetown Test with injury but was back in full force in this second Test at Port-of-Spain. It made the West Indian bowling even stronger.

Pakistan had never made anything close to 372 in the fourth innings of a Test. Our highest fourth innings score at the time was 301 (after being set 442 to win), made against the West Indies at Kingston in 1976-77. It was the only time we had crossed 300 in the fourth innings of a Test match.

But this was a different Pakistan team and we took on the challenge. I understood my obligations to the team. The way I saw it, they went well beyond just making runs. I was nervous about the target we faced, but I had to appear confident. There's nothing like the determination of the senior players to lift a team's morale.

We nearly won. When the twenty mandatory overs began in the final hour of play, I was still at the wicket and getting good support from Ijaz Ahmed at the other end. Then luck deserted us. Ijaz was stumped off Richards's off-spin for 43, and soon afterwards, Richards caught me off Ambrose after I had made 102. It was deeply disappointing. I tried to take it in my stride: If you win some, you have to lose some as well.

West Indies surely smelled blood after taking my wicket, but we never gave up the fight. Our final pair of Ijaz Faqih and Abdul Qadir hung on and we drew the match making 341 for 9, which remains the highest fourth innings total ever by Pakistan.

Then on to Bridgetown, Barbados, for the third Test. One-up in the series, we couldn't lose the series from that point, but this made no difference to us. We were always going to play to win. We wanted total victory above anything else.

Things remained neck and neck. Richards put us in and we made 309 in the first innings. West Indies responded with 306. Then Marshall took 5 for 65 as we set West Indies a fighting fourth innings target of 266.

We got them down to 207 for 8, and would've wrapped up the game, but a couple of crucial umpiring decisions robbed us of a deserved victory. West Indies eventually achieved their target and tied the series 1-1.

It was a great boost to have Imran back for this series. He bowled some fine spells and led from the front. I think that series also lifted Imran's spirits and made it easier for him to continue playing international cricket for the next few seasons— the seasons in which Imran oversaw the development of Wasim Akram and Waqar Younis to whom he passed on the torch.

Umpiring interventions aside, those three Tests in the West Indies in the spring of 1988 were a phenomenal series and attracted a great deal of media attention from around the world. It probably represents some of the best cricket that's ever been played anywhere.

CHAPTER 15

In Search of 365

I was well into my Test career by the mid-1980s, but I still had critics who said I was only good for home wickets and couldn't score outside Pakistan. The criticism was difficult to bear. I took it as a challenge. I decided I would not rest until all my critics had been convinced otherwise.

Cricket is the best game in the world. It is a game of skill and strategy, but most of all it is a game of character. The difference between a good and a great cricketer is not one of skill but of character. A number of qualities have to come together for this. It takes a lot more than just knowing how to handle bat or ball. You have to understand the game and know what it means, but ultimately you have to understand yourself and be true to yourself. That's the way to excel at cricket. And once you've really excelled at cricket, what else is there?

To be a good batsman, you have to get into the bowler's mind. You have to figure out his plan and the pattern of his reactions so that you can always stay one step ahead of him. Brilliant shots happen when a batsman has been able to predict a bowler's moves and correctly anticipate the trajectory of the deliveries almost before they have even been bowled.

I used to get away with playing risky shots like cuts, late-cuts and reverse sweeps because I had figured out the bowler's thinking and knew the next ball he was going to bowl. It is the ultimate batting weapon to get into the bowler's mind, because then you can start playing with his head. For example, if someone kept up a nagging off-stump line against me and it was starting to bother me, I would expose my leg stump and make him change his line to try and upset his rhythm.

You've always got to keep the fielding side unsettled, too. The fielding captain should never be allowed to feel satisfied with the field he's set for you. As a batsman you have the power to move the fielders around. If you want a position opened up, you can play in a way that will deceive the fielding captain into thinking his man there is being wasted. I would sometimes play uppish shots in a vacant area just so the field would get adjusted, which sometimes opened up a part of the ground I was hoping to score in.

You've also got to have a very good idea of your own limitations. If you come across a bowler in top-flight who is going to get you out, you have to accept that reality and take calculated risks to maximize your scoring prior to the inevitable dismissal.

A good batsman has to be creative and must never stop thinking. If you think fast enough, no one will be able to figure you out and fielding and bowling traps will be ineffective.

I strongly feel that great batsmen are born, not made. Training can make an average batsman into a good one, but training alone cannot make a good batsman great. Greatness requires instinctive gifts. But even instinct and inspiration alone are not enough, though. You have to develop your gifts in the right way. Allah bestows talent on many, but not everyone knows what to do with it.

Cricket is ultimately an unequal game with respect to bowlers and batsmen. In a way, bowlers have it easier than the batsmen. As a bowler, you get many chances to do well. If you bowl a bad ball and get hit for a boundary, there is always an opportunity to try and make up for it by doing better with the next ball. There is no such luxury for a batsman. In batting, one mistake and you're gone.

Another thing about bowling is that you don't have to bowl at seasoned batsmen all the time. Sooner or later you'll get to bowl at a tail-ender, who will be much lighter opposition. Batsmen, in contrast, have to face regular bowlers always or almost always. The game's rules require everyone in the team to bat, including those who bat poorly, but not everyone is required to bowl. Indeed those who bowl poorly don't have to bowl at all. Yet every player has to bat, regardless of how well they can or can't do it. So while bowlers enjoy the concession of bowling to poor batsmen, batsmen never have the opportunity to face the poorest bowlers in a side.

Batting also involves luck to a greater extent than bowling does. It is very unusual for a great delivery to be put away for a boundary because it will invariably trouble the batsman. But a great shot doesn't always get runs. You could play the most attractive shot in the book, but it can always be unpredictably plucked out of the air by an athletic fielder who's having a good day. What you felt was a beautifully timed square-cut could end up being responsible for your dismissal.

These realities make it harder for batsmen to earn recognition compared to bowlers. Don't get me wrong—bowling is very hard work and it obviously takes great skill to pull off a notable bowling feat such as a five-wicket haul. But you could have made a number of errors along the way, and still if you just manage to send down five unplayable balls, that would be good enough for you to end up with your five-wicket haul. A comparable feat in batting would be to make a century, but that typically takes four hours of concentrated effort, during which no mistakes are allowed. There are many more chances to fail if you're a batsman, than if you're a bowler. It is a delicious inequality in the two major departments of the game.

I would not be the one to say if I was a talented or accomplished batsman. That is for others to decide. But good batsmanship is something I always aspired to, and I wanted to use it in the service of my country.

As a batsman, one sometimes goes through a lean patch, when nothing seems to work. You use the same technique and try your best to concentrate and learn from experience, but still you keep struggling. At other times, everything seems to come together nicely and you start to wonder what all the fuss was about.

My best period as a batsman came in the years 1987 through 1989, ten years after I had made my Test debut and after I had lost some of the impetuosity of the early years. I was older and perhaps my reflexes were not as sharp as before, but experience gathered against the best bowlers of the day may have made up for that.

A lot of my batting ambition during this time came from wanting to create a new world record for the highest individual score in Test cricket, which at the time was Gary Sobers's 365 not out made as long ago as 1957-58.

I had in fact dreamed about this king of all cricket records from my earliest playing days. But after I had been forced to end my innings at 280 not out against India in 1982-83, I realized for the first time that this achievement could actually be within my grasp. Declaring that innings closed was the best favour Imran Khan ever did for me. It gave me that extra hunger for huge innings.

After that knock of 280 not out against India, the next time I felt that 365 was within reach was when I made 260 at the Oval against England in 1987 (Chapter 12). A relative run drought had preceded that score, as I had gone the previous nineteen innings without making a hundred. Then, too, I wasn't getting any younger. After the Oval innings, I knew I had to keep trying for 365, but I also knew I couldn't keep trying forever.

For nineteen months beginning with the Oval Test, I made 1,431 runs from sixteen innings at an average of 89.44, including seven 100s, of which three were double centuries. This was the sequence:

260	fifth Test vs. England at the Oval, 1987
65	first Test vs. England at Lahore, 1987-88
19	second Test vs. England at Faisalabad, 1987-88
4	third Test vs. England at Karachi, 1987-88
114	first Test vs. West Indies at Georgetown, 1987-88
18 & 102	second Test vs. West Indies at Port-of-Spain, 1987-88
14 & 34	third Test vs. West Indies at Bridgetown, 1987-88
211	first Test vs. Australia at Karachi, 1988-89

43 & 107	second Test vs. Australia at Faisalabad, 1988-89
27 & 24	third Test vs. Australia at Lahore, 1988-89
118	first Test vs. New Zealand at Wellington, 1988-89
271	second Test vs. New Zealand at Auckland, 1988-89

I have already gone over that intense series in the West Indies in the spring of 1988. I had no commitments for the summer of 1988, and I spent it in England playing league cricket.

In September 1988, Australia visited Pakistan for three Tests. I was made captain because Imran declined to play. The series was hastily arranged and accommodated the Australian schedule by taking place before the start of the regular season in Pakistan. Imran took the stand that it should never have happened. I think an important reason for Imran's inflexibility was that his relations with the Pakistan Cricket Board had soured. This emerged later, when the Board asked me to continue as captain following that Australian series.

We won that three-Test series 1-0. But, as had become the pattern in Pakistan cricket, a winning captain was changed yet again. The Board asked me to continue, but Imran wanted the captaincy back. Things could have turned ugly. I had stepped aside before to accommodate Imran and I did so again.

It was a strange arrangement, but I had become used to this charade while captaining Pakistan. Imran was always able to call on me when he was captain; but when I was captain, I didn't have the same luxury. Imran played in only 13 of the 34 Tests that I captained. Yet I played in all but 2 of the 48 Tests in which he led the team. Yet both of us won the same number of Tests for Pakistan—fourteen. I was present in each one of Imran's Test victories, but he was present in only five of mine. All of his wins came from a full-strength team, while more than half of mine came from a team with a second-string bowling attack from which our best bowler was missing. One of us had the pick of his team; the other had to make the most of whatever he was given, and yet we both won the same number of Tests.

It was a strong Australian side that visited Pakistan that season. Border was captain, and he was leading some star players including Geoff Marsh, David Boon, Dean Jones, Graeme Wood, Steve Waugh, and Bruce Reid. Australia's great Ian Healy, who would go on to become the most successful Test wicketkeeper ever, made his Test debut in that series. Yet one got the feeling that the Australians' heart wasn't in the game. It was as if they had just come to pass the time.

In Imran's absence, I decided to have spinning wickets prepared. We won the first Test by an innings. My 211 from that Test is the highest individual innings at Karachi, my hometown. We had made 469 in the first innings but had batted into the third day. We needed to have the Australians follow on if there was going to be any chance of a victory.

Wasim Akram was unfit, so Aamer Malik and Mudassar Nazar opened our attack with military medium.

Our real bowling strength lay in spin, in the form of Iqbal Qasim, Abdul Qadir and Tauseef Ahmed. These three were bowlers of exceptional class and it was a joy to direct them. I saw it as a marriage of my mind and their bowling arms. I would set the field with great attention to detail, and tell them what I wanted them to do—where to pitch, how much to flight, when to mix in their variations—all depending on how I was reading the batsman and his reactions. These spinners were professionals of the highest calibre and complied with my plans beautifully. It brought results for Pakistan.

Iqbal Qasim was at his best in that Test; of his nine wickets in the match, all but one belonged to top-order batsmen, and he conceded only 84 runs in the process. Qasim's great talent was laser-accuracy, as he could repeatedly pitch the ball at the same square-inch of turf, delivery after delivery after delivery. It could be sheer torture for the batsmen.

Tauseef Ahmed was extremely accurate too, but spinning in the other direction. He bowled finger-spinning off-breaks that were the mirror image to Iqbal Qasim's orthodox left-arm spin.

Tauseef was a shining example of Pakistan cricket's disregard for system and procedure. In the 1979-80 season, he had walked into the Pakistan Test side literally as a nobody off the street. In the build-up to an Australian visit for a three-Test series that season, a training camp had been held at Karachi. It was going to be my first series as captain (narrated in Chapter 5).

As the camp got underway, a friend of mine Riaz Malik, called to say he had come across an amazing bowler and wanted to send him over to play in the nets with the Pakistan team. One often receives such solicitations, and they are usually disregarded. But I knew Riaz to be a successful businessman and a keen cricket enthusiast, who was also managing a competent club side in Karachi, so I told him to send the boy over.

The next day Tauseef took the bus from his home in Karachi's Faisal Colony and arrived at the National Stadium. I put on pads and took guard in the nets to see what he was all about, and right away he started beating my bat. That was enough to win him a spot in the team for the first Test.

We thought we would break the news of Tauseef's selection to him gently. We worried it might be a bit of a shock for him. So after a couple of days of nets, I casually suggested he might as well stay with the Pakistan team at our hotel, and so avoid the trouble of taking the long bus ride from Faisal Colony. I think that gave him the clue he was about to make his Test debut.

Tauseef justified my confidence in him and went on to become a fine bowler who served Pakistan with honour and distinction.

I digress, but any discussion of lateral entry into the Pakistan Test side cannot be complete without the story of Wasim Akram.

I came across Wasim Akram one day in late 1984 during nets with a youth team in Karachi. I had gone over one afternoon to get some batting practice. One of the bowlers was Wasim Akram, aged eighteen. He was completely raw and had yet to make even his first-class debut. He came in with a whippy left-arm action and moved the ball about, and I knew I had just seen a future star in action.

When the Pakistan team left for a tour of Australia and New Zealand a few months later, I insisted Wasim accompany the team. Before the team left, Wasim came to me and asked how much money he should take along. He was so green and so enthusiastic, he hadn't even expected to be paid!

The rest, of course, is history, and best recounted in Wasim's own autobiography, *Wasim* (Piatkus).

It takes a knowledgeable eye and a bold decision to pick and then back a cricketer who may be a diamond in the rough. If you know what you're doing, the return on your bold investment can be limitless. In Wasim's case, it has turned out to be a haul of 400 Test wickets and another 400 One-Day International wickets. I thought I made a good call on that one.

To get back to that first Test against Australia in 1988-89, in response to our total of 469, the visitors folded up for 165 in their first innings and 116 in the second, as the three spinners split the wickets amongst them.

The second Test was drawn, though I took the opportunity to make another century. The third Test was drawn as well, although not before Australia gave us a fright and had reduced us to 153 for 8 by the end, after having set us a target of 269 in the fourth innings.

By 1988-89, the limited-overs revolution had completely taken hold of international cricket and schedules everywhere were packed with one-day matches. Following that home series against Australia, we participated one after the other in three One-Day International tournaments.

First up was the Champions Trophy in Sharjah, where we lost in the finals to West Indies. Next was the Asia Cup in Bangladesh, where we failed to make the finals. Finally we travelled Down Under to be the third team in Australia's limited-overs triangular series that also featured the West Indies. I had a good time with the bat throughout that tour and made several 50s, but we didn't get to the finals in the triangular either. After the triangular, we went to New Zealand for a two-Test series.

Imran wasn't with the team in Sharjah or Bangladesh, but returned as captain for the tours of Australia and New Zealand.

In New Zealand, the two Tests were due to be played at Dunedin and Wellington, but the first scheduled game was washed out without a ball being bowled. The Wellington match effectively became the first Test and a new Test was added at Auckland.

I batted well in both Tests, yet it is with a profound sense of disappointment that I remember that series. My innings in the second Test at Auckland is the best chance I ever got to overtake 365, though it was not to be.

It is something I still regret. Circumstances could not have been more perfect. Eden Park, Auckland, is a small ground with a short boundary on all sides. The pitch was excellent, and conditions remained ideal for batting. The New Zealand bowling attack, although by no means mediocre, was probably the least threatening of all the teams then playing Tests, including Sri Lanka.

I had been enjoying a rich streak of form leading up to that series. I had always relished making runs against New Zealand and for a long time had been looking forward to the batting opportunity provided by this 1988-89 trip to New Zealand. Tests against New Zealand were my favourite hunting arena—my career average against that country is 80.

In the Wellington Test I made 118, and was involved in a 220-run partnership with Shoaib Mohammed who made 163. We didn't get a chance to bat again and the match was drawn.

At Auckland, everything felt right as Imran won the toss and we started batting. I was due at my trademark no. 4 spot, and came in at 44 for 2. Immediately, I felt in rhythm and had soon crossed the 50 mark and was batting freely.

John Wright, the New Zealand captain, had to go on the defensive. He was forced to set a limited-overs field, with no slips and no close-in fielders in front of the bat. I soon realized I could do exactly as I pleased. The pitch was completely predictable and offered nothing to the bowlers. I was able to send virtually any delivery anywhere I liked.

I felt sorry for the spinners, whom I plundered almost at will. Left-armer Stephen Boock was the workhorse, going for 229 runs from 70 overs. John Bracewell's off-breaks went for 138 from 37 overs.

I ended the first day not out on 154, sharing an unbeaten stand of 245 with Shoaib, who had also made a hundred. The next morning I started from where I had left off. It had been a seamless transition from the day before, and as I crossed 250, the target of 365 was firmly in my sights. I felt like a ruler with everyone doing my bidding at Eden Park. The batting had become so effortless, it didn't matter where the bowlers pitched. I was hitting the ball wherever I wanted to. I told myself all I had to do was just keep my head.

But the batting had in fact become so easy, it made me complacent and overconfident. Eventually, this complacency caught up with me. I played an outgoing delivery from Ewan Chatfield towards the slips area. It was a ball I could have played anywhere; I deflected it towards the vacant slips region for no reason other than to be cheeky. That was finally my undoing.

Ian Smith, who would retire as New Zealand's most successful wicketkeeper, was standing behind the stumps. He threw himself at the ball and it stuck in his hand—Miandad c Smith b Chatfield 271.

The record mark of 365 had been there for the taking. I knew Imran had learnt from his mistake in abandoning me on 280 not out back in 1982-83, and he was not going to risk declaring our innings closed again with me having crossed 250. I had remained untroubled by the bowling from the very beginning. None of the New Zealand bowlers had come even close to threatening me. I still fluffed the opportunity. It had come to the point that the only person who was going to get me out was myself. Unfortunately, that is exactly what I managed to accomplish. There was a reason that Sobers's record had stood for so many years—it simply took a lot to try and approach it, let alone go past it. The moment I got out, I knew I had lost the chance of a lifetime.

That Eden Park innings of 271 represents my sixth—and last—double-century in Test cricket. Only Donald Bradman and Walter Hammond have more.

Each time I crossed 250—at Hyderabad in 1982-83, at the Oval in 1987, and at Auckland in 1988-89—I had thought that 365 was within my reach. I am proud of these scores, but each of these innings also represents for me an unfulfilled dream. Getting out at 271 hurts the most as that innings really was my best shot at what to me remains the ultimate batting prize.

The king of batting records has an interesting history. It includes some of the truly great batsmen and starts at the very beginning of Test cricket. In history's first Test match, Australia versus England in 1876-77, Australian Charles Bannerman made 165 not out that stood as the highest individual score in Test cricket for several years. This record was overtaken by another Australian, W.L. Murdoch, who made 211 against England in 1884, nearly twelve years and fifteen Test matches after Bannerman's innings.

Murdoch's record stood for nineteen years, during which time another sixty-two Test matches had been played. The record fell when Englishman R.E. Foster made 287 against Australia in 1903-04.

Foster's record was broken by another Englishman, Andy Sandham, who made 325 against West Indies in 1929-30. Foster's record had stood for twenty-six years and 115 Test matches.

Sandham's glory was short-lived. Donald Bradman took the crown when he made 334 the following season, against England in 1930. Two and a half years later, Walter Hammond had taken over the top spot from Bradman after making 336 not out against New Zealand in 1932-33.

Hammond's record stood for nearly six years. In 1938, Len Hutton surpassed him by making 364 in a Test against Australia. A long reign for Hutton's record followed. Nearly twenty years later, Gary Sobers went past him with 365 not out made in a Test against Pakistan in 1957-58.

Sobers still owned the king of batting records when I started playing Test cricket, in 1976-77, and his achievement was the one I kept aiming for. It was finally another West Indian, the talented Brian Lara, who exceeded Sobers's record when he made 375 in a Test against England in 1993-94.

Sobers's 365 had reigned supreme for an unbelievable thirty-six years, from 1957-58 to 1993-94, a time span during which 809 Test matches were played. It was one difficult nut to crack. Who can say how long Lara's record will stand? Pakistan's Inzamamul Haq came close to bettering it in his innings of 329 against New Zealand at Lahore in 2001-02. I had dearly hoped to see Inzi take the crown, but in the end I wasn't surprised that he too faltered and fell short. Many have perished trying to go where no man has gone before.

CHAPTER 16

Top of the World

The pain of failing in the 1987 World Cup eventually faded, and we started looking ahead to the next World Cup, scheduled for early 1992, to be played in Australia and New Zealand. In the years building up to that tournament, the Pakistan team went through a period of mixed fortunes.

The 1988-89 season had ended with the second Test against New Zealand at Auckland, in which I had made 271. We started in 1989-90 by winning the Champions Trophy in Sharjah featuring India, West Indies and ourselves. After that we lifted the Nehru Cup in India in a limited-overs tournament involving all the Test-playing nations except New Zealand. In November-December of 1989, we hosted India for a dull series of four drawn Tests. In the third Test of that series, at Lahore, I made 145 and shared a 246 fourth-wicket partnership with Shoaib Mohammed, who got a double century. To end the season, we went to Australia for three Tests and the Benson and Hedges Triangular but didn't do well, losing the Test series 0-1 and losing to Australia in the finals of the Triangular.

In 1990-91, we played just two Test series, both at home. We completed a 3-0 whitewash against New Zealand under my captaincy and then drew 1-1 a three-Test series against West Indies.

The World Cup was the following season, in 1991-92. We began that season at home, winning a three-Test series against Sri Lanka by a 1-0 margin. After that, all eyes were on Australia and New Zealand.

The World Cup title has become the biggest prize in international cricket. If you win it, you're at the top, and it doesn't get any better than that. Take it from a member of Pakistan's victorious 1992 World Cup team: being on top of the world is a very special feeling.

A great deal is at stake, but the World Cup isn't something you can prepare for easily. In one-day cricket, you have to take things one day at a time. If you do well today, it improves your chances of doing well tomorrow. You still have to go day by day, step by step. To my way of thinking, this is the recipe for World Cup preparations, because winning the World Cup ultimately depends on how well your team comes together on the day. In a high-stakes limited-overs game, all the planning and preparation can come unstuck if the other team is having a better day than you are. Indeed, a good deal of the outcome of the cricket World Cup comes down to luck. This is why the cricket World Cup has a well-earned reputation for being a graveyard for predictions. Except for 1979 and 2003, when the favourites retained the title, the pre-tournament favourites have never won the championship.

Pakistan cricket is never dull and even before we had left the country, our World Cup campaign had caused some excitement. By this time in my career I had represented Pakistan in 112 Tests with a record that I, for one, felt proud of, and had come to think of myself as more or less an automatic selection for the Pakistan team. However, when the Pakistan Cricket Board announced the World Cup tournament squad, my name wasn't in it. It was a shock to most of the cricket-following public in Pakistan. It should have been a shock to me, too, but I had been around long enough and nothing surprised me anymore.

In the Test series against Sri Lanka that preceded the 1992 World Cup, Imran had suggested changing my position in the batting order. In the first Test at Sialkot he sent me in at no. 5, after Saleem Malik had come in at no. 4. I wasn't happy about this. I had been a career no. 4 batsman and made clear to Imran I had no intention of batting at any other spot. But Imran— never an easy man to dissuade—insisted I be tried at no. 3 or no. 5 or 6. In the second innings of the third Test at Faisalabad, he sent me in at no. 3, with Saleem Malik again coming in at no. 4.

These discussions about my batting position continued into our World Cup training sessions. Imran's argument was that I was too 'precious' to be risked at no. 4 because if I got out cheaply, a Pakistan collapse was likely to follow. That may have been so, but elementary cricket logic dictated that the team's batting anchor come in at no. 4, and in my mind at least, there were no doubts as to who ultimately anchored Pakistan's batting.

I had confidence in my ability to do well when it mattered. I had done it for Pakistan before, and I knew with certainty I could do it for Pakistan again. I had learned a thing or two about the game and about myself by this time, and that gave me great mental comfort in my abilities. I had learned to play according to the demands of my team, my country and the situation in which I found myself at the batting crease. I knew when the time came I would give 200 per cent.

I saw something else behind this pressure to switch me around in the batting order. I couldn't help feeling it was an attempt to somehow bring me down a notch, to try and diminish whatever stature I had managed to earn as the Pakistan no. 4. It was hard to shake off this feeling. Years in the Pakistan side had taught me that I wasn't surrounded by well-wishers.

Questions about my batting in the Pakistani press were not helping the situation either. The newspapers were suggesting that I was past my best for Pakistan and had little to offer now.

The piece that really stung was a prominent newspaper article by Imtiaz Sipra, one of Pakistan's veteran sports writers, the gist of which was that Miandad was finished and that we should forget about him. That hurt me very deeply. It upset me that one of Pakistan's seasoned sports writers could misjudge me so completely. I knew better than anyone that I still had a lot to give Pakistan. I took it as a challenge to prove Sipra wrong.

Then during our pre-tournament training camp, my detractors were given an excuse to try and write me off from the 1992

World Cup altogether. During a physical training session, I strained my back. I had had trouble with my back off and on, but nobody understood my back better than I did, and I knew that with just ten to fifteen days' rest, I would be fit again. Still it became an issue to be used against me. Although the back strain happened a good four weeks before the World Cup was to begin, already the vultures had started to circle.

Despite the injury, I understood from the captain, Imran, and the manager, Intikhab Alam, that I was going to be in the side. Then the official squad was announced. I had fully expected to be a part of it, and thought that my name would appear, but it would probably be qualified by the words 'subject to fitness'. In fact, my name was nowhere to be seen. I was even expecting to be named vice-captain, but the vice-captain announced was Saleem Malik. My exclusion from the World Cup team reinforced my suspicions that there were forces in Pakistan cricket working desperately against me.

I was angry at being left out, especially after the assurances from Imran and Intikhab to the contrary. I thought about calling Imran to vent my frustration, but decided there was little point. Instead, I called up Intikhab and let him have it.

'How could I be dropped like this after all that I have done for the team over the years?' I asked Intikhab. I told him if fitness were an issue, I should still have been selected—subject to fitness—as we were still weeks from the tournament's opening game. I challenged Intikhab to justify my exclusion from the World Cup squad, but he remained quiet; there was no justification, and Intikhab knew it.

So the team flew off to Australia without me. I was disappointed and hurt, but I knew there was still a fair chance I would get a call-up. My back was getting better and I knew it would be fine in time for the tournament. Just wait for the team to be put to the test in Australia, I told myself; they'll soon be calling for Miandad.

That is exactly what happened. The team arrived in Australia well in advance of the tournament to help get acclimatized to the local conditions. The Pakistan Cricket Board had arranged for our team to play a number of warm-up games ahead of the World Cup. Right away, the side's weaknesses were exposed. Most of these preliminary matches were with semi-professional club sides, but even against such second-string opposition, the team was performing dismally.

It was all very predictable. Back in Lahore, I started getting urgent calls from the Board's top officials asking me to pack my bags for Australia. Of course I was going—there was no question about it. I was aware that 1992 could well be my last World Cup, and after the 1987 tragedy in Lahore, I was desperate to make the most of this new opportunity and try and win the World Cup title for Pakistan. I agreed to go and join the team in Australia. Shahid Rafi, the Board Secretary, asked me to prove my fitness to a Board-appointed panel, which I did without difficulty.

Before leaving for Australia, I happened to run into Imtiaz Sipra in Lahore. I was still simmering about his dismissive newspaper piece and I confronted him about it. I told him if he was right about my batting, I would give up cricket, but if I proved him wrong and was successful in the World Cup, I expected him to give up journalism. Sipra tried to laugh it off but I told him I was dead serious. He had openly challenged my ability to bat for Pakistan and to me it was no laughing matter. So he agreed that if I helped bring the World Cup to Pakistan, he would give up his sports writing career.

Australia is a fair distance from Pakistan, and there are no direct flights. In Karachi, I boarded a plane for Singapore, from where I was to take a connecting flight to Canberra. The travel arrangements were rudimentary. There was an eight-hour stopover in Singapore, which I spent hanging around the airport, unsuccessfully searching for some comfort. I eventually reached Canberra late in the evening local time. The next day Pakistan were scheduled to meet South Africa in a friendly unofficial match. Imran wanted me to play in that game, but I was dog-tired and jet-lagged, and politely but firmly declined.

The unofficial game with South Africa was to be followed by a friendly against Sri Lanka. This one I did play, and made 89.

My back was better and now I had also made some runs in a practice match. I was ready for the World Cup to begin.

The tournament was to be played as a Round Robin League, in which all the teams play each other once. There being nine teams, this meant a total of thirty-six matches in the preliminary stage. The top four teams would then progress to the semi-finals.

The competition's rules called for each team to name a fourteen-member squad at the beginning of the tournament, after which no changes would be allowed except in the case of injury. Pakistan's fourteen-strong contingent was a mix of experience and youth. Imran was captain and I was asked to be vice-captain, which I accepted. A demoralizing omission was that of Waqar Younis, who had been diagnosed with a stress fracture of the back and was unavailable for the duration of the tournament. Waqar was by this time one of the frontline fast bowlers in the world, and everyone felt his absence was a significant blow to our chances.

A number of our players were in mid-career. Players like Ramiz Raja, Saleem Malik, Ijaz Ahmed and Wasim Akram had already participated in the 1987 World Cup and they combined talent with a good deal of international experience. For other players—Aamir Sohail, Moin Khan, Aaqib Javed, Mushtaq Ahmed and Inzamamul Haq—it was to be their first World Cup. These were promising youngsters and much was expected of them. Inzamam, especially, was very green and had made his One-Day International debut only a couple of months before. He would play a memorable role in our World Cup campaign even though at the start of the tournament his limited-overs career was only seven matches old.

Imran by this time was 39 years old, and I was 35. We were among the oldest players in the tournament. We were also the most experienced in World Cup terms: Imran and I were the only two players in the entire competition who had played in each of the previous four World Cups.

At the start of the tournament, Australia were the favourites. The Australians certainly had a solid team and would be playing with home advantage. They were also the World Cup title-holders, having lifted the Cup in the 1987 final at Calcutta. One of the Australian newspapers published an analysis that since the 1987 World Cup, Australia had won 75 per cent of their limited-overs international games, which was a winning percentage far ahead of the other teams. It was an impressive statistic, but many of us knew that the World Cup tournament had little respect for such predictive reasoning.

Besides Australia, the other teams being mentioned as favourites were England and Pakistan. And after the tournament's opening match, when New Zealand comfortably defeated Australia by thirty-seven runs, everyone sat up and took notice of them too. New Zealand had come to the competition with method, strategy and singular determination, and it forced everyone to treat them with great respect.

Our own World Cup got off to a terrible start. Of our first five matches, we lost three—one each to West Indies, India and South Africa. We would also have lost a fourth match, against England, but for rain. The only game we won in that early phase was the one against Zimbabwe, who were not yet a Test side. The way we played in those initial games, it seemed we wouldn't even manage a semi-final spot.

Our team appeared to be going through the World Cup matches as if they were just in another practice camp. Team morale was extremely low and no one seemed to be playing with any passion. Waqar was already unavailable, and now Imran too had a shoulder injury. All of a sudden our bowling was looking very ordinary indeed.

After losing three of those first five matches, we squared off against Australia at Perth on 11 March 1992. The final was scheduled exactly two weeks later at the MCG. To lift the World Cup title from that point, we would have to win every single game, and even then our chances of getting into the semi-finals would depend on the outcome of other matches that didn't involve Pakistan and over which we had no control. There was no longer any room for error, and even if we played perfect cricket from then on, we would still be at the mercy of things beyond our control. By the time of our Round Robin match against Australia—our sixth match—we had reached the point where it was no more just up to us—we were in need of divine intervention.

Beginning with that game against Australia at Perth, Pakistan's fortunes underwent a dramatic transformation. The outcomes of matches between other teams also played out in our favour, and the permutations ended up securing a semi-final berth for Pakistan.

I have a firm belief that this miraculous turnaround for Pakistan was Allah's answer to the heartfelt prayers of millions of our compatriots. Then, too, March 1992 was no ordinary time for prayer. It happened to be Ramadan, a time of great blessing and the holiest month in the Muslim year.

In fact it was heavenly intervention—quite literally—that had kept our chances alive even up to the time we met Australia. Had we not split a point each in the game against England (our fourth match of the competition), we would no longer have been in contention.

Rain had saved us. This Round Robin match against England was played at the Adelaide Oval on 1 March. England won the toss and put us in without hesitation, on what appeared to be a dangerous seaming track. Imran was injured for that match and I took over as captain.

The wicket lived up to our expectations, and more. The sky was overcast and the conditions suited England's seam and swing attack perfectly. We were down 2 wickets for 5, then 4 wickets for 20, and were at one point 7 down for 42, in danger of eclipsing Canada's record of 45 as the lowest One-Day International innings in history.

We eventually managed 74, in the process establishing a couple of low-scoring records. This figure remains the lowest total by a Test-playing country in World Cup matches, and was at the time our lowest-ever innings in limited-overs cricket.

A target of 74 in a One-Day International match is for all purposes a mere formality. Our innings had finished well before lunchtime. England came out to bat before lunch and had reached 17 for 1 by the interval.

Then the skies grew dark and the heavens opened. It was quite unexpected. It hadn't rained in Adelaide for the previous three months, but now it was coming down in torrents. Soon the outfield was sodden and the match had to be abandoned. Despite batting like an inept school team, we had still managed to garner a crucial point from this match and it kept us in the running. Give any explanation you like, to me it was the Hand of God that saved us.

Three days later, we met India at Sydney. It was the usual tense affair, with both teams out for each other's blood. Our World Cup campaign was up against the ropes and it made us nervous and edgy. Meeting India had of course its own set of anxieties. All these things kept us from playing up to our potential in that game.

Many people, myself included, remember that match for a testy exchange that went on between the Indian wicket keeper, Kiran More, and me. More was appealing for everything in sight, and was being a real nuisance. His incessant ranting was making it difficult for me to concentrate. I complained to one of the umpires, who instructed More to zip it up.

Of course this only managed to get More even more worked up. His frequent appealing was bad enough, but it was the constant chatter he kept up whenever he wasn't appealing that got to me. He would go on about what the Indians were going to do, how they were going to overwhelm us, and how all my efforts were going to amount to nothing. It was all delivered in rather colourful Urdu, and it was making it impossible for me to concentrate. We had been set a target of 217, and I had walked in with our innings at 17 for 2. I had a difficult job to do as it was, but More's antics made it harder than it needed to be.

I finally turned around and confronted More.

'Talk and appeal all you want, Kiran,' I told him, 'but stay quiet once the bowler has taken his start and I have settled into my stance.'

For a while after that, More put a lid on it, but then he started again. It was extremely annoying. Obviously, words—from myself as well as from one of the umpires—hadn't got through to More. So I decided to make fun of his antics and jumped around the wicket like a kangaroo to ape how excitable he had become. It was captured by all the TV cameras and by a number of photographers. It became one of the images of the 1992 World Cup.

I made 40 in that game and shared an 88-run partnership with Aamir Sohail that took us from 17 for 2 to 105. But after Aamir left, the rest of our batting began to collapse around me. We lost our last 8 wickets for just 68 runs and fell short of the Indian target by 43. The Indians were naturally overjoyed. We slunk back to our hotel to lick our wounds.

Our next match was four days later, against South Africa on 8 March. On 5 March, however, the day following the match against India, I started experiencing stomach pains. At first I thought it was just stomach flu, and didn't pay much attention. The team had to travel to Brisbane for the game against South Africa and I went with them. When we got to Brisbane, I began vomiting and the pain in my abdomen was so severe that it was obvious I needed medical attention.

Initially, the problem couldn't be diagnosed. Then after an endoscopy test it was diagnosed as gastritis—inflammation of the stomach lining. The gastroenterologist explained that the pain medication I had been taking for my back was to blame. That medication, while very effective in controlling my backaches, had as one of its major side-effects stomach inflammation and bleeding. Unfortunately, I had been taking the medicine rather liberally and had developed this complication.

The medical advice was to rest and to start a new medicine that reduced acid production in the stomach. I had been slowly internally bleeding, and was consequently feeling very weak. Reluctantly, I followed the doctor's orders and sat out the match against South Africa.

Ramiz Raja was also missing from that match because of a sore shoulder. Even though our batting was depleted, we still felt we had a fair shot against South Africa, who were re-entering international cricket after two decades in the wilderness due to the apartheid boycott.

This time, though, the rain worked against us. Set to chase 212 from 50 overs to win the match, our reply was interrupted by rain with our score at 74 for 2 in the 21st over. When play resumed, the target was revised to 120 from just 14 overs. Before the rain, our asking rate had been 4.76 per over; after the rain interruption it became an astronomical 8.57 an over. The revision was based on the most expensive overs bowled by us in the South African innings, as dictated by a rule being followed in that particular competition.

It was a silly rule—there is no other way to describe it. On this occasion, it helped South Africa, who went on to win that match as we inevitably faltered in our chase. (But if you live by the sword you die by the sword too. Applied to its ridiculous extreme, the same rain rule would keep South Africa out of the tournament final after they had nearly beaten England in one of the semi-final matches.)

It was now do-or-die for us. Our next match was against Australia on 11 March, in the Western Australia city of Perth. We had to win it outright otherwise we would be on a plane to Karachi. I was still feeling very weak and suffering from intermittent stabs of pain, but I was needed by the team and was determined to play.

Our morale had now slipped to rock bottom after our continuous defeats. We kept getting word from Pakistan that the public's mood was turning nasty. Newspapers back home were apparently full of interviews and opinion columns roundly criticizing our efforts. It didn't sound pretty, and it made us all the more desperate for a victory.

We came out against Australia with our backs to the wall. It was going to be a gladiator fight because Australia were also facing elimination. We batted first and made 220. I managed 46, the second highest score in our innings, but remained in great discomfort throughout the match because of my stomach. We then restricted Australia to 172 as Aaqib Javed and Mushtaq Ahmed took 3 wickets each.

It was one brawl of a match, with tempers flaring on both sides. But with this victory against Australia, we gave ourselves some breathing space. Four days later, on 15 March, our campaign gathered momentum as we defeated Sri Lanka, also at Perth. Although we won with just four balls to spare, we had never been in real danger of losing that match and it was ultimately a comfortable win. I topscored with 57 and picked up the Man-of-the-Match award.

Only three matches now remained in the Round Robin League and an extremely interesting situation had been set up in the points table. South Africa, England and New Zealand had already qualified for the semi-finals, but the last semi-final spot was still up for grabs.

It would be decided on 18 March, when we took on New Zealand at Christchurch. The same day, Australia would meet the West Indies and England would meet Zimbabwe.

For Pakistan to make the semi-finals, we not only had to beat New Zealand, but the results of the other two matches also had to go a certain way—our semi-final berth would not be secure unless Australia defeated the West Indies that day and Zimbabwe defeated England.

The odds were heavily against us. To begin with, no one had thus far managed to beat New Zealand, who were enjoying the tournament's only unbeaten streak. Then, between Australia and West Indies, the Australians had won only three of their previous seven games while the West Indians had won four and had greater momentum. Of course the least likely outcome was of England being defeated by Zimbabwe. Zimbabwe were not yet a Test side and had lost each one of their previous seven matches coming into that last Round Robin game against England.

Maybe one or two of these matches could have gone against predictions, but the chances that all three would go against the odds were minuscule. Incredibly, though, that's just what happened.

In our match against New Zealand at Christchurch, we bowled the opposition out for 166 and then Ramiz Raja played a fine innings of 119 not out (the highest score of the 1992 World Cup) to steer us to an easy 7-wicket victory with six overs to spare.

Soon after that match, we received word that Zimbabwe had downed England at Albury (near Melbourne). It was such an unlikely outcome to begin with, but it had seemed even more unlikely when Zimbabwe had been bowled out for 134 after being put in to bat by England. But Zimbabwe rallied and won by 9 runs in the game's final over.

Two down, one to go. When our match against New Zealand ended in Christchurch, we still didn't know if we would be in the semi-finals. The match between Australia and the West Indies was a day-nighter at Melbourne and its result was not going to be known for another few hours. We showered and changed, and went back to our hotel to follow the Australia-West Indies match—and our fate—on television.

I don't think any of us have ever followed a match on television with such interest. We were crowded around the TV sets in each other's rooms and could barely move. Every ball was being followed closely, our fate unfolding before our eyes.

Australia had batted first and posted the rather modest total of 216. At one point it looked as if the West Indies would win the match, but Mike Whitney tore out their middle order in a spirited spell taking 4 for 34 and they were eventually 57 runs short. When the last West Indian wicket fell, our joy erupted. We hugged each other in elation and celebration.

One by one, each step had fallen in place to complete the circuit for Pakistan to enter the semi-final round. It was enough to make us feel we were being specially guided towards a great destiny.

The tournament was now down to the last four. On 21 March, we would square off against New Zealand in the first semi-final, played at Eden Park, Auckland. The second semi-final would be held at Sydney the following day, between England and South Africa.

We arrived in Auckland with great hope and a sense of mission. I had played for Pakistan in three previous World Cup semi-finals—1979, 1983 and 1987—and my team had remained unsuccessful each time. It was a frustrating legacy. Would 1992 be our year to reach the final?

New Zealand, too, had played in previous World Cup semi-finals—against West Indies in 1975 and against England in 1979. Like us, they too had yet to play in a World Cup final. It was clear that 1992 had so far been New Zealand's best World Cup. By the end of the Round Robin stage, New Zealand were in fact the team of the tournament, coming into the semi-finals with the best record of any team, with seven wins from eight matches and the best net run-rate.

We were acutely aware of New Zealand's strengths. They had stuck to a well thought out plan in every match, and so far it had worked beautifully for them. In Mark Greatbatch, New Zealand had an exciting opener who had been taking full advantage of the fielding restrictions in the early overs. In Chris Harris and Chris Cairns, they had two talented all-rounders, and in their captain, Martin Crowe, they had the best batsman ever to play for New Zealand. The New Zealand bowling had been amazingly on target as well. Each bowler had bowled to his field with great discipline. The off-spinner Dipak Patel had been especially tight and had the best economy rate of the tournament.

We had just beaten New Zealand in our final Round Robin game, which was a tremendous confidence booster, but the semi-final was the crunch match and we knew it would take something special to overcome the formidable momentum that New Zealand had managed to generate.

New Zealand won the toss and batted, and put up an imposing 262, built around a sterling 91 from their captain Martin Crowe. Even though Eden Park has a short boundary, 263 from fifty overs is a demanding target under any conditions. We had, in fact, never reached that total batting second in World Cup competition. It made us very nervous.

In reply, we lost our first wicket at 30 and the second at 84. I walked in at 2-down and put on 50 for the third wicket with

Imran, before he fell for 44, making us 134 for 3. Then Saleem Malik walked in. Much was expected of him, but after scoring just a single, he planted a drive straight into the hands of Rod Latham at short cover and we were 140 for 4 in the 35th over.

It was a deep, deep crisis. The asking rate had climbed above eight an over from the last fifteen overs and the top order was gone. New Zealand had us in a stranglehold, and they were squeezing tighter.

As I waited for the next man to come out after Saleem Malik's departure, I kept going over the match situation in my head. We faced a steep task, but I felt confident we would pull it off. I tried to think of it as just another limited-overs match. I had been in such situations for Pakistan before and I knew very well that all it takes are just a few good overs to turn a one-day game right around.

We still had Inzamam, Wasim Akram and Moin Khan, each capable of powerful hitting. The way I saw it, two things were critically needed: The asking rate desperately needed to be brought down, and I had to stay at the wicket right to the last ball. My plan was to hold up one end and limit myself to high-percentage shots while one of these big-hitters fetched us some boundaries. That would keep us alive until the final overs, when anything could happen.

I was expecting Imran to send out Wasim, but Inzamamul Haq came out instead. He was young and inexperienced and had yet to play a Test match, but he had already displayed a talent for fluent strokeplay in the match against South Africa and we knew he was a quality player headed for big things. Inzi walked up to me for advice. He seemed nervous and overawed and looked like he had seen a ghost.

I tried to put him at ease. I told him that he had to put the crisis situation out of his mind and to just play his natural strokes. He nodded, but didn't say anything. I think he was so overwrought that he could barely get any words out. As soon as he faced his first ball, it was clear that he was in fine touch. Right away, Inzi began middling the ball and finding the gaps, and the New Zealand bowling started looking like a mediocre club attack. I realized immediately I needed to give Inzi as much strike as possible. He went on to play one of the great World Cup innings, overturning the course of a semi-final.

Inzi got to his 50 from just 31 balls and was eventually out for a brilliant 60 from 37 balls. He was run out, which was the only way he looked like getting out.

Inzamam and I put on 87 for the fifth wicket from ten overs. When he left we were 227 for 5, needing another 36 from the last five overs. The asking rate had come down to seven an over, and Wasim Akram was coming in to take strike. I sensed panic in the New Zealand ranks. They were without their captain Martin Crowe, who hadn't come out to field after having pulled a hamstring while batting. John Wright had taken over and had done fine—until Inzamam walked in and made a mess of New Zealand's bowling plans. For the first time in that semi-final match, I began to smell victory.

Wasim was out for 9, but it was a minor hiccup. Moin Khan came in and clobbered a six onto the grandstand balcony. He also hit the winning run, from the last ball of the 49th over. I finished not out on 57. The match had seemed all but out of our grasp when Saleem Malik got out and when we needed 8.2 runs an over from the last fifteen overs. Then Inzamam came in and played out of his skin and we had found our way into our first World Cup final. It was a sweet, memorable victory, and one that I will always savour.

I was again reminded that Allah was watching over us. We were in the middle of Ramadan, the Muslim holy month of fasting. I did not fast on the days we were playing matches, but I did fast every day in between. I also prayed the five daily prayers and, as I had done for the last so many Ramadans, was reading passages from the Holy Quran every day. Through our darkest days in the competition, I had found strength in my faith. Now that we had found a winning streak, my belief sustained me more than ever.

Elated as we were, I did, however, feel a great deal of sympathy for New Zealand. They took the loss very hard and many of their players were fighting back tears. The Eden Park crowd was in mourning. Having been in the Pakistan side that lost that greatly hyped-up World Cup semi-final against Australia in 1987, I identified with the New Zealand team. I was sad for them and for the New Zealand public, who had been such a great part of their team's momentum in that World Cup and must surely have felt this was going to be their tournament all the way.

But someone has to lose, and on that day it was New Zealand. They ran a lap of honour around the stadium, thanking and bidding farewell to their supporters. It was a moving and sad moment to watch and they bore their loss with great dignity.

Our berth in the final secure, we waited patiently for the other semi-final to be played the next day at Sydney, which would decide whom we would encounter—England or South Africa—for the World Cup title.

Having been frustrated semi-finalists three times, getting into the final was a very big achievement for us. At one point we had nearly been knocked out of the tournament, and now here we were, just one match away from taking the coveted title. We felt as though we had already won the trophy.

In the second semi-final, England defeated South Africa to enter their third World Cup final. I am sure England fancied their chances against us. They had an edge in World Cup playing experience, having made it to the finals in 1979 and 1987. And they had all but beaten us in the washed out Round Robin match we had played against them three weeks earlier. Like us, England had never won the World Cup either. They were just as hungry for it as we were.

I say 'just as hungry', because I can't imagine they would have wanted the World Cup title any more desperately than we did. Our team meeting before the final was passionate and intense—we simply had to win the World Cup. Defeat was not an option. We were peaking at the perfect moment and there was a great sense of energy and confidence. We firmly believed we were going to win.

South Africa ended up being the unluckiest side of the tournament. They deserved to be in the final with us, and who knows, they might well have won. A brief rain interruption saw their ask of twenty-two runs from thirteen balls revised to a farcical twenty-one runs from one ball in the semi-final against England. But what a fairytale re-entry they had made into international cricket. For twenty-eight years they had wandered in the wilderness of the apartheid boycott. Yet they were still able to come back and resume almost from where they had left off. It was true that many of their players had remained active in high-quality cricket through participation in English league and county cricket as well as with the 'rebel tours' in which international players periodically violated the official ban. But ultimately it showed how deeply institutionalized cricket had been in South Africa that even close to three decades of sporting sanctions had not dented its mettle. Their performance in the 1992 World Cup had been nothing short of a tribute to the South African nation and its cricket.

On Wednesday, 25 March, we faced England in the 1992 World Cup final at the MCG. Imran won the toss and we batted. Winning the toss was a positive start for us because our strength was in setting targets, not in chasing them. It was a day/night game, and our innings started at 2 p.m. in the afternoon. The sun was out, the weather was hot, and there was a slight breeze. We dearly hoped for a stable, productive opening stand from our openers, Aamir Sohail and Ramiz Raja, both of whom were in good nick and had scored centuries earlier in the tournament. If we got off to a good start, the middle-order would be able to play without pressure, and we would be ideally placed to post a daunting total.

But things didn't exactly proceed according to plan. We first lost Aamir Sohail with our score at 20, and then four runs later Ramiz also got out. Both openers had fallen to Derek Pringle, who was taking full advantage of the breeze and bowling lively swing and seam.

Imran had come in after Aamir Sohail's dismissal, and at 24-2, I walked in to replace Ramiz. Imran had first decided to bat at no. 3 in our Round Robin game against Sri Lanka, and had done so again in the semi-final match against New Zealand. He and I were the most experienced batsmen in the side. Imran at 1-down was an effective solution to the brittleness of our inexperienced middle-order, which was always vulnerable to pressure situations.

I came in and took guard. Imran was at the other end but we barely exchanged a glance. I felt no need to talk because it was obvious what needed to be done. We had been here before. Both of us knew the loss of another wicket would trigger a batting collapse. The plan was simple. We absolutely had to bat out our full fifty overs. We would pull down the shutters and settle into a long third-wicket partnership. I made up my mind to still be at the crease when the fiftieth over was bowled.

The key to our plan was discipline and complete and total focus on the situation at hand. There was so much riding on our partnership—we had the opportunity to crown our careers with Pakistan's first World Cup title, an opportunity we had fluffed in 1987—but I let none of that enter my mind. Cricket logic dictated I was to hold on to my wicket at all costs, and that is all I focused on.

The only way to ensure we wouldn't lose any wickets was to not take any risks. Even the bad balls were to be played cautiously. We were going to just nudge the ball around for a while and keep getting ones and twos, but we were not going to go for any boundaries. It meant the scoring rate would drop, but that was a price we were willing to pay for a while.

We eliminated risks and the run-rate slowed down. But we weren't worried, we were in charge and we were confident, knowing exactly where we were headed. Imran and I had decided to stay together until the 35th over or so; if we were able to hold on to our wickets until then, players like Inzamamul Haq and Wasim Akram would be able to play without pressure and be able to throw their bat about and we could end up with a respectable 240-250.

For a while we scored at the average of barely above two runs an over. It was fine with us because at that time our top priority was simply to hold on to our wickets.

At one point early in my innings, I had a close call that had me genuinely worried for a moment that I might be given out. Derek Pringle got one to rap me on the pads and immediately he threw his arms up in a big roar of an appeal. I always know precisely where my off-stump is, and I knew that Pringle had hit me just outside the line. But I was covering the stumps, and I wasn't sure if the umpire too realized that the ball had hit me outside the line of off. The thought gripped me with sheer terror, because I simply could not have imagined losing my wicket then. Fortunately, the umpire at the bowling end was none other than Steve Bucknor, who has a well-deserved reputation for competence. He hesitated a moment, and I saw in his eyes that doubt had entered his mind. I turned away in relief and the moment passed.

As we approached the 25th over mark, we became conscious of the need to push up the scoring rate. Imran came up to me and said he was going to go for his shots, but he insisted that I had to keep one end secure. I was in full agreement with him; the time had come for Imran to open his shoulders. In the 28th over, he lifted Illingworth for 6. That took the score to 83 for 2, and pushed our run rate up to 3 runs an over. I continued picking the gaps at the other end and kept the scoreboard turning with regular singles, which was no problem for me. It was something I could do easily, without taking any real risk at all.

As we went past the 30th over, I decided to accelerate as well. I, however, had a harder time trying to force the pace. The problem was that my stomach had started to act up again. I managed to bring up my fifty, but by this time I was fighting away jabs of pain and the batting was fast becoming unbearable.

I had to call for a runner, but despite that I knew I wouldn't be able to go on much longer. How I had wanted to see Pakistan through to the 50th over, but this time it was not to be. The younger men would have to take over. My stomach was killing me and the severe, constant pain had sapped all my energy. I was exhausted and felt I would collapse any minute.

I knew my time at the crease was limited and I wanted to go out with a bang. We were in the 40th over, with our score close

to 160. Ray Illingworth was bowling orthodox left-arm spin. I
wanted to hit out against him. If I tried a conventional slog
towards mid-on or mid-wicket, I didn't have the energy to clear
the field. I thought I would try the reverse sweep instead. It was
a shot I knew well. I would be playing with the turn, and aiming
to clear the off-side cordon, which was closer in compared to
the on-side field.

Illingworth bowled one at the off-stump that pitched the right
length for being reverse-swept, and I saw it early. But I had no
power left to hit. I made feeble contact and the ball sailed into
the hands of Ian Botham fielding at point. I was out for 58. My
third wicket partnership with Imran had yielded 139. We were
now into the final stretch of overs, still with seven wickets in
hand. Imran went a couple of overs later, trying to hit Botham
out of the ground but only finding Illingworth in the deep.
Wasim Akram then came in to join Inzamamul Haq and the two
batted with abandon to take us to 249, our eventual score.

It was a defendable target, but England were still very much
in the match. Any team that includes batsmen like Graham
Gooch, Ian Botham, Allan Lamb, Graeme Hick and Alec Stewart
would be considered an outstanding batting side by any
standards.

I was, nevertheless, very pleased with our eventual score. At
24 for 2 we had been in danger of collapsing in a heap, but
Imran and I were able to arrest the slide of wickets. I thought
we were fortunate to have eventually reached 249.

One of the most pleasurable features of batting in that final
match was the tremendous crowd support we received. The
MCG is a huge stadium and crowd attendance in the 1992 World
Cup final was documented at 87,182, which remains the largest
official attendance at a One-Day International ever. The
atmosphere was unbelievable. It was a discerning crowd, and
they knew when to be silent and when to scream.

The best thing about that crowd was how it had made a
connection with our team. For the several overs when Imran
and I were just quietly going about defending our wickets, the
crowd had remained eerily silent, almost as if they were holding

their breath. Then when we started to accelerate, they literally cheered every run. It made us feel as if we were playing in Karachi or Lahore—such was the total crowd support for Pakistan at the MCG that day.

It must have been very galling for the England team, but we all know how the Australians hate the English. I think we became the beneficiaries that day of this age-old hostility.

The crowd support became even more vocal when we came out to field. I was laid up with a burning stomach and didn't come out with the team, but it was such an intoxicating atmosphere under the lights at the MCG, I never felt I was away from the action.

Wasim Akram rose to the occasion that evening and bowled us to victory. He had been given his battle orders, which were to get an early breakthrough at all costs. Gooch and Botham had come out to open the innings. England had just put 6 runs on the board when Akram bowled one to Botham that pitched just short of a length and exploded off the pitch, taking the outside edge of Botham's bat for a catch at the wicket. The umpire gave him out caught behind for a duck. Botham made a bit of a show about not being pleased at the umpire's decision, but I am not sure what he was going on about because there was a clear nick.

The one umpiring decision in that match that did appear a little strange came shortly after Botham's dismissal. Aaqib Javed moved one away in a perfect trajectory and got the ball to clip Alec Stewart's bat on its way to Moin Khan's gloves. But Stewart refused to walk and for some reason Umpire Brian Aldridge judged him not out as well. It was quite inexplicable.

But wickets fell steadily for England in the early overs. Mushtaq Ahmed dismissed Gooch and Hick with his leg-spin and Aaqib Javed repeated his wicket-taking outswinger to finally get rid of Alec Stewart, and England had been reduced to 69 for 4.

But just when we looked like running away with the match, Allan Lamb got together with Neil Fairbrother and they started cobbling together a partnership. They painstakingly took the score to 141 for 4 as England started to slowly claw their way back into the match.

Something needed to be done, and Imran did it. He called on Wasim Akram to bowl a second spell.

In one of the defining moments of our cricket history, Wasim took the ball and in the space of two unplayable deliveries, all but secured the World Cup for Pakistan.

The first unplayable ball got rid of Lamb. It was a rocket of a delivery pitching a perfect length on middle and leg and straightening up just enough to beat the outside edge and hit the top of the off-stump. There wasn't much anyone could have done with that ball, except perhaps Bradman. It almost certainly would have gone past my defences.

Chris Lewis then came in to replace Lamb. A 24-year-old who had been included as an all-rounder, Lewis was expected to be able to bat a bit. Wasim sent him back for a first-ball duck with an in-swinger that swung a mile, sliced Lewis in half, and clipped the bails. Wasim seemed like a man possessed and went mad with jubilation. Those two wickets had completely knocked the wind out of England and their innings wilted away.

The match ended in the final over of the England innings when Imran had last man Ray Illingworth caught at mid-off by Ramiz. The winning margin was 22 runs.

It was an incredible achievement for Pakistan, and its scope overwhelmed us. Many of our players prostrated themselves in front of Allah and bowed their heads on the MCG turf. I came out of the dressing room and ran on to the ground to celebrate with my teammates, hugging and kissing whomever I came across. I tried to look for Imran in the throng of Pakistan players. When I finally spotted him, he had his back to me. I patted him on the shoulder so he could turn around and see me, and we locked in a long embrace. There was so much to say, but neither of us spoke. I suppose it was the kind of moment too great for mere words.

Imran, in fact, would perhaps have been better off staying quiet the whole evening. As the winning captain, he was required to make a speech during the trophy presentation ceremony, but he ended up making a real hash of it. Imran has been heavily criticized for that victory speech in the 1992 World Cup. I can understand the criticism because it was quite a silly speech in which Imran forgot to thank the crowd and—more importantly—completely neglected to mention his team. He just mumbled his way through some words of commiseration towards the England team and then made Pakistan's World Cup victory sound like little more than just another step in his cancer hospital's fund-raising campaign.

But I, for one, sympathize with Imran on this count. His public-speaking skills were modest to begin with, and now he was asked to deliver such a high-profile speech when he had just crowned his cricket career with the accomplishment of a lifetime. I know Imran meant well and he had genuinely wanted to say all the right things, but it was an intense emotional moment for him. I should know, because it was an extremely intense moment for me as well. I had a huge lump in my throat—but at least I had the option of not having to speak. Imran's state of mind could not have been much different. At a time like that one can hardly think straight at all, much less sound articulate and sensible.

The World Cup victory ignited Pakistan. From a position of being nearly knocked out, we had emerged at the head of the pack. Our cricket public can be merciless in defeat, but they know how to show their appreciation for a great accomplishment. Nothing compares to the feeling of an entire nation pouring out its love and respect to you.

After our victory, I also met up with my writer friend Imtiaz Sipra. He had been in Australia reporting on the World Cup and had followed all our games closely. I reminded him that he had agreed to give up journalism if I got runs and brought home the World Cup. He smiled and said he accepted that I had proven him wrong, and could I just let it go at that, which of course I did.

There was a general feeling in Pakistan that while the young stars had played their part, ultimately Imran and Javed had won the World Cup for Pakistan. There is no doubt that, with ten World Cups between us, Imran and I brought experience to the side. But the heroics of the rising Pakistanis—Inzamamul Haq,

Wasim Akram, Mushtaq Ahmed, Aaqib Javed, Aamir Sohail, Ramiz Raja and Moin Khan—were really the crucial balance in the equation. Without their brave performances, our team could not have become champions.

For someone who had not even made it into the original selection, I thought I had ended up doing quite well. In nine matches, I had made scores of 57 not out, 89, 3, 40, 46, 22, 30, 57 not out and 58, for an average of 62.43 and at a strike rate of over 62. It was the second highest aggregate in the entire competition (19 runs behind the leader, Martin Crowe). And it had all been managed despite the agony of a bleeding stomach that could produce searing pain without warning. I had never lacked for critics in Pakistan, but I thought this might keep them quiet for a while. After nearly two decades in Pakistan cricket, I was finally learning it is best to let your bat do the talking.

It is a great competition, the cricket World Cup. It is deeply satisfying for me to have been part of a team that brought the World Cup to Pakistan and I pray I will live to see the World Cup come back to Pakistan again and again. We had been certain that 1987 would be our year, but fate had other plans. How I had hoped then that I would get another chance at helping Pakistan secure the championship, and now it had come to pass. What does one do with such largesse but bow his head in supplication to his Maker.

CHAPTER 17

Imran and I

Victory in the 1992 World Cup was a glorious accomplishment for Pakistan. It was also the crowning achievement in my long association with Imran Khan. I was fortunate to have seen Pakistan become a world-class team during my playing career; it would not have been possible without Imran. It may seem strange for a cricketer to be devoting in his autobiography an entire chapter to another cricketer. But Imran is no ordinary cricketer; he is one of cricketing history's greatest. This chapter is my tribute to him.

At the height of his career, Imran Khan ruled Pakistan cricket. He was like a general whose orders could not be questioned. He got to be that way, to some extent, because of his education, bearing, and the family name (two cousins—Majid Khan and Javed Burki—had been former Pakistan captains). But what really accounted for his strong grip on Pakistan cricket was that he was an irreplaceable bowler.

Pakistan had been producing elite batsmen without too much difficulty, but producing elite bowlers, especially fast bowlers, had seemed to be the prerogative of just England, Australia and West Indies. Imran was the first bowler produced by Pakistan who was accepted into the top echelon of bowlers. Even more impressive, he ranked among the best not only with his own generation but also in history.

It is not possible to be a dominant Test side without the services of a world-class fast bowler. In fact, the more frontline fast bowlers you have, the greater your chances of world dominance. History's best Test side—in my opinion the West

Indians of the 1980s—had a virtual assembly line of such fast bowlers, and they ruled the cricket world like no other team before or since.

Imran was first recognized as a genuine paceman after Pakistan's historic win against Australia at Sydney in 1976-77. Shortly after that, he played along side the world's best in Kerry Packer's World Series Cricket, and troubled all the top batsmen. Around this time, Imran participated in a competition of bowling speeds with the world's other fast bowlers. Pitted against names like Lillee, Thomson, Holding, Roberts, Le Roux, Mike Proctor, Croft and Garner, he was placed second-fastest (after Jeff Thomson). This highly novel and interesting competition captured the cricket world's imagination and enthroned Imran as an exceptional fast bowler. This competition also convinced Imran himself, beyond any shadow of a doubt, that he was one of the very best, and his confidence became unshakeable.

When Imran emerged as one of the world's leading fast bowlers, the star of Pakistan cricket rose with him. Imran's importance to the team and indeed to the country increased exponentially.

When Imran became the Pakistan captain, he led from the front and created an atmosphere in which there was no room for mediocrity. He made selection strictly performance-based. Everyone feared for their place in the side, and it motivated them to give of their best. Secure in his own abilities, Imran feared no one. This made everyone, the players as well as the cricket establishment, fear him even more.

Imran and I played our best cricket together for Pakistan. He handled the bowling obligations and I did my best to anchor the batting. For many years both of us also shared the Pakistan captaincy. It is said in Pakistan that my collaboration with Imran brought a new dimension to Pakistan cricket. Naturally, it is impossible for me to be objective about such an analysis. But I do know that it has been a great privilege for me to have found in Imran a partner with whom I could do much more for Pakistan than I could ever have done on my own. When I look back on my career, this makes me feel extremely fortunate—that I played for Pakistan at the same time as Imran.

I have often been asked about my relationship with Imran. The impression I have is that cricket followers in Pakistan—and perhaps abroad—are very curious about this.

I have never thought of myself as being irreplaceable in any way. I played some of my best innings under Imran's captaincy and I think he came to value my contributions as a batsman. I also frequently gave Imran suggestions—about bowling changes, field settings, batting orders. I know he valued these suggestions because he usually implemented them.

Imran was born Imran Khan Niazi on 25 November 1952, in Lahore. He enjoyed an upper middle-class upbringing and was exposed to cricket very early on, playing with other family members in Lahore's Zaman Park and then at Aitchison College, an English-style public school in Lahore with colonial origins.

During high school, Imran left for England, where his proper cricket foundations were laid. He spent his formative years playing for Worcestershire County Cricket Club and Oxford University. This is the period—the years following high school—when a young man seeks to define himself, and casts his hopes and desires into the ambitions of his later life. Imran's idea of who he was, what his cricket meant to him, and where it would take him, were all shaped in England during this time.

The reason Imran became such a fine cricketer is that he made the most of his exposure in England. He worked hard, intensely hard. He was gifted to begin with, and in his formative years in England he built on this through diligence, focus and intelligence. He learned all the right things about playing and the correct approach to cricket that, at least back in those days, it was only possible to learn in England.

Imran's capacity for hard work is an example to all aspiring cricketers. It is an example, in fact, to anyone who seeks rare accomplishment in any sphere of life. Early on in his playing days, Imran had developed a strict routine of physical training that he adhered to without fail throughout his playing days. He would run and perform his demanding aerobics daily, with no exceptions. Every day, he would bowl 6-8 overs without fail. He wouldn't be bowling to any batsman but would just be on his own, bowling at a single stump. There would be a popping crease, and 22 yards away there would be the solitary stump. In that setting Imran would bowl his 6-8 overs every day without fail—just Imran and the craft of bowling, with the rest of the world completely blocked out.

In those days, there was not the coaching culture that developed in the 1990s and later. There was very little guidance, and you had to seek help on your own. In his own writings, Imran has downplayed this aspect of his cricket education, but it needs to be acknowledged that he largely taught himself. He had complete confidence in his own physical abilities and mental skills, and it paid him great dividends. It takes a very strong mind to be able to teach yourself to become world-class at anything. This side to Imran's personality sometimes gets mistaken for arrogance, but it is really just strength of mind.

As an eighteen-year-old, Imran was selected to tour England with the Pakistan team in 1971. After that tour, he stayed back in England to attend Worcestershire Grammar School. This marked the beginning of his cricket education in England. Had he returned to Pakistan at the end of that 1971 tour, he would not even remotely have been the cricketer he eventually became.

After graduating from high school, Imran went on to Oxford University. Oxford was crucial to Imran's cricket development. It was a relaxed environment with all the right elements to bring out the best in a talented cricketer. At Oxford, Imran was head and shoulders above all the other players. This fetched him a great deal of attention and at the same time left him free to develop his cricket. He made the most of the opportunities and worked himself tirelessly.

After Oxford, Imran started playing for Worcestershire County. The Worcestershire cricket programme was more regimented than Oxford's, but Imran had the cricket intelligence to know what he should be paying attention to and what he should ignore. He was in an exponential phase of growth as a bowler and had to take what he needed from Worcestershire but stay clear of any influence that would inhibit his development.

Bowling instructions in English county cricket can be very unimaginative. There is this dominant need to maintain a 20 overs-an-hour over rate, which means you have to get through your over in just 2 to 3 minutes. A true fast bowler needs at least 4 to 5 minutes for an over, but the instructions for any newcomer are invariably to go for line-and-length and get through your over quickly. Had Imran fallen into this trap, his genius would have been lost to the cricket world forever.

From Worcestershire, Imran moved to Sussex, where he and I were club-mates for two seasons. We lived in separate apartments in Hove, but spent a lot of time together, often getting together in the evenings. We travelled together and shared accommodations whenever we had to play away from Hove. By this time the two of us had of course been playing together for Pakistan, but my friendship with Imran really began around this time in 1977 when we came together at Sussex.

At Sussex, I saw Imran mature under the guidance of England's celebrated fast bowler John Snow. Here his talents were duly recognized and understood. He developed fearsome pace and acquired a formidable reputation on the county circuit.

He was also now a very clever bowler. He learned to do things that batsmen would least expect, such as bowling from wide of the crease yet moving the ball away. Somewhere around this period Imran picked up his Midas Touch—the art of reverse-swing—that he developed to perfection and that in years to come he would use to help himself to scores of wickets.

The combination of pace, guile and reverse-swing made Imran absolutely lethal. He started predicting his wickets, and whenever the tail was exposed, he seemed almost to be able to take wickets at will. He would often tell us he'd spotted a weakness in the batsman and how he was going to get him next ball. And sure enough he would. He had become that good with his pace and control.

Imran was never one to rest on his laurels, and so he never stopped growing as a cricketer. Having mastered fast bowling, he turned his attention to batting. He approached batting like a genuine batsman, with great method and application. Again, the county system served as his tutorial. He started batting in the lower middle-order for Sussex and emerged as a responsible batsman with orthodox technique. He would go on to became a complete batsman and play many a great innings in the service of Pakistan.

As I have noted elsewhere in this book (Chapter 22), Imran became the best all-rounder of his time. That is a huge statement when you consider that his contemporaries included Kapil Dev, Richard Hadlee and Ian Botham. Imran was the best batsman amongst them, and as good a bowler as any. He was also the most successful captain. The English media especially have canonized Botham as the ultimate all-rounder, but they are wrong. With the minor exception of slip-catching, Imran was superior to Botham in every aspect of the game.

Imran finished his career with 362 Test wickets, but he is really an honorary member of the 400 Club. He was unable to bowl for a couple of years because of a stress fracture of the shin. Those were his peak years as a bowler, and who knows how many wickets he would have taken had the injury not occurred.

Imran's injury was a great disappointment for the Pakistan team and Pakistan's cricket supporters, but imagine the effect it must have had on Imran himself. He had been robbed of two crucial years of bowling at his best. It depressed and demoralized him, but he was a great fighter and he shook it off with characteristic strength of will.

Imran was the kind of person who never, ever gives up. When we went to Australia for the World Cup in 1992, he injured his shoulder, but he was undeterred. He decided even if he couldn't be at his best as a bowler, he would compete and excel as a batsman—and he did. If he had not been there at the other end batting with me in the final, I doubt we would have won.

Imran was a very successful captain for Pakistan, but he was also a lucky captain. He would try a number of risky things, and they would often work. He was also, at least in my experience, a listening captain. I would be in regular consultation with him on the field and he always considered what I had to say.

He was, most of all, a very demanding captain. He had high expectations from everyone, including himself, and was never afraid to let you know if you didn't measure up. His favourite word for a strong performer was 'tiger'. It was a colourful image that inspired and motivated the players, and everyone wanted to be a 'tiger' for Imran. He dispensed criticism freely but, I thought, largely appropriately. There was something about the way he admonished the players that they took it positively. Rather than make them sulk and brood, a chastising from Imran often spurred the boys to do better. It was an extremely effective gift for a captain to have.

I feel overall that Imran was a sound judge of player merit. Sometimes he would see something special in a player and he would then support and promote that person even if the player had failed to perform. A well-known case in point is that of batsman Mansoor Akhtar, whom Imran continued to include in the Test side despite a string of disappointing performances. There is a feeling that Imran had become unreasonable in his support for Mansoor and it suggested a certain stubbornness in Imran's personality. If you ask me, I think Imran was correct in this strategy. Mansoor was a very good player with the right technique and it made good cricketing sense to persevere with him. That Mansoor never quite clicked is bad luck, but he certainly had all the ingredients to become one of Pakistan's best batsmen. I credit Imran with following his judgement and not bowing to public pressure on this one.

Captaincy also brought out strong likes and dislikes in Imran. He usually took time to form an opinion about a player, but once he had done so, it was very hard to dissuade him. There are some players who feel their careers for Pakistan were prematurely terminated because they could not curry favour with Imran. There definitely was this negative side to Imran, if he had decided you were somehow deficient, it was next to impossible to get him to revise his view. However, whatever faults Imran may have had as a captain, they went largely unchallenged. The team rose to new heights under him, and no one was going to question a formula that was working so well.

Every now and then, I too would come up against this obstinate side to Imran. There were occasions when I felt Imran was wrong and I feared that his intransigence was going to cost us a match. At times like these, I knew I just had to get my way—and I did. The best example of a situation like this was before the Bangalore Test against India in 1986-87, when Imran had made up his mind to play Abdul Qadir rather than Iqbal Qasim. I knew that Qasim would be far more effective on that track, and urged Imran to change his mind. It became a testy exchange and I finally ended up invoking God and country before Imran relented. I can't imagine Imran regretting it, because Qasim bowled us to an historic victory.

One of the questions that keeps coming up is whether there was any element of professional jealousy between Imran and myself. I think this is a silly question because, really, how could there not be? We were both committed performers who strove to excel at all times. It was natural to feel a competitive edge with each other. Indeed this kind of feeling has been common among most of the leading players in the Pakistan side and, I am sure, in other teams as well. Others may deny it, but you can take it from me that it exists.

The important point to recognize is that this sense of professional rivalry was just that and nothing more, and it was not allowed to spoil our relationship at a personal level. I was always conscious not to let these feelings spill over into the personal arena, and as far as I can tell Imran has been careful about this too.

There remain of course all kinds of rumours about the nature of my personal relationship with Imran. It has been variously described as 'difficult', 'stormy', 'troubled', even 'prickly'. It is interesting that the newspapers and tabloids have always seemed to know more about this than I do. The truth is that Imran and I have always got along fine. Yes, we have had our differences—how could we not, considering the stakes, the circumstances and the pressures that surrounded our association? The important thing is that these differences have not invaded our personal interaction with each other. Over time, the differences have either been resolved or set aside, and our friendship has survived intact.

After his retirement, Imran put his entire efforts into completing the cancer hospital he had been building in Lahore in memory of his late mother. The Shaukat Khanum Memorial Cancer Hospital and Research Centre is now a leading cancer care facility in Pakistan, and it has kept its promise of never turning away a patient who couldn't afford to pay.

Imran had initially announced his retirement from international cricket after our failed campaign in the 1987 World Cup. He was disheartened after our semi-final defeat to Australia. This 'retirement' didn't last long and he was back to lead Pakistan on a tour of the West Indies late in the 1987-88 season. Imran shouldn't have retired in the first place because there was still a lot of cricket left in him, but I also think he really returned to international cricket because he realized it would help raise funds for the cancer hospital project, which was fast becoming his obsession.

Remaining active in cricket certainly helped the hospital's cause because it maintained Imran's high profile and allowed him to attract funds. It also made available to Imran the services of the rest of the team.

Indeed, the Pakistan cricket team has had a big hand in making Imran's dream of a cancer hospital a reality. Our team donated all kinds of prize money—from team awards as well as cash from Man-of-the-Match awards—to the hospital. On one occasion, one of the players was awarded an automobile, which was also handed over to help with the hospital.

Many of us directly helped with the fundraising. I tried to do my part towards this noble cause and was able to convince many resourceful individuals to support the project generously.

Some reports appeared in the press that the team was being coerced into giving up its prize money to Imran, but this is a misrepresentation. Certainly the force of Imran's personality was a factor in getting the players to donate, and no one could deny the value and moral dignity of building a cancer hospital. The prize monies would be donated with everyone's consent; there was no coercion. Often the prize money would be promised to the hospital even before it had been won. We felt that Allah would help us to victory if the prize money were already promised to a charitable and noble cause.

Since setting up the cancer hospital, Imran has put his weight behind an effort to solve the problems of the Pakistani nation. He has entered politics and launched a new party, the *Tehrik-e-Insaf*, or Movement for Justice, and managed to get elected to Pakistan's parliament. I wish Imran every success in politics, because Allah knows Pakistan can use an honest politician. But I hope he also enjoys it. When I met him a couple of years after he had started his party, he told me by way of personal advice to never get into politics.

Personally, I remain surprised that Imran harboured political aspirations. He used to be one to always shun politics and I never thought it would be his calling. If politics is now his chosen path, I wish him the best in it. It can't be easy going, but Imran has the ability to pull through anything.

My own dream has been for Imran and I to continue to do for the cause of the Pakistani nation what we did for the cause of the Pakistan cricket team. I look forward to one day collaborating with Imran on economic, social and development-related projects, helping our country any way we can, through media projection, fundraising, coordination, or any other way in which our services might prove useful.

Pakistan has been good to both Imran and I. We owe Pakistan our careers and a debt of gratitude that can never be repaid. I am humbled by what Pakistan has given me, and I am sure Imran feels the same way too, because Pakistan has not given him any less.

A couple of years ago a Cricket Hall of Fame was set up at Lord's, in which we were told that three Pakistanis had been inducted. I feel privileged to be named in this group, along with Imran and Hanif Mohammed.

Imran's is a famous name in cricket, but the great thing is that it also remains an untarnished name. There have been no scandals, no allegations of him being anything less than impeccably honest. It is a pristine legacy, unsullied and unblemished. This reputation has also made Imran a great ambassador for Pakistan, and what greater achievement can there be than to enhance the name of your country through the shining example of your own person.

CHAPTER 18
A Difficult Retirement

Al things eventually come to an end. Of course I knew that my playing days would not last forever and I would have to retire some time. I had hoped that when the end came, it would be dignified, smoothly handled, and free of controversy.

The administrators who presided over Pakistan cricket in the early 1990s had other ideas. They tried to prematurely push me into oblivion. No one deserves to be treated the way they treated me. I was hurt by the events surrounding my retirement at a personal level. I was also hurt because the Pakistan team suffered as a consequence.

After our 1992 World Cup victory, I took over the leadership from Imran. I knew the Pakistan side better than anybody else and I had a vision and a plan for where I wanted to take the team over the next few years. I wanted to pass on my experience in all areas of cricket and hoped that the momentum we had been able to generate would not go to waste.

Following the World Cup success, I led Pakistan to a 2-1 victory in the five Test series in England. After that we went to New Zealand for a one-off Test at Hamilton where I made 92 and captained the team to victory even after we had conceded a 48-run first innings lead and had set New Zealand a fourth innings target of only 127.

With these victories overseas, my long history of honest and sincere service to Pakistan, and my record of leading Pakistan over the years to fourteen wins from thirty-four Tests as captain—second to none in the country's history—I contemplated Pakistan's cricket future. I was looking forward to an uninterrupted period of captaincy in which I would have the freedom to consolidate on the foundations Imran and I had built for Pakistan cricket in the preceding decade.

Imagine my surprise when, upon my return from New Zealand, I found a Pakistan Cricket Board with a new attitude altogether. All the top Board officials I met were distant and unfriendly, and none of them said anything positive to me about my leadership or my future. It didn't take an Einstein to figure out that I was no longer the Board's favoured choice for captain.

A move was afoot to unseat me and make Wasim Akram the new captain of Pakistan. The origins of this move could ultimately be traced back to Imran, whose influence was still very strong. Imran was close to all the top Board officials including the chairman and the secretary, and had formally been retained as a Pakistan Cricket Board advisor.

I don't know what Imran's motives were; I can only guess at them. Perhaps he felt an undisturbed Miandad captaincy would overshadow his legacy. Imran had not formally retired after the 1992 World Cup. He had injured his shoulder during the World Cup and it was more or less understood that by then he had played the last of his international cricket. Just before I departed for England for the Test series, the Pakistan Cricket Board Secretary, Shahid Rafi, assured me that I was going to remain as captain of Pakistan for as long as I continued to play. Imran, he said, was not in the picture at all.

Imran was very much around in England when I took the team there at the beginning of the 1992 summer. He was writing columns and articles in the English press and wrote a few pieces where I thought he was trying to disclose our weaknesses and our strategy. In one of his columns he wrote that the Pakistani batting would be most exposed on seaming wickets. It wasn't as if he was revealing state secrets to the enemy, but it wasn't the sort of thing you expected from your immediate past captain.

During that tour, Imran was also in contact with several members of the team, especially the younger ones. He even threw a party in which he invited the entire team with the exception of three people—Ramiz, Saleem Malik, and myself. I found this strange. Here was a man who just a few months ago was captaining from a lofty perch, unwilling to give the team's youngsters even the time of day, now he was reaching out to these very same lowly youngsters and inviting them to dinner. Something was wrong with this picture.

My guess is that Imran's efforts were aimed at trying to create an intrigue against my captaincy. I had a fabulous tour of England in 1992 and had no fears for the captaincy then. At the time these actions of Imran's had not seemed important; but it all made perfect sense once I had seen my dreams of uninterrupted captaincy go up in flames after returning from New Zealand in 1992-93.

As I have said, part of the reason behind Imran's behaviour was I think his fear that I would obscure his legacy. I think part of it, too, was resentment at the way the final days of his own captaincy had played out. We had won the 1992 World Cup under him, but he was not a universally admired man within that team. He was a fine cricket leader and no one doubted that, but the players' patience with his obsession for the hospital fundraising had started to wear thin. The players had nicknamed him 'Meter', implying a money counter that was always ticking. Imran was well aware that none of the players was sad to see him go.

As I said, I am only guessing at Imran's motives, though I am certain he played an important role in my final ouster from the captaincy.

After I returned from New Zealand in January 1993, it was not long before the Board's true intentions surfaced, and Akram was named the new captain. At that point, I confronted the Board Chairman Justice Nasim Hasan Shah and the Board Secretary Shahid Rafi.

'Today you have destroyed Pakistan cricket,' were my words to both of them in a face-to-face meeting. I let my feelings be known about their decision to appoint Wasim Akram in my place. It was not that Akram was not a deserving candidate. He just didn't deserve the captaincy at that point in time. I felt very strongly that I should have continued in the interest of the team's stability.

After I was removed, all the capital we had painstakingly built up in terms of the team's steadiness and dependability was squandered and the team went into a tailspin. The decision-makers of Pakistan cricket had gravely misread the situation, and it was our cricket that paid the heavy price for it.

Starting from the West Indies tour in 1992-93 up to the end of the decade, when England visited Pakistan in 2000-01, the Pakistan captaincy lost any meaning and became a game of musical chairs. In this period the leadership switched fourteen times between seven individuals—Akram of course, then Saleem Malik, then Ramiz Raja, then Akram again, then Saeed Anwar, then Ramiz again, then Akram again, and on and on. It was a circus, with Rashid Latif and Aamir Sohail also being tried as captains, followed by Moin Khan in 1999-2000. Waqar Younis was then given the job in 2001. There would be times during these years when more than half the team consisted of ex-captains. For thirteen years Imran and I had shared the Pakistan captaincy with only a brief interruption from Zaheer Abbas. And then this.

Naturally, it is the cricket that has suffered. To give an idea of the decline in performance, during these years we have lost a Test series at home no less than six times, twice to Sri Lanka and once each to South Africa, Australia, England, and Zimbabwe. And this is not to mention the 0-3 defeat to Australia in 2002-03—technically a 'home' series but played in Colombo and Sharjah—during which the Pakistan team hit rock bottom in all respects, including innings totals of 59 and 53 in the same Test match.

What a staggering turnaround! Prior to the first of these home losses, to Sri Lanka in 1995-96, Pakistan had lost at home on only four previous occasions in its entire Test history going back to 1952.

In a way, worse was still to follow, and it came in the form of the 2003 World Cup, in which a hopelessly casual approach brought about Pakistan's worst showing in a cricket World Cup ever. True, we had had a first-round exit before, in 1975, but not before coming within a hair's breadth of defeating the West Indies, the eventual champions. Then, in 1979, 1983 and 1987, we had finished as semi-finalists. In 1992, we were champions. In 1996, we were quarter-finalists; and in 1999, finalists. In 2003, we hardly came to the party, only managing apologetic victories over unranked Holland and Namibia and rolling over in front of the ranked sides in our group.

Pakistan is a great cricketing country and no doubt, its fortunes will rise again. However, I cannot help feeling that if the Pakistan Cricket Board had only listened to me back in 1993 when I pleaded with them not to play around with the captaincy and to let me finish the job, this sorry mess may well have been avoided. We had set out in the 1980s to make Pakistan one of the game's top teams, consistently victorious, talented and feared. The talent continues to pour forth—no one can stop that—but the team has not acquired anything even remotely resembling consistency. People have come to say that Pakistan can beat anyone 'on their day'. That basically describes a team of talented underachievers whose 'day' hardly ever comes.

I never thought it would ever happen that my heart would no longer be in cricket. When the Board removed me from the captaincy for the final time, I knew they had done lasting damage to Pakistan cricket and it hurt me deeply.

I was so disheartened then that I wanted to quit everything. I didn't want to go on playing and nearly announced my retirement. The Board subjected me to emotional blackmail saying that I should still play because Pakistan needed me. The situation was such that if I had gone ahead and quit, it would have appeared that I selfishly coveted the captaincy and would only serve Pakistan if I were captain. As I could not tolerate the slightest blemish on my unquestioned record of loyalty to Pakistan, I went along as a regular player under the captaincy of Wasim Akram.

Wasim's first assignment was to lead Pakistan on a three-Test tour of West Indies. It ended up being a complete disaster.

The series was lost 0-2. I was not in the right frame of mind to play and failed with the bat, averaging only 24 overs 5 innings.

On the beach in Grenada, some of the boys got mixed up with a drug possessions charge. When the police got involved, it became a huge mess and arrests were made. A couple of English girls were arrested as well. It didn't help matters that one of the accused happened to be Wasim Akram, the new captain. Everyone—the team manager Khalid Mahmood, the other players, even the PCB Secretary Shahid Rafi—were turning to me for guidance. I had never realized my name carried any influence in the Caribbean, but it certainly helped us negotiate our way with the Grenada authorities. I called on some local contacts and helped arrange legal counsel, after which the charges were dropped. It was quite a scandal.

This was highly improper conduct by the players, but our Pakistan Cricket Board tackled it very feebly. Later a couple of the involved players sold their stories to the local tabloids; the Board remained ineffectual even on this infraction.

We returned from West Indies in May 1993 and I had a quiet summer. In October, I went with the team to play in the Pepsi Champions Trophy in Sharjah, which also included West Indies and Sri Lanka. We lost in the finals to the West Indies.

Pakistan's next major commitment was to host Zimbabwe for three Tests and three One-Day Internationals beginning December 1993. I had a recurrence of my back problem and there was some question about my fitness. Nevertheless, I was keen to play and made myself available to the Selection Committee. Neither the selectors nor the PCB officials seemed interested and I sensed that they had decided to do away with me altogether. I saw through their game—the lack of fitness was going to be a convenient excuse for them to finally axe me from the Pakistan Test side.

If the Board was going to drop me, I wanted them to come clean about it. I didn't want any fitness problems diluting the Board's culpability. I forced the issue and insisted on being given a fitness test.

Reluctantly the Board agreed, eventually asking me to appear for a fitness test at the Pakistan Cricket Board headquarters in Lahore. At the time I was at my mother's home in Karachi, but flew to Lahore and was at the PCB office precisely at the appointed hour.

I arrived to find the place unexpectedly quiet. There was no activity, no panel of doctors, no indication that a fitness test had even been arranged.

I sent word to the Secretary's office that I had arrived, but nothing happened. I waited and waited. An hour passed, but still nothing. I felt insulted at being treated in this offhand manner and became very upset. The PCB had hoped to drop me from the team under the cover of fitness issues. I didn't want them to get away with it. I had insisted on taking a fitness test, to which they had agreed, but they were now playing games. It certainly wasn't the treatment I had expected from the Board after serving Pakistan with all my heart and soul for so many years.

Enraged and upset, I found my way to the Board Secretary's room. An assistant was hovering outside and tried to stop me. I told him to let the Secretary know I was waiting. The assistant stuck his head into the Secretary's office and delivered the message, to which the Secretary Shahid Rafi responded, 'Tell him to wait.'

The moment I heard this, I pushed the assistant out of the way and barged into the Secretary's office.

Inside, there was a cosy little party going on—people smoking and laughing, enjoying each other's company in a genial atmosphere. Shahid Rafi was at his desk with the others seated around him. Selectors Haseeb Ahsan and Waqar Hasan were there, as was a doctor I recognized, Dr Aamir Aziz. There were also a couple of other people whom I didn't know. Everyone seemed to be having a grand old time. This, apparently, is what I had been made to wait for.

I just exploded. All my frustrations with the Board's high-handedness came pouring out, and I let them have it. 'I am not dying to play cricket,' I told that crowd assembled in the Board Secretary's office. I told them if they wanted to drop me they should do it openly without trying to hide behind some fitness issue. I also let them know I hadn't expected to be treated like this.

I was livid. I remember shaking my finger at Shahid Rafi: 'You were the ones who set the time and asked me to come for this fitness test, and now you are making me wait around like a schoolboy.' I accused them of never having had the intention of evaluating my fitness.

'I've played this game a long time and I can see through your charade,' I said, shaking with anger.

Everyone became very quiet and pulled themselves up in their seats. For a brief moment, no one said anything. Haseeb Ahsan was the first to speak. He got up and came towards me and began apologizing, the others joining in. Haseeb's tone was very conciliatory. He said they had just been talking about me and pointed to the presence of Dr Aamir Aziz as evidence that a fitness test had indeed been planned.

Whether the Board was serious about giving me a fitness test that day, I don't know. What I do know is that the effect of my rage was such that after only a cursory examination by the doctor, I was declared fit and was invited to join the team's training sessions. I think they had no real answers for me, and my outburst had caught them off guard.

It was ironic that in fact I was not completely fit. I knew, however, that I was going to be all right provided I got a few days rest. I had expected that at the fitness test the doctor was going to find me less than 100 per cent, and I would then ask for one week's rest from training. The way things happened, though, the doctor hardly examined me, and I was declared fit even though I didn't feel 100 per cent.

After all the fuss I made, I didn't want to give the Board even the slightest excuse to remove me. I wasn't going to ask for any rest and joined the training camp, even though I was still struggling a bit with my back.

The training camp proved another unpleasant experience. The selectors said they wanted to see me bat in the nets. I got padded and gloved, put on a helmet, and got ready to face our bowlers.

Right from the first delivery, I began facing bouncers—all hostile, ugly and short-pitched. The selectors had apparently given our bowlers a game plan that they hadn't shared with me. The bowlers—Wasim, Waqar, Aaqib Javed—had difficulty looking me in the eye. It was obvious the selectors had forced them to do this. After the first few bouncers, the bowlers began apologizing, but still they kept digging them in short.

I was incensed, I threw off my helmet in a fit of rage and challenged the bowlers to aim for my head. That finally shamed them into improving their length. This was the attitude that I had to put up with in the practice camp.

We played the first Test at Karachi on 1 December 1993. It was the inaugural Test for Karachi's second Test centre, Defence Stadium. Akram was injured and Waqar was made captain. I made 70 and 12 (run out) even though a stiff back was hindering me. Waqar was in his element and recorded his best match analysis (13 for 135) as Pakistan won the Test by 131 runs. In the second Test I made 20 and 10, and in the third Test I made 31. I got a chance to bat in two of the three limited-overs games, and scored 19 and 55.

After that series, I was dropped from the Pakistan side. It came as a rude shock.

I was being forced into premature retirement. I had it in me to keep batting for Pakistan, and who knows I may have crossed 10,000, perhaps even 11,000 Test runs. Compared to my earlier playing days, the quality of bowling in the 1990s had deteriorated. If anything, this transition in opposition bowlers had improved my chances of batting success. But there were forces in Pakistan cricket wanting to deny me my achievements. They overlooked the fact that any feats I might accomplish would ultimately be a credit to Pakistan as well.

To my utter amazement, the news that I had been dropped from the Pakistan team triggered a wave of public protests in Pakistan. People came out on the streets in mass agitation and launched hunger strikes.

After Zimbabwe's visit, Pakistan had been due to tour New Zealand in the latter part of 1993-94. When the selectors announced the touring party, my name wasn't in it. Akram had been named captain for the tour but many of the players rejected his leadership. Saleem Malik emerged as the new captain. New Zealand had been my favourite hunting ground and I could have offered our young team a great deal there with the bat as well as with my experience, yet I had been overlooked.

After the New Zealand tour, the team was headed to Sharjah to participate in the third Austral-Asia Cup. I wasn't selected for that trip, either. I decided then that there was no need to prolong my humiliation and so I made up my mind to retire.

I had came in to bat on 9 October 1976, with Pakistan 55 for 4 against New Zealand at Lahore. Now, after seventeen years and 124 Tests in the service of Pakistan, I decided that I had finally played the last of my Test cricket. My last Test was the third Test against Zimbabwe when I made 31 at Lahore on 16 December 1993. In 189 innings, I made 8,832 runs at an average of 52.57 with twenty-three 100s, including six double centuries. It is also been pointed out that my batting average never dipped below 50 at any time in my career, which is a feat no other batsman has been able to match (not even Sir Donald Bradman, who scored 18 and 1 in his first Test match). I am proud of my career record, which sits on the top of Pakistan's batting figures, but I look forward to the day when another Pakistani will surpass it.

I had decided to retire from cricket the moment I saw that I had been overlooked for the Sharjah trip. I kept this decision to myself and didn't inform even my closest friends. I didn't want anyone leaking the information as I wanted to announce it myself in a press conference. The only people I shared this decision with prior to making it public were my wife Tahira and my elder brother Bashir.

I invited the press to a meeting at the Karachi Press Club. I told them I would be making a press statement but the invitation didn't give details. The evening before the press conference, I went to see Muneer Hussain at his residence in Karachi. Muneer Sahib has been one of the great personalities of Pakistan cricket—a cricket administrator, commentator and magazine editor—and I consider him one of my dear friends. He was instrumental in helping to arrange the press briefing and we went over the preparations one last time. I had told Muneer Sahib I would be saying things about the cricket administration in Pakistan and the workings of the Pakistan Cricket Board. Right up to the last minute, I said nothing about my retirement. I just couldn't bring myself to do it.

The press meeting was very well attended. I had planned on giving a preamble before coming to the announcement of my retirement, but soon after I began speaking, my emotions overwhelmed me and I broke down. I tried to fight back the tears but I was helpless. It is very hard when you've done something you love for years and then have to call it quits. I was also very sad at the way my retirement had come about. The Board was misguided about Pakistan cricket, and in their ineptitude and ingratitude they had ignored and insulted me. This is not the way I had expected to go. With a knot in my stomach, a lump in my throat and with tears flowing, I told all the assembled reporters and newsmen that my cricketing career had come to an end.

The news was met with even greater protests in the streets. I thought and hoped it would all soon die down. Days went by, yet the newspapers remained full of accounts of people marching in the streets, protesting with banners and demonstrating in front of the PCB headquarters in Lahore, refusing to see me go. Some people were threatening to set themselves on fire if I didn't take back my announcement. I was already torn up inside about retiring, and now this. It was extremely unsettling.

At first I thought the protests were just coming from Karachi, my hometown and the place where I learned my cricket. Then incidents started happening all over Pakistan. I got word that even people outside Pakistan wanted me to reconsider my decision. During those days I got a call from BBC Radio in London asking for an interview. They said people had been calling their Urdu Service offices in tears to record their grief over my retirement announcement. All this was very difficult for me. I was greatly moved at the outpouring of emotion from so many fans, but I was helpless at trying to ease their frustration.

This passionate admiration that I received from my fans overwhelms me whenever I think about it. Retirement is normally a time when one is gradually forgotten, but when I said I was going to retire, people came out on the streets. I would get telephone calls from desperate wives saying their husbands were refusing to eat if I didn't come out of retirement so could I please take it all back so that everyone could get on with their lives.

I always knew I had a solid fan base, but it was my retirement that made me realize how large and how intense this support really was. I owe a great debt of gratitude to these fans and supporters, without whom my cricket would have been meaningless. The respect my fans have given me makes me feel the most fortunate person in the world.

I had decided long ago that I would retire from Test cricket while I was still doing well. Greg Chappell had made 182 in his last Test match, at Sydney in January 1984. It was a Test against Pakistan that I had been part of. Chappell's parting shot made a great impression on me. I decided that I, too, would say my goodbyes while I was still at the top. It became my ambition to also make a hundred in my last Test innings.

I was only 36 years old and still had a lot of good cricket left in me when I was dropped following that series against Zimbabwe in 1993-94. I know I would have got that last-innings hundred if they had only let me play on. I had made 55 in my last innings in that series, in the third One-Day International at Lahore, and still they dropped me.

This loud public outcry over a cricketer's retirement was unprecedented in Pakistan's history. It became such a problem that the government had to get involved. A number of members from the National Assembly, Pakistan's parliament, urged me to reconsider my decision to retire. Their constituents were all up in arms about it, they said. Some of them thought I needed to continue playing and reach 10,000 career Test runs.

I tried to reach out to my supporters through some public forums. One of these was a public meeting organized by *Jang*, Pakistan's leading Urdu language newspaper. I went over the events leading up to my retirement announcement and tried to explain the way it had all played out. I wanted to help people reason through their disappointment, but my efforts in these public forums had the opposite effect. People began talking about bringing the Pakistan Cricket Board to justice over the way it had mishandled its dealings with me.

The matter caught the attention of the highest levels of government in Pakistan. I was invited to meet with Farooq Leghari, then President of Pakistan. One doesn't get called to meet one's head of state every day; it was a major event for me. I went to see him at Aiwan-e-Sadar, the President's official residence in Islamabad.

I had no idea what President Leghari was going to say and the anticipation made me nervous. The President began by saying he thought I wasn't in the team because I had a 'slipped disc'. That gave me some idea of how badly misinformed he had been. I clarified the situation for him, and when he realized that I was fit and eager to play, he asked me to reconsider my retirement. He said he spoke for the whole country in wanting to see me play and to bring greater glory for Pakistan. I politely declined.

Shortly after that I received a call from Asif Zardari, husband of then Prime Minister Benazir Bhutto. Asif was a sports fan and a colourful personality. He insisted that I return to international cricket. 'You've got to come back,' he would keep saying. Asif was very persuasive but I was hesitant, as my decision to leave cricket hadn't been taken lightly.

Then finally one day I was summoned to see Prime Minister Benazir Bhutto herself. The meeting was arranged in the VIP Lounge at Karachi airport. The Prime Minister was extremely welcoming and gracious. She began by speaking highly of my career and achievements. I was overwhelmed. It was also quite embarrassing. She said she wanted me to take back my retirement and play again for Pakistan.

'Javed,' Benazir Bhutto said, 'I want you to return to the team and go past 10,000 runs. I want it to happen during my government's tenure.' She said it was a personal plea from her.

I tried to express my reservations, but she would have none of it. I struggled with the choice I faced, but in the end, I was unable to refuse her. I also wanted to put an end to all the protests and unrest from my supporters and realized I would finally have to give in to all the pressure and come out of retirement.

The pressure was really crushing, and it had become simply impossible to maintain my state of retirement. I withdrew my previous announcement and once again made myself available to be selected for Pakistan.

By this time it was July, the middle of the summer in Pakistan. A tour of Sri Lanka was coming up in the start of the 1994-95 season, for which I had now made myself eligible.

The Selection Committee had changed from the previous season and was now headed by Imtiaz Ahmed, Pakistan's former wicketkeeper-batsman and captain from the 1950s and 60s. The selectors announced that all eligible players would be asked to appear in a trial match. This was fine by me. A trial match was duly arranged at the United Bank Sports Complex in Karachi. It was being described as a trial for all the players involved, but I knew the real focus of attention was going to be nothing other than my batting. Conditions would be hot in July, but I was used to doing my training routine in the mid-afternoons in Karachi, and I felt I would be up to it.

In that trial match, I scored a century. It ended up being a very one-sided match and was finished within two days. Despite the heat, I held up fine. Several of the other players were not so lucky and were badly dehydrated. Once I went out to bat and became set, the selectors left the ground and didn't return. As I had suspected, they had been interested in evaluating no one else but me.

Soon afterwards, I was named in the team to tour Sri Lanka.

However, what Allah does not wish to happen, can never come to pass. Fate had determined that I had played the last of my Test cricket on 16 December 1993. And fate would let no one—not the fans, nor the President or Prime Minister, not even the force of my own will—change that.

In August 1994, a couple of weeks after the trial match, I was fooling around playing football in the pre-tour training camp at Gaddafi Stadium in Lahore. It was in the morning and we had just finished our warm-up exercises. Someone thought it would be a good idea to kick a football about. When the ball came my way, I pivoted around to try and kick it, and immediately felt my knee snap. I could barely walk after that and knew I had been ruled out of the upcoming tour, at the very least.

I underwent MRI scans of my knee in Karachi and was diagnosed with a torn cruciate ligament. After that I went on to England for arthroscopic knee repair. I am indebted to two doctors who helped me through this difficult injury. Dr Aamir Aziz took me to England and introduced me to Dr David Rees, a Welshman and a fine orthopaedic surgeon with an outstanding reputation. Dr Rees was a cricket fan, and said he had admired my batting. He waived his professional fees for me. I insisted on paying, but he came back with a disarming answer: 'If I can do a good job with your knee and see you bat again, that would be more than enough fees for me.' He was that kind of a man.

Dr Rees operated on my knee and then handed me over to Leslie King, a sports physiotherapist who understood her craft thoroughly. Leslie was amazing. She worked with me over six demanding but inspiring months at the Crystal Palace training facility in London. I made a steady recovery under her expert guidance and gradually the knee healed. By the time I left London, it was as though the injury had never happened.

By the spring of 1995, I had regained full fitness. Pakistan's international cricket calendar for 1995-96 included limited-overs tournaments in Sharjah and South Africa, as well as Test series against Sri Lanka and New Zealand. After the meeting with Prime Minister Benazir Bhutto the previous year, I had come out of retirement, and so was technically available to play.

I was put under great pressure to join the team—from the fans and supporters as well as from senior PCB members like Arif Abbasi—but the moment had passed. Too much had happened with me over the last couple of seasons. The convalescence from the injury had been a long and quiet six months, which had finally given me refuge from the all the ups and downs surrounding my retirement. It had all been nothing less than an emotional roller coaster ride. I was tired now, and resisted all the offers to return to the team.

Something special, however, was coming up around the corner. In early 1996, the sixth World Cup was being staged in Pakistan, India and Sri Lanka. I had expected that the pressure to play in the tournament would be intense, and it was. I had hoped to resist it, but when it became a question of serving Pakistan in its quest to retain the World Cup that we had brought home in 1992, I had to give in.

If I stayed out of the tournament and Pakistan lost the title, the public would never forgive me. That was the straightforward argument I used to convince myself to play for Pakistan again.

We had a very good team for the 1996 World Cup and should have won it, but the outfit failed to come together as a team. I don't think I was alone in feeling out of it; there was just no spirit in our campaign. In 1992 we had played out of our skins; in 1996, we just went through the motions.

It wasn't at all easy for me because all through that tournament, I felt like an unwanted member of the team. I was being sent in to bat at no. 5 or no. 6 even though I had played at no. 4 all my life. The captain, Wasim Akram, and the team management knew they were under-utilizing me, but they didn't do anything about it.

After the league matches, we ran into India at Bangalore in one of the quarterfinals. Wasim Akram pulled out at the last minute citing a side strain. Everyone was expecting him to be the captain and this was a shock for all of us. We didn't know he would be stepping down until the last minute.

Akram had strained his side in our last league game, against New Zealand at Lahore. That had been three days before the quarterfinal. At that time he told everyone he was '75 per cent fit' and expected to play at Bangalore. If he had any reservations about playing in the quarterfinals, he certainly didn't take the team or the management into confidence about it. At the very

least, he should have identified a potential substitute captain.
No such thing was done.

There is no doubt that Akram should have made it clear well
in advance if he feared he was unfit and might be missing the
game. We were playing the quarterfinal of the World Cup. If
there was any chance the captain wouldn't be available; an
alternative strategy should have been devised.

The morning of the match, Akram came up to me clutching
his side. He said he had taken a painkiller injection but it hadn't
helped. He then tried to bowl a few deliveries in a practice session.
The quarterfinal was going to be a floodlit game and was not
going to start until 2 p.m. Even as the time for the toss approached,
we still thought Akram would be captain. Imran was at the ground
and I noticed Akram chatting with him, though I have no idea
what they talked about. Around 1.30 p.m., just shortly before the
toss, Akram told us he was unfit and would not be playing.

Aamir Sohail was made the substitute captain in Akram's
place when in fact I should have been asked. I would have
offered all the experience I had accumulated over a twenty-year
career in all kinds of situations and at all levels of the game,
including as captain. I had started captaining Pakistan when
Aamir Sohail had not even made his first-class debut. Sohail
was in fact the team's vice-captain, but this was no ordinary
game—it was a battle to the death against India in their home
arena, in front of a sell-out crowd of hostile fans. It was too
much for Sohail, who had never captained an international match
before. India racked up 287 for 8 as Sohail mishandled the
bowling changes and proved an amateur at field placements. He
was simply out of his depth. As the Indian innings flourished
and our bowling floundered, I kept expecting Sohail to seek my
counsel, but not once during that match did he ask me for advice.
I don't think he knew how to.

I had spent a career getting in and out of tough situations and
I knew a thing or two about strategy, but I found no takers that
day for the things I had learned over a lifetime. I was just
wasted in that match. Had it been up to me, I would have come
in to bat at no. 3 and tied up one end. After the openers had

given us a flying start, we were then required to consolidate, but instead the wickets fell steadily. I was held back to come in at no. 6, which was really pointless. The whole thing was typical of our approach in that tournament—devoid of any plan or strategy, we came to each match just hoping for the best.

We were knocked out of the tournament, and with that quarterfinal match I finally said good-bye to international cricket. However, the good-bye that really mattered to me had already come a few days earlier, at Karachi on 3 March 1996.

I am a Karachi product if I am anything. It is my hometown, the place where I learned to bat. I have naturally always felt a deep bond with the city and its people, and whenever I have played at National Stadium, it has always felt as if I was playing in my own backyard.

When I first saw the 1996 World Cup's list of fixtures, the date of 3 March jumped out at me. The date of our group match against England, it would mark my last appearance in an international match at Karachi.

We were batting second in that game and I came out to bat in the final stages. By that time we needed another 36 runs to win, with 7 wickets in hand and more than enough overs left. There was no reason to be anxious, yet the intensity of that moment is still with me years later. Throughout my career, I would always get a special cheer from the Karachi crowd, but this time the cheers that welcomed me were deafening. Inzamam was in great form at the other end and knocked off the target quickly, and we headed back to the pavilion having won the game.

All the players must have realized I was doing this for the last time, because they all stayed back and let me walk ahead. The crowd rose to their feet and started chanting my name and waving madly. I had never experienced such an overwhelming outpouring of affection and it moved me deeply. As I entered the pavilion, I was struggling with my emotions and I would be the first to admit that my eyes were moist. I wanted to look back at the cheering crowd one more time, but before I knew it I was back in the dressing room and it was all over. My cricketing love affair with Karachi had ended and would soon pass into memory.

Six days later, on 9 March, we played the quarterfinal against India at Bangalore, after which I returned home to join my family in Lahore. On 17 March, Sri Lanka met Australia in the final played under lights at Lahore's Gaddafi Stadium. I watched that match as a spectator and had a relaxed and restful time sitting on the other side of the fence. People kept coming up to me and showed me such warmth and affection, and were extremely generous with their praise. I was overwhelmed at the respect I received just walking around the ground and following the cricket from the stands that warm Lahore evening.

I had nothing to hide and nothing to fear. The other members of our team apparently saw it differently. They stayed away from the public eye and slunk away to different parts of the country. A rumour started that Wasim Akram had been bribed by the bookies to miss the quarterfinal. I had no personal knowledge of this and as far as I could tell it was just a rumour, but the public seemed convinced and vented their fury and frustrations by pelting Wasim's house with stones and garbage.

It was a fabulous World Cup final and Aravinda de Silva's name was written all over it. He took three wickets as Australia batted first, and then played a gem of an innings to make 107 not out. Earlier in the tournament, the Australians had refused to play in Sri Lanka due to security fears. It was ironic they were now defeated in the final by the same team whose hospitality they had spurned. We all cheered as Sri Lanka steered themselves to a well deserved victory.

I had finally stepped out of the international spotlight and cricket began to recede from my mind. There were things I had to catch up with. I looked forward to being with my family; my children were growing up, and I longed to spend more time with them and with my wife, Tahira. Perhaps at the time I thought about coaching or doing something in cricket administration, I don't remember what, now. All I remember from that time is that I was looking forward to a long, indefinite break from the pressures of the cricket world.

CHAPTER 19

Mr Controversy

I have done nothing discreditable in my career and have nothing to apologize for. Yet at some point in my cricket life—I am not sure when exactly, but it happened quite early on—I became labelled a controversial person. People tried to discredit me and to cast me in a negative light. This happened abroad, in countries like Australia and England, but I have also received this treatment within Pakistan, at the hands of my own teammates and countrymen. Whatever the reasons for this, the label has stuck and I have accepted it as something that I cannot change. I am what I am and don't intend to change just to accommodate some people's need to escape the truth. If others find me controversial, it is their problem not mine.

I suppose controversy happens when expectations are violated. In advanced cricket-playing countries like Australia and England, people expect cricketers from Third World countries to behave in a certain subservient way. We are expected not to challenge anything, not to make a fuss. If a wrong is done, people expect us to accept things and meekly get on with it. They don't want us to make an issue of anything because that can often turn out to be embarrassing for them.

Someone like me who speaks his mind and refuses to shy away from the truth will obviously be considered a troublemaker in this setting. Speaking your mind openly can be disturbing for others, but if you can also back it up with good cricket, the whole package becomes too hot to handle.

Those who try to conform are better tolerated. I suppose if I too had gone partridge shooting in the English Midlands, or had been photographed in a morning dress at Ascot, people would have found me more palatable. I am proud of who I am and where I come from and I have no reason to try to be something other than what I am.

Test cricket started in England and Australia and for years these two countries dominated the game and its administration. The Asian countries were never taken seriously and certainly never respected in the same way as England and Australia respected each other. This climate prevailed even when I began international cricket but I have never accepted it. After the 1980s and 1990s, with the spectacular rise of cricket in Asia, the equation is finally changing.

There is now a huge market for cricket in Asia. Most of this is due to the enormous population of India, which is the single largest cricket market in the world. But there is also a great cricket following in Pakistan, Sri Lanka, Bangladesh and Sharjah, and it exceeds the popularity of the sport in other cricketing nations. Sponsorship and publicity have followed the emergence of the Asian market, causing the cricket world's centre of gravity to shift towards this part of the world. Today, Asian cricket is self-sustaining and financially robust. Countries like India and Pakistan can sustain their cricket markets even if they limit themselves to only playing each other. One can no longer say this of Australia and England. Cricket would die there if these countries played no one but themselves.

I may have made mistakes in my career, but I would do nothing different were I to live through it again. I would like to explain what it is about me and my cricket that makes people put a negative spin on my behaviour and motives.

One factor behind my controversial image is undoubtedly my aggressive approach to cricket. Unfortunately, my aggression has been misunderstood. It has been misconstrued as something negative and troublesome. In fact, aggression in sports should be respected as an expression of a fighting spirit. This is how I had hoped my hard-nosed attitude to cricket would be viewed.

My aggression didn't follow the rules of submissiveness prescribed for Asian cricketers in the 70s and 80s. This resulted in some controversial incidents over the course of my career.

During the first Test at Perth on the 1981-82 Pakistan tour to Australia, I was involved in an unfortunate incident with Dennis Lillee. Sledging, or abusive verbal harassment, was routine fare in Australian cricket in those days and it created an especially charged atmosphere for touring teams. I have never been one to take any kind of harassment lying down and have always believed in giving as good as I got. I would never initiate abuse but if ever any was directed at me, I was not going to shrink from responding in kind. Far from turning my back on confrontation, I am the sort who insists on puffing out his chest and inviting more of the same.

That 1981-82 trip to Australia was my first tour as captain of Pakistan. It was a difficult time for our team as we were trying to regroup after being battered in a home series loss by West Indies the previous season in 1980-81, as I have described earlier in Chapter 5.

It was an especially trying time for me personally. The problem was not the demands of captaincy, as I have always relished the challenge that comes with the job and, in fact, my record as captain of Pakistan is second to none. The real issue was the timing of my appointment. The more senior players in the side felt I had been appointed out of turn and some of them thought this meant that the job was lost to them forever. Whether that was true or not, my position was straightforward: the Pakistan Cricket Board had made me captain and it was every team members' professional obligation to obey me in that capacity. Instead of displaying professionalism, though, some of the more experienced players went around looking unhappy, which disturbed team morale. It was a distraction I didn't need on this important debut tour as captain.

To make matters worse, our hosts scheduled the series opener to be played at Perth.

If you've never played at Perth, you don't know what you're in for. It is the fastest and bounciest track in the world. A regulation delivery that pitches on a length and heads for the top of the stumps on any ordinary wicket explodes off the pitch and shoots up past your shoulder at Perth.

By the time we got to Perth, Dennis and I had already been going at each other for a while. In one of the side matches, a four-day game against Queensland at Brisbane, I had scored a hundred and Dennis had been frustrated at not being able to get me out. We had already exchanged a few 'pleasantries'.

I don't think Dennis or any of the other Australians had expected to see a Pakistani player like me who simply refused to back down. For years, Pakistani teams on foreign tours had found it difficult to shake a sense of inferiority. Perhaps we were embarrassed to be from a Third World country that not too long ago had been ruled by white colonialists. These mental shackles had kept us from reaching our true potential overseas. Of course, none of this made an iota of a difference to me. As far as I was concerned, cricket was war and I was at war whenever I played. Retreat was not an option and I was never going to back down.

Dennis was a naturally hostile fast bowler, without doubt one of the very best I have played against. I respected his skill, but I was in no mind to step away from it.

That Perth Test started out well for us as our fast bowlers Imran and Sarfraz bowled Australia out for 180 in the first innings. When our turn came we couldn't handle the pace of the Perth wicket and our response was disastrous. At one point we were 26-8, and eventually managed 62, at the time Pakistan's lowest ever Test score. Australia then piled up 424-8 declared, leaving us a target of 543 with nearly two days to spare.

The encounter with Lillee happened when I was batting in the second innings. The crowd was worked up and was chanting 'KILL, KILL, LILL-EE' each time Lillee ran in to bowl. I had come in at 27-2 and was painstakingly trying to rebuild the innings in a third wicket partnership with Mansoor Akhtar. With the score 78-2, I played a delivery from Dennis towards the square-leg umpire and pushed off for a single. About three-quarters down the pitch, I collided with him as he had stepped back at the last minute to block my path. Since I had to make my ground, I just pushed him out of the way and got to the safety of the non-striker's end. As Dennis passed me on the way back to his run-up, he kicked me on the pad and swore at me. Almost in reflex, I turned around and threatened him with my bat.

Dennis's was an outrageous gesture but obviously he contemplated it because he thought he could get away with it, or at least get off lightly. We were after all only from Pakistan and he felt he could take liberties with us. Had I been captain of England, I wonder if the idea of retaliating with a kick on the pads would even have entered Dennis's mind.

The Australian media compounded the situation. They really played up the incident and their incessant coverage made the whole thing much bigger than it deserved to be. I was projected as a miscreant because after Dennis had kicked me, I had swung around and threatened him with my bat. What was I supposed to do, bend over and ask for more? The media ran riot. They tried to suggest I was responsible for starting the whole mess in the first place and tried to seal my guilt by referring to the brandishing of my bat. In fact, I had tolerated a volley of abuse from Dennis and my threatening him with my bat should have been seen in the context of that abusive exchange and the heated atmosphere in which it had taken place.

When the dust settled, Dennis received a censure from the Australian Cricket Board and a fine of (Australian) $200. To my great astonishment, certain individuals in the Pakistan team lobbied with our own team management for me to get a fine or some other kind of punishment. These players' reasoning mystified me. I was first blocked from completing a run and then provoked into anger, and for that I needed to be punished?

These finger-pointers should have paid attention to people with better judgment than their own. The highly respected former Australian leg-spinner Bill O'Reilly, in an opinion column in the *Sydney Morning Herald*, noted, 'Lillee should have been instructed to leave the field, temporarily at least. If the [Australian Cricket] Board is prepared to do its job, Lillee is due now for a long holiday.' O'Reilly also termed 'utter eyewash' the suggestion from some quarters that I had somehow been 'baiting' Lillee.

I will say again that the media coverage is what gave this story a life of its own, one that it didn't deserve. The press made it out to be some horrible, ugly scandal that would stain cricket forever. In a way, I sympathized with Dennis. He was a loudmouth who played top flight cricket, and the press loves to skewer such people whenever they seem to falter. Even then I knew, as is now clear, that the media reaction was unjust and the hype was overblown. Dennis and I have never formally talked about that incident. Soon afterwards when we met off the field, it was as if nothing had happened. We had a few photographs taken afterwards, shaking hands amiably in a gesture of peace, but that too was media-driven. Dennis and I are friends now and have been for a long time, and I have the greatest respect for him. The incident itself has quietly receded away and very few people think of it now.

I was also involved in another controversial incident in Australia, this one during the first Test at Melbourne on the 1979-80 Pakistan tour. That was a much happier Pakistan team, with Mushtaq Mohammed as captain, in which I was a relatively junior member. We were fresh from a series victory in New Zealand, and were still savouring the famous home series win against India the previous season, in 1978-79.

The incident happened when, in the Australian first innings, fast bowler Rodney Hogg was batting and I ran him out. Apparently Hogg saw it differently.

We had batted first and made 196 in our first innings. In reply, Australia were struggling at 167-8 with Hogg and opener Graeme Wood at the crease. Hogg played a defensive shot to a ball from Sarfraz Nawaz and the ball trickled out towards silly point, which was vacant. I was fielding at short-leg and stepped across to pick up the ball.

Meanwhile, Hogg decided to leave the batting crease. I had my back towards the pitch and was partly blinded, so I couldn't see if Hogg was actually going for a run. All I could see was the empty batting crease. So I turned around and clipped the bails. Hogg was out of his ground and the square-leg umpire gave him out.

I was portrayed as having done something crafty or underhand, but as far as I was concerned Hogg was out of his ground and that was the end of it. Hogg, however, appeared unconvinced. Television replays showed that he had taken a few steps down the pitch to do some 'gardening'. I suppose he felt that as he wasn't going for a run and the ball had become 'dead' after he had played it, he should not be out. Fair dinkum (as they say in Australia). But the umpire had reached a decision and cricket's code of conduct required Hogg to obey it. He should have respected the judgement and walked off without a fuss.

Our ever-astute captain Mushtaq Mohammed saw through the confusion and decided to retract our appeal and recall Hogg, but the umpires would have none of it. Hogg had been ruled out—end of discussion. In frustration, Hogg smashed the stumps before finally walking away.

In my opinion, technically, Hogg was out—and umpire Mick Harvey obviously agreed. The umpire is the final judge of play and it is part of cricket that sometimes you just have to grit your teeth and accept an umpiring decision that you may not like. There was certainly no need for Hogg's petulant behaviour.

A third controversial incident that also attracted a good deal of media coverage happened in Sri Lanka, during the second Test at the Colombo Cricket Club Ground on the 1985-86 Pakistan tour to Sri Lanka.

The umpiring had been highly disappointing throughout that series, and the match was being played in an atmosphere of open acrimony between the two teams. In the second innings, I was given out to a pathetic LBW decision, but I swallowed my anger and headed towards the pavilion.

As I started walking back, I realized someone from the crowd was pelting stones at me. Up to that point on the tour, we had put up with questionable umpiring, a highly one-sided Sri

Lankan press, and a bitterly partisan crowd. But now to be pelted with stones ... this was just too much!

So I jumped the fence and ran into the crowd to put an end to it. I spotted the culprit, but he ran away as soon as our eyes met. In the meantime, some of my teammates also ran over to be with me and calmed me down. The security forces finally came around and I let them know exactly what I thought of the 'security' they were providing.

Then of course there is that infamous incident between Mike Gatting and Shakoor Rana in which I, being the Pakistan captain, was involved by default.

The incident happened in Faisalabad during the second Test of the 1987-88 England tour to Pakistan. English teams visiting Pakistan have tended to have the attitude that Pakistan is a backward and underdeveloped country, and this particular touring party was very much of the same view. This attitude amazes me because some of the facilities we have had to endure in England, either during Test duty for Pakistan or on the county circuit, have been rather underwhelming. I have been on tours to England where it was not unusual for us to be put up in a modest bed and breakfast and to have to wait in line just to take a shower. These second-rate accommodations are no match for the deluxe five-star comfort and hospitality that we provide touring teams in Pakistan.

English teams visiting Pakistan have also tended to have an arrogant demeanour towards support staff, such as waiters, porters and other helping hands—and sometimes even towards the fans. Not all the players are guilty of this, but there are enough of them for it to have been noticeable.

While the third Test of that 1987-88 series was going on, an ugly incident happened at Karachi's five-star Pearl Continental Hotel with an autograph hunter, whom I happened to know personally. This young man went after Graham Dilley and Philip DeFreitas in search of an autograph and followed them to their hotel room. The players displayed their displeasure by slamming their door on him with such force that the poor fellow's hand was crushed and he sustained multiple fractures of his fingers. I was also staying at the Pearl at the time and the man was brought to me in terrible shape, his hand bleeding profusely. We immediately sent him to the hospital and I went over to give Dilley and DeFreitas a piece of my mind.

While we had been fuming at the English team's presumptuousness, the English team itself was under strain during that trip. The series was taking place right after the 1987 World Cup and I am sure Gatting must have been sore at having presided over England's second loss in a World Cup final.

What sparked off the incident was a basic disagreement where Umpire Shakoor Rana thought Gatting was moving a fieldsman back without notifying the batsman (Saleem Malik), while Gatting felt he had given the batsman proper notice. Saleem had earlier played a hook shot and had been shocked to find that after he had settled into his batting stance, the square-leg fielder had moved from his usual position and gone deeper. Saleem had pointed this out to Umpire Rana, who warned Gatting and decided to keep an eye out for more of the same. When it happened again, Rana confronted Gatting, and Gatting blew his stack. A terrible row followed in which Gatting and Rana screamed their heads off within kissing distance of each other. Rana demanded an apology and the match could not be continued until one was tendered the next day.

I was in the dressing room at the time and didn't hear the exchange firsthand, but Rana later told me that Gatting was openly swearing and kept pointing his finger at Rana's chest. 'Get your finger out of the way,' Rana told him, but Gatting seemed possessed and could not be reasoned with.

In my opinion, Gatting was wrong, terribly wrong. He showed an extreme lack of respect for the umpire, which is simply unbecoming of any cricketer, let alone an English captain. Regardless of the merits of Umpire Rana's decision, Gatting was required to respect it as the ultimate judgement on the field of play. He put neither cricket nor his country first. When the exchange happened, England were in a commanding position as we had been reduced to 106-5 in response to their first innings total of 292. Gatting's childish refusal to apologize for his mistake held up the game for over a day and the match slipped out of England's grasp.

It is often claimed that I was the one who urged Shakoor Rana to demand an apology from Mike Gatting. This is absolutely true. 'You must insist on an apology,' I told Umpire Rana when he asked for my opinion on the situation. I felt that offering an unconditional apology was the least Gatting could have done after his ridiculous behavior.

I wanted the apology not as the opposing captain but as a Pakistani. Gatting's audacity in yelling at Umpire Rana was an insult to Pakistan. Can you imagine what the English would have demanded had I berated an English umpire the way Gatting had Shakoor Rana? They would probably have asked for my head, at the very least. We were just asking for an apology.

I fail to understand why Gatting was so stubborn. Had he apologized promptly and allowed the game to continue, he would have become a hero. Instead, the dark memory of his row with Shakoor Rana has permanently disfigured Mike Gatting's reputation. When he eventually did apologize, after play had been held up for over a day and a half, it was too late.

Astonishingly, at one point the Pakistan Cricket Board tried to accommodate Gatting. As both sides appeared deadlocked, the Board considered removing Shakoor Rana from the game and asking another umpire to officiate in his place. Thankfully all the other available umpires also refused and that idea went nowhere.

The only good thing to come from this incident is that it forced the cricket establishment to take a stern view of on-field misbehaviour, which is now closely policed by the system of match referees. The ICC has empowered match referees to haul up players for even looking at an umpire the wrong way, which in my opinion, is as it should be.

I have often not seen eye-to-eye with the English. Considering this, it is surprising that my tours to England have not been marred by any major controversies. I think this is partly because the English are a subtle people—in everything including insults.

Also England, being a mini-Pakistan with strong immigrant crowd support, disarms the subcontinental visitor.

Another reason is that once you have put up with the county circuit, Test cricket in England seems like a class in manners. Once in a county game, not long after I had started playing for Sussex, I lifted Ray Illingworth straight behind his head for six. To my utter surprise, he turned around and called me a 'black bastard.' This was an England I had neither heard of nor expected, but I soon came to realize these kinds of verbal exchanges were not unusual in county games. I don't believe Ray's expletive was meant as a racial slur, and I certainly didn't take it as such. He was simply giving vent to his competitiveness.

The one incident in England I was involved in that did receive a good deal of media attention was the situation between Aaqib Javed and Umpire Roy Palmer. This happened at Old Trafford during the third Test of our five-Test 1992 tour to England, when I was captain.

Aaqib Javed was a talented fast bowler for Pakistan who could bowl a menacing outswinger. He was one of our leading bowlers in that series. We had batted first and made 505. In reply, England had reached 379 when their last pair came together. At this point, Aaqib started pitching short to Devon Malcolm, who had come in to bat at no. 11.

Umpire Roy Palmer felt Aaqib was bouncing Malcolm and he warned Aaqib about intimidatory bowling. Both Aaqib and I disagreed with the umpire's interpretation. Though pitched short, Aaqib's deliveries were not getting up above waist height. I don't care which way you look at it, that's just not a bouncer. This is the point I made to Umpire Palmer.

Many people felt I was unnecessarily confrontational in that incident. This is a regrettable misinterpretation. I was trying to make a point, albeit forcefully. Aaqib was right and Umpire Palmer was being unfair to him. As captain, I was obliged to defend and stand up for my players, especially when in my opinion they had done nothing wrong.

The notorious incidents of my career have happened on a backdrop of an East-West culture clash. Underlying cultural differences are always a fertile ground for misunderstandings. The situation can get worse by the minute, and before you know it the whole thing has acquired a life of its own. Today, a good deal of mutual cultural respect has developed amongst opposing teams from different backgrounds—England's 2000-01 tour to Pakistan being a perfect exhibition of this—but you can still sense the distinct fault line between Eastern and Western perceptions.

Perhaps many of the incidents I was involved in would never have become controversial had we been playing a team that shared our culture, like India. I know this sounds paradoxical because India is such an archrival, but it makes sense to me. Looking back, many of the things I did on the field in India could well have been blown out of proportion had they happened in Sydney or Manchester.

On our 1983-84 tour to India, we played the first Test at Bangalore where I made 99 in the first innings. During this innings, I scored many of my runs against the Indian left-arm spinner Dilip Doshi. Dilip is a gentle, good-natured fellow but nobody likes to be hit for runs and I could see that Dilip was getting increasingly frustrated. He responded by trying to peg me with a nagging leg-stump line. After a while of this leg theory, I said aloud within earshot of several Indian players including Dilip, 'I know only two creatures that can hold on to a leg like this—one is a dog and the other is Dilip.'

Doshi was livid! His frustration had already peaked and my witticism pushed him over the edge. Several of his Indian teammates, though, saw the humour in this and started laughing. This disarmed Dilip and immediately defused the tension between us. I am not sure if he also saw the humour, but the light-hearted reaction of his teammates clearly helped him deal with his mounting frustration and the matter didn't escalate into an incident.

Another situation that was on the verge of turning messy happened in the third Test at Jaipur, during our 1986-87 tour to

India. Sunil Gavaskar had become the highest run scorer in Test cricket around this time and I was in a mood to needle him. Sunny is a great friend but I never pass an opportunity to take a dig at him. In that particular Test, India won the toss and elected to bat; Sunny came out to open the innings and to face the first ball. As he walked up to the wicket, I made some comments about his superstar status.

'So you've become a really big player, Sunny,' I said from my position in the slips. When he ignored me, I told him it didn't matter how big he had become because he was going to be out first ball and I was going to take his catch.

Maybe it was what I said or the way I said it, or maybe it would have happened anyway. But—unbelievably—Gavaskar edged the first ball of the innings from Imran to me in the slips. The look on his face was one of utter disbelief. As for me, I went crazy with joy and started gloating and jumping around like a mad man. Sunny managed to keep ignoring me and quietly walked back, and soon afterwards everything was forgotten. In Jaipur, nobody made an issue of it, but you can imagine how this would have played out at a place like Lord's.

To me, cricket is war. Just like a soldier defending the borders of his country, I was always focused on the battle in front of me. This is true of every game I have played in, feeling the intensity of battle whenever I was on the field. I always took care, though, not to carry this intensity off the field. After the game, our opponents became our friends and we enjoyed cordial relations. When we returned to the field of play, it was back to war.

I hated bowlers and batsmen who did well against me and my team. I loathed batsmen helping themselves to runs at our expense, and I simply despised bowlers who managed to take my wicket or did damage to our batting line-up. Poor performances and losses have been very hard for me to tolerate, as I really hate losing. The hatred, however, has been limited to the field of play—the theatre of war—and never carried off the field.

No bowler has ever been able to intimidate me. They have tried hard, pitching short, trying to stare me down, saying nasty things to try and upset my rhythm and my confidence, but I matched their aggression at every step, punch for punch. I refused to take any form of bowling intimidation lying down. I knew if I didn't respond this way, it was an automatic victory for the bowler. I never held back, for doing so would only have inspired the bowler further. Whenever a bowler got too fresh, I made it amply clear that I wasn't amused and that I was going to sort them out. Cricket is as much a mental game as a physical one and you can never let your opponent think they may have got the better of you.

Intimidatory verbal exchanges suit my personality. They help me concentrate and elevate my game. Players who tried to threaten and bully me probably didn't realize they were doing me a favour. Their attitude emboldened me and intensified my fighting spirit. When you make sharp comments and retorts, you are then forced to back it up with good performance because your honour is on the line. Ultimately this is what has made me a fighting player.

My headstrong attitude has also defined my relationship with the broadcast and print media. Many of the incidents I was involved in became controversial because of the way they were seized upon by the media. I don't really blame the media for this, as they have a job to do and need to be aggressive to do it well. Instead of fretting and fuming over the negative way I was being portrayed in the press, I used the press to try and advance my performance. Whenever I had done well, whatever praise appeared in the press was irrelevant to me and I never bothered with it, but whenever I saw myself being censured or criticized, I took it as a provocation and my fighting instincts automatically pushed into top gear.

The media have tended to cast me as a troublemaker and an instigator of disruption. I have never bothered with trying to contest this image, but I want to make it clear that this is not an accurate portrayal of my personality. I sometimes have a confrontational approach, but it is only because I refuse to have myself or my country belittled and castigated.

I can also be a peacemaker and a conciliator. Those attributes, however, are not very newsworthy and so have received little media attention.

My peacemaking efforts have been active away from the public eye, in otherwise trivial events that threatened to become huge media infernos but which went unnoticed because the problem was nipped in the bud.

Once during a Benson and Hedges Triangular one-day series in Australia, both the West Indian and Pakistani teams were together on an airline flight. During the flight, someone from the back rows started throwing paper wads at Curtley Ambrose, who was seated in the front section. For a while Curtley tried to ignore it, but the miscreant was persistent and eventually Curtley snapped.

As Curtley got up from his seat and turned around to look down the aisle, the first person he spotted was Abdul Qadir, seated just a couple of rows back. For some reason, he got it into his head that Qadir was doing the mischief. Without any words or ceremony, he just walked up to Qadir and punched him square in the jaw. Naturally, Qadir went berserk. I was seated nearby and couldn't believe my eyes. Without regard to the obvious physical mismatch, Qadir jumped up and started throwing punches at Curtley, with both of them shouting obscenities at each other. It was clear that a major diplomatic row between Antigua and Pakistan was in the offing. I stepped in and calmed them down and soon had them apologizing to each other and making up. Viv Richards also came over and before long it was as though nothing had happened.

Once I also averted a fight between Imran Khan and the England-based Pakistani cricket writer Qamar Ahmed. For a variety of reasons, Imran has never liked Qamar. All the same, though, Qamar has befriended both Imran and myself and, back in the days when we were both playing for Sussex, we used to stay in Qamar's flat whenever we were in London.

It was during one of those early seasons that Imran took offence at something Qamar had written. When we next saw Qamar in his flat, Imran's anger peaked and he became acutely aware of everything he disliked about Qamar. Admittedly, Qamar's was a bachelor apartment and not the tidiest, but Imran let loose on the 'pigsty' we were having to put up with. Reference to pigs never goes down well with Muslims and Qamar lost his composure. All of a sudden, the two men were screaming four-letter words at each other and Qamar was sticking out his chest urging Imran to take a swing. It had got very ugly very quickly, but I stepped in and put an end to it.

These kinds of incidents never made the papers and nobody knows about them. They are important to me because they describe the other side of my personality.

During my playing days, things would invariably get ugly on the field. In later years, I and my competitors from other countries learned to look back on our bitter rivalries and appreciate them for the worthy battles that they were, hard fought, with honour, effort and commitment.

Regrettably, though, such appreciation from within Pakistan's cricket circles has been hard to come by.

Many of my former cricket competitors from other countries are now media men and broadcasters and they often go on record with laudatory comments about me that both honour and humble me. When I was in New Zealand as national coach with the touring Pakistan team in 2000-01, I heard Martin Crowe, Ian Smith and Jeremy Coney talking about me on TV and saying that Javed Miandad was the one cricketer who believed in pointing out and learning from his own mistakes. Similarly, in the West Indies I have heard commentators, many of whom are themselves legendary former Test players, say that I had the capacity to take complete command of a game, that I could alter the course of a match on demand.

Similar statements are made about me in other parts of the cricket-playing world, including England, Australia and India. I have heard the cricket intelligentsia in these countries describe me as a model batsman, even by some as a cricketing genius.

The point of elaborating these comments is not to claim that I am something special, for I am nothing except whatever God has made me. The point rather is that such generous recognition is coming from outside Pakistan rather than from within Pakistan. As someone who is fiercely proud of whatever he has done for his country, this is a disappointment to me.

The trouble with Pakistan cricket has been that we have had more than our share of small-minded personalities. Both our players and our administrators have often been lacking in personal calibre and maturity. The inevitable sad result has been a lack of vision in our cricket, both as a game and as a national institution.

I am mystified by the 'bad-boy' image I have in Pakistan. Even after all that I have done for my country, many of my own compatriot players and media figures think nothing of trying to put me down as some kind of a pest or a menace. The same people who relied on me for team victory, who knew that Javed would save them, now go on about my 'difficult' attitude. The same people who pinned their national hopes on me when I was batting, are now experts on my 'problem personality'. 'So long as Javed is batting, we've got a chance,' these people used to say; all of a sudden I am nothing to them but a magnet for controversy. This is really perplexing.

Part of the reason behind this misrepresentation is, perhaps, professional jealousy, for many of these people have found frustration in their own cricketing aspirations. Even though this is a perfectly natural reaction, it still surprises and disappoints me.

I have always tried to help my team with whatever insight and experience I have gained. If someone was having a problem that I thought I had figured out—an issue of technique, a question of strategy, field-placing dilemmas, anything—I dispensed the information without reservations. If my batting partner was feeling shaky, I made sure he was protected from the bowling. I would tell them not to worry—they were guaranteed to receive only the occasional ball in an over until they felt more set. I have never sought to withhold information that might be of value to someone, for I believe it is in helping others that one ultimately helps oneself and one's team.

It is particularly irksome how many people in Pakistan try to undermine my social background and the urban setting of my childhood. I am often called a 'street-fighter,' a label that has a pejorative quality, as it seems to suggest my personality has been shaped by running around wild like a street urchin. I have already described my home and family; we enjoyed a middle-class lifestyle and all my brothers and sisters earned college degrees. Of course I played cricket on the streets; in Karachi, everyone does.

I remember after my well-known innings of 200* for Glamorgan versus Essex on an impossible wicket at Colchester in 1981 (Chapter 10), Peter Roebuck wrote that I had batted like a rickshaw driver negotiating the streets of Karachi. This is a perfect example of how something negatively perceived within Pakistan is often seen as a positive, distinguishing quality outside Pakistan. Unburdened by the preconceptions of Pakistani society, Roebuck had generously compared my batting to the versatility of a rickshaw on a crowded street. I appreciated Roebuck's comment for what it was, an honest appraisal of how the dynamics of my urban background had formed my cricket.

Outside Pakistan, my modest background adds value to my career; within Pakistan, it is used to detract from it. Buried within this paradox is the class-consciousness of a post-colonial society like Pakistan's. I could have been born to a prince, but I wasn't. I was born into a modest middle-class household. I had no control over the matter, it is what God willed. I didn't go to any elite schools and I don't have an Oxford BA but I'm still a human being. Let that define me and my cricket. That is all I ask.

CHAPTER 20

Coaching Pakistan

I n the summer of 1998, officials of the Pakistan Cricket Board approached me to ask if I would be interested in coaching the national team. I gave them a conditional response, but the truth is it was a welcome offer. I had been away from international cricket for nearly five years, but the retired life was not suiting me. I had been hoping to get involved with Pakistan cricket again in some capacity—perhaps administrative, perhaps something else.

The years of my retirement coincided with the rise in importance of coaching in top level cricket. In my own playing days, cricket coaching at the Test and One-Day International level didn't exist. It was assumed that if one enters the national side, you had already mastered the basic skills and attitudes that coaching provides. Further development as a player was expected to come from one's own gifts and initiative, or under the guidance of a senior role model in the team.

A lot more cricket began to be played through the 1990s and those following the game also increased enormously in numbers. Teams came under pressure to use all possible resources to make the most of their potential, and the value of good coaching began to be recognized. It was already understood in many other sports—such as football, basketball, baseball, tennis—that a good coach can do wonders for an individual or a team even at the game's highest levels. As usual, cricket had been slow to catch up with this trend, but eventually it did. Through the 1990s, prestigious coaching jobs became available with all the Test-playing teams.

The philosophy behind coaching is straightforward: no matter how good a player has become, there is always room for improvement and one can always learn something new. It is the job of the coach to keep striving for such improvement in his players with the aim of creating a competent, consistent outfit.

Ever since my retirement, the Pakistan team had become very inconsistent. A number of gifted players were still in the team, but the outfit had ceased to play to its potential. The captaincy was changing virtually after every series. The Board had made some coaching appointments, but they were short-lived and no one had settled into the job. The position had received little or no attention from the public or the media.

As far as I can tell, it was only after my appointment to the position that the coaching job with the Pakistan cricket team acquired a high profile stature. The call conveying the Board's interest in me came from Khalid Mahmood, who in 1998 was the Chairman of the Pakistan Cricket Board. The Board wanted to appoint a capable coach with a long-term mandate, he said, and everyone was unanimous in the opinion that I was the right man for the job. He told me that Majid Khan—who was then the Board's Chief Executive—was also behind this offer. Khalid Mahmood was very persuasive and said that my appointment was going to lift the nation's spirits. He wanted me to name my terms and conditions so they could move the process along and make my appointment public.

I was delighted at the thought of being a part of the Pakistan cricket unit once again, but I didn't have much confidence in the Board's ability to recognize one's true worth. When Khalid Mahmood conveyed the Board's offer to me, the national coach was Mushtaq Mohammed, employed for the sum of 50,000 rupees per month (then around US $1,000). This was a paltry arrangement as far as I was concerned. I also knew that Mushtaq had requested a raise but had been turned down, which in my view was ridiculous.

In my written response to Khalid Mahmood's offer, I told the Board that I was ready to devote everything in the service of Pakistan cricket once again. As for my terms and conditions, I simply wanted my true worth to be recognized and rewarded accordingly. I told them that if the Board wanted to pay me the same amount they had been paying Mushtaq, then I would rather give my services for free. The issue had little to do with money. I was just seeking due recognition for all that I felt I had worked hard to achieve and become. The Board had been remiss in giving me my due in the past, especially in the events surrounding my retirement, and I would have no patience if they were going to be up to the same old tricks again.

The Board's response turned out to be satisfactory; in fact, it was quite generous. The appointment was made public and was welcomed in the press. I was back in the eye of the storm, and it was a great feeling.

This was August 1998, and we took the team to Toronto, to play India in five One-Day Internationals for the Sahara Cup. Aamir Sohail was captain. We lost the first game but then went on to win the next four in succession, and ended up trouncing India 4-1 in the series. The team had come together wonderfully and the players were all following my ideas and instructions to a man. I felt it was the perfect beginning to my coaching tenure for Pakistan.

We returned to Pakistan to host Zimbabwe, who were visiting for three Tests and three One-Day Internationals. Regrettably, we found the cricket atmosphere back in Pakistan to be corrosive. Almost as soon as we landed, petty disputes broke out between the players and the old infighting began again. Quarrels emerged over player selection, with people trying to outdo one another through intrigue and manipulation. There was also a match-fixing inquiry underway in Pakistan at this time and it was weighing heavily on everyone's minds. The rumours had got stronger and stronger and could no longer be ignored. The Board had finally taken it up at an official level and started an investigation.

The match-fixing inquiry was an internal matter that the Board had undertaken in private, but that didn't stop the newspapers from printing all kinds of innuendo, with oblique references to many of the leading players and how they may have succumbed to greed. It created a very negative atmosphere that undercut team morale. Inevitably, the Pakistan side was terribly distracted when it finally met Zimbabwe in the first Test at Peshawar. We were playing four seamers—Wasim, Waqar, Aaqib Javed and Azhar Mahmood—and as per instruction, the groundstaff at Peshawar's Arbab Niaz Stadium had prepared a greentop wicket. Our bowlers failed to stay focused and could not take proper advantage of the surface. Our batting also lacked application, and the side was bundled out for a meagre 103 in the second innings after being ahead on the first innings by 58 runs. We ended up losing by seven wickets to hand the African nation its first Test victory overseas.

Of course the series was still far from over, and with two Tests still to go, we were confident of bouncing back and winning—or at the very least equalizing—the rubber. The weather, not usually a factor in Pakistan, prevented us from doing so. In the second Test at Lahore we had posted a sizeable first innings lead, but because of foggy conditions the match had to be abandoned. The third Test, scheduled for Rawalpindi, could not be played at all, again because of fog. So Zimbabwe ended up taking the series 1-0.

No disrespect to the Zimbabweans, but a home series loss to such an inexperienced team was quite an embarrassment for Pakistan. As the post-mortem began, the players started throwing blame and accusation at each other and the infighting reached new levels. A few players sensed that Aamir Sohail was about to lose the captaincy and they started jockeying for position to claim it for themselves.

Chaos within the team overflowed into the ranks of the management. As the player infighting reached fever pitch, cracks began to appear in the Board itself. A power tussle erupted between the Board chairman Khalid Mahmood and the chief executive Majid Khan. It precipitated a constitutional crisis within the Board. All this couldn't have come at a worse time for Pakistan, what with a match-fixing inquiry, a home series loss to Test novices, player rivalries, captaincy intrigue, and now an organizational meltdown in the game's administrative structure. I didn't think things could get much worse for Pakistan cricket than they did in those dark days following the Zimbabwe visit in 1998-99.

The one person who emerged untarnished from this mess was Majid Khan. Mud was flung at him but it never stuck. As the Board's chief executive, he was at the centre of the chaos, but in my opinion his no-nonsense, precise management style was an asset for the Board. Had someone like him not been in a central position in Pakistan cricket at that time, things would probably have descended into total chaos. In fact, had he received the right kind of support from the other administrators—notably the Board chairman—the troubles may have been avoided altogether.

In the event, the power clash between Majid Khan and Khalid Mahmood forced the Board's organizational structure to be revised. Constitutionally, the chief executive had been invested with greater powers, but Khalid Mahmood managed to garner greater support for the chairman's position and he eventually prevailed. As happens so often in life, a straight-talking man like Majid Khan who preaches common sense could find few supporters. The crisis has had a lasting impact because the position of the chief executive was thereafter done away with altogether and the Board chairman invested with supreme executive authority. The chief executive's position was watered down to the post of 'director of operations,' a person with authority to supervise the operational activities of the Board but who is completely answerable and subservient to the Board chairman.

Khalid Mahmood too was a good friend of mine, but he had his flaws. He would sometimes approach the players directly and discuss with them matters of technique and temperament, and it made me conscious that my authority as a coach was being by-passed. Like a manager bringing together his subordinates, he would often collect the players, captain and coach alike to form a discussion group that he would then try and inject with his wisdom. It was annoying because his insights were superficial and these meetings interfered with my ability to do the best coaching job that I could do.

After the Zimbabweans left, Australia visited Pakistan for a three-Test series. We lost this series as well, by a 0-1 margin. It was a tough Australian side led by the highly competent Mark Taylor, but the reason for our defeat was simply that our players under-performed. There is no doubt they could easily have done much better in that series. For reasons I can only guess at, they seemed indifferent and unmotivated. I would have exhaustive sessions with the players going over strategy, technique and tips, but when they went out into the middle, it was as if I hadn't said a word to any of them. I never saw any of my instructions followed, and the players didn't seem to be taking my advice seriously during that series. It rendered me ineffective as a coach.

It was a series we really should have won without much trouble, because psychologically Australia had been on the defensive even before they landed in Pakistan. They had not won a Test in Pakistan since 1959-60, when they took a three-Test rubber 2-0 under the captaincy of Richie Benaud. Since then, Australia had visited Pakistan five times, played 16 Tests, lost 6 and won none. They had, in fact, lost the last four series they had played in Pakistan, beginning with the three-Test rubber in 1979-80 (which also happened to be my first series as captain).

The Pakistan team showed no signs of motivation this time around, and the Australians took full advantage of it. Against this Pakistani side that included some of the best bowling talent in the world, Mark Taylor managed to hit an unbeaten triple-century. I don't mean to take anything away from Taylor's knock—a triple-century in Test cricket is a superlative achievement no matter what—but one cannot ignore the fact that our bowlers were capable of much better. One expects top-level international bowlers to at least have learnt control of line and length. They may not take wickets, but I don't think it is too much to ask that at least the line and length should be right. All of a sudden in this series experienced Pakistani bowlers with hundreds of international wickets under their belt were bowling like beginners when it came to the simple matter of controlling line and length.

I tried to work with the bowlers in the nets but couldn't shake their casual attitude. I would insist that our seamers assume match conditions and come in to bowl with their full run-up, yet they would keep bowling off a two-step start.

The indifferent attitude of the bowlers also extended to the limited-overs games. In the One-Day International at Lahore, we failed to defend a total of 316, as Australia equalled the record (with India) of making the highest total to win a One-Day International batting second. The batsmen were equally at fault, showing minimal application and no ability to concentrate. Their shot selection was horrible and they were misjudging line and length like amateurs. I really have no idea what these players were up to—all I know is that they were giving far from their best.

Normally, a player who under-performs should be dropped from the side, but the Pakistan selectors had become suddenly very shy of dropping well-known players from the side even if they were performing badly. In effect, they had given these chosen players a license to play poorly. This was a ridiculous situation. As far as I am concerned, when you are representing your country, there is simply no excuse for giving anything less than the very best. Players guilty of doing this are actually guilty of short-changing their country; it really is a kind of treason. At the very least, the punishment must consist of being dropped from the playing side—no fuss, no arguments.

There is, after all, little point to even having a domestic cricket set-up and grooming promising youngsters if we are not prepared to drop under-performers and make room for new people who are going to be more devoted to the task of representing their country. Once selection is firmly linked to match performance, merit and justice will prevail—two elements that have traditionally been scarce in Pakistan cricket. You cannot be a consistent, world-class team if your players don't fear for their place in the side. It is as simple as that.

During the series against Australia, I also discovered another cancer eating away at the fabric of the Pakistan team. It was the notion that the senior players were entitled to greater privileges simply on account of their years of service. Not facing the risk of being dropped from the side was part of this sense of entitlement. Another absurd expectation was that they should not be reprimanded for a poor performance. If one of these so-called 'senior' players had made a cricketing mistake—got out to a careless shot, or misjudged a catch perhaps—I didn't hesitate to point it out to them. I wanted them to understand what they had done wrong so they would work at the problem and try not to repeat it in the future. It was little more than standard coaching practice. But the prima donnas—the 'senior' players—found this insulting. They seemed offended that their behaviour and performance was being questioned. In the most obvious way, they lacked the ability to handle criticism.

This idea of seniority was at odds with my own views. To me, seniority signifies honesty of effort and maturity of temperament. It brings a greater sense of responsibility towards the team and creates higher expectations from the player of superior performance in the field. In this Pakistan team, the idea of 'seniority' was as an excuse to slack off. This kind of thinking was poisonous to my hopes of transforming the players into a team of world-beaters.

Another spin-off from this 'seniority' complex is the attitude that one has mastered all there is to master in cricket. It is an attitude that makes the self-entitled 'senior' players feel that they are above being challenged or questioned. This mind-set is hilarious as much as it is sad. It betrays a fundamental misunderstanding, indeed a disrespect, of the game. Cricket is a deep, deep sport, certainly the most complex game played on a field ever devised by man. It is a game in which you are always learning. A cricketer is a perpetual student. One can always learn more about cricket, and about using one's own talents in its service.

Had there been a limit to mastery in cricket, it would certainly have been achieved by Sir Donald Bradman, but even The Don was out for a second-ball duck at the very end of his Test career, after a lifetime of batting far above any other player before or since. Just imagine—a player like Bradman, after 79 Test innings played at an average of 101.39, he could still have learned a thing or two about playing the googly. The moral of the story is that you never stop learning in cricket; if you do, you're just wasting your God-given talents, which makes you a fool and an ingrate.

I approached coaching the same way I approached playing—with honesty, sincerity and 110 per cent effort. I feel I have managed a reasonable understanding of cricket over the course of my playing career and in the process I think I might have picked up an insight or two that could help other players. This was the ethic that I brought to my coaching position—to help my team with whatever insight and experience was at my command.

As the Pakistan coach, I was devoted to helping my country succeed, and in the spirit of sharing and serving the game, I gave advice whenever it was sought, by Pakistani and non-Pakistani alike. It was interesting that at the same time as my words of advice to the Pakistani players under my charge appeared to be falling on deaf ears, people from around the world were approaching me for coaching advice.

Once when I had accompanied the Pakistan team to Sharjah as the national coach, Sachin Tendulkar came to ask me for some batting advice. 'Javed bhai, I need your help with a problem,' he said in his polite, unassuming, unaffected way. He had been getting out cheaply by playing inside the line. We talked things over. I helped in whatever way I could, and he was smart enough to figure the rest out for himself.

Another time, I received a call from Bob Woolmer while he was coach of the South African team. He wanted insights on playing spin. South Africa were headed for a tour of Australia and the boys were all terrified of facing Shane Warne. To the best of my ability, I told Bob what to do with the spinners and why they had never troubled me.

After the defeat at home at the hands of Australia in 1998-99, Aamir Sohail lost the Pakistan captaincy and Wasim Akram took over. Two major assignments now loomed up in front of us, both involving our old foe India. First, we were due to make a two-Test tour of India. This would be followed by the Asian Test Championship involving ourselves, India and Sri Lanka, in which we would be facing India at least once.

It was a very serious undertaking. A tour of India can never be taken lightly by any team, least of all one from Pakistan. This tour was particularly significant for two other reasons. First, this was the first time in ten years that the two countries would be meeting in a Test match and the first time in thirteen years (not since 1986-87 with our famous victory at Bangalore) that Pakistan was touring India. Second—and this was a bigger issue as it went well beyond cricket—we were not welcome guests in the eyes of many Indians with right-wing political views.

Armed with a new captain and with the seriousness of our assignment in India before us, I tried to forge a new attitude within the team. In this regard the home defeats to Zimbabwe and Australia had actually proved useful. The humiliating experience seemed to have brought the players to their senses and I found the team with a new sense of responsibility, receptive and ready to listen.

Wasim Akram had been captain before—he had, in fact, been captain when I had toured the Caribbean as a player back in 1992-93—but to my great and pleasant surprise, he turned out to be the most attentive player of all. He was open to all aspects of strategic advice that a coach can give, and made it clear to me that he was completely prepared to do as I said. It was a welcome change from my dealings with the previous captain.

Wasim and I developed an excellent working relationship during that series. We talked selection and strategy in detail. He sought my advice constantly and I made myself available at all times. During matches, he would ask whom to bowl, when to bowl them, and what field to set. We would discuss batting orders and declarations. I would sometimes send out instructions on to the field while play was underway, and invariably saw them implemented.

Pakistan's weak point—indeed the traditional Achilles' heel of South Asian teams—has always been the fielding. When I took over as coach, I was determined to work on this deficiency. Good fielding takes a great deal of hard work and practice, and its rewards are neither immediate nor dramatic. The rewards also don't come to the individual as much as they come to the team as a whole. Good fielding can, however, be the only difference between an average team and a successful one. Right from the beginning of my coaching assignment, my intention had been to organize gruelling sessions of fielding practice and insist on sharp fielding from everyone, all the time and without exception.

It had been hard to implement this programme during the Zimbabwe and Australia series at home in Pakistan, but now in India I led long sessions of fielding practice in which all seventeen squad members participated. I made myself part of the drill with the players, and worked up as much of a sweat as anyone else. They were intense and demanding workouts, and I know they couldn't have been to everyone's liking, but with the coach himself running around just like everyone else, there was no opportunity for anyone to complain.

The boys had a fantastic series and played outstanding cricket on that 1998-99 trip. The cricket was tense and exciting. Sadly, though, the real tension was to come from off the field.

Diplomatic relations between India and Pakistan have never been trouble-free. In late 1998, as our tour approached, extremist Hindu groups began expressing anti-Pakistan sentiments in India and threatened demonstrations and unrest if our cricket tour went ahead. The Pakistan Cricket Board had been carefully monitoring the situation in India and it was suggested at one point that the tour be cancelled out of safety concerns. We had already committed to the tour and our conscience would not let us renege on our promise to our Indian counterparts. Security assurances were then sought, and received from the Indian government, and that was good enough for us.

I had no idea, however, that the Indian government would have to go to such great lengths to ensure our safety. I can't imagine even a head of state requiring the kind of elaborate security detail under which we made that tour. Wherever we went, streets would be cleared well in advance. Not only were the streets *en route* emptied, but up to three adjoining streets on either side would be cleared of traffic as well, with the aim of completely eliminating any security threats. Military units would be standing in front of houses and building exits to prevent people from coming out and getting near us. The hotels we stayed at would be cleared of all guests except us. It was all very unnatural, a side to India that I had never before seen. It is certainly something that I hope never to experience again.

We drew first blood in the series by winning the opening Test at Chennai. It was a tremendously exciting match in which the boys played with great application. After conceding a first innings lead of 16 runs, we set India a target of 271 to win in the fourth innings. The bulk of our second innings total had come from a mature 141 by Shahid Afridi, whom I had been after to temper his impetuosity and wait for the bad balls, and it seemed for once that he had listened. India started poorly but Sachin Tendulkar steadied the innings with a masterly 136; in the end, though, his effort wasn't good enough. At one point India were 254-6, needing just 17 more for victory with 4 wickets in hand and Tendulkar at the crease, but they seemed jittery. I sent word out to Wasim not to panic. The boys remarkably held their nerve as Saqlain took 3 of the last 4 wickets to fall, including Tendulkar's. We won by the wafer-thin margin of 12 runs.

India equalized in the next Test, at Delhi, winning by 212 runs and tying the two-Test series 1-1. We then met India in a Test match at Calcutta's Eden Gardens. Separate from our series with India, this Calcutta Test was the first match in the Asian Test Championship, in which Pakistan, India and Sri Lanka were to play one Test each against one another, with the top two teams contesting the final to be played in Dhaka.

The Calcutta Test included a number of fine performances. Moin Khan made a fighting 70 after we had been reduced to a pathetic 26 for 6 after choosing to bat first. In our second innings, faced with the task of setting India a final target after being 38 behind on the first innings, Saeed Anwar batted his heart out for an unbeaten 188. It wasn't a chanceless knock because he was dropped with his score at 5, but he took full advantage of the mistake and made India pay dearly. There was also an outstanding Indian performance in that match, Javagal Srinath returning match figures of 13 for 132.

What makes that Calcutta Test truly memorable—for Pakistan at least—is Shoaib Akhtar's dismissal of Sachin Tendulkar for a first-ball duck (the only one in Sachin's career). It was not just a classic fast bowler's delivery but a classic Pakistani fast bowler's delivery—an inswinging yorker delivered at screaming pace that curved in like a guided missile and uprooted Sachin's middle-stump.

Eventually set 278 to win, India started promisingly, with a century stand for the first wicket, but after that the slide began. Later in the innings Tendulkar was the victim of a freak run out, and it made the crowd very restless. With India struggling at 214 for 6, the crowd rioted and play had to be abandoned for the day. The following morning—the last day of the Test—crowd trouble persisted. Then the most amazing thing happened. The authorities cleared the Eden Gardens stadium—one of the largest in the world—of all spectators. The match resumed in front of empty stands. It was one of the most bizarre and eerie experiences I've ever had in a Test match. The playing arena felt like a ghost town. When the crowd had rioted, Saurav Ganguly was the only person standing between Pakistan and victory. Soon after play resumed, Wasim had him caught at slip for 24. Not long afterwards Pakistan took the match by 46 runs.

The other two Tests in the Asian Test Championship (India versus Sri Lanka and Pakistan versus Sri Lanka) were drawn. Pakistan and Sri Lanka—the two undefeated sides—met in the Championship final at Dhaka. This match was all Pakistan. We annihilated Sri Lanka by an innings and 175 runs as Inzamamul Haq and Ijaz Ahmed both posted double-centuries.

It was now March 1999 and I was seven months into my coaching job for Pakistan. Things had started to look very good for Pakistan and I was having a ball, both with coaching and being with the boys.

All eyes were now on the World Cup in England, set to begin two months later, in May. We were considered one of the favourites for the tournament, and I was in cautious agreement with that view. I personally thought we had a better than even chance, though it would take a lot of discipline to get past Australia and South Africa. I was looking forward to the challenge. Allah was giving me a chance to bring a second cricket World Cup home to Pakistan.

Before going to England for the World Cup, we were due to participate in a limited-overs tournament in Sharjah. It was the Coca-Cola Cup, involving England, India and Pakistan, comprising six matches and a final, all in April 1999. I welcomed the opportunity—it would be a good rehearsal for the World Cup.

We eased through our first two games with imposing totals— 323 for 5 in a 90-run victory over England, followed by 279 for 8 in a 116-run victory over India.

In our third match, however, the batting unexpectedly collapsed. Our bowlers had done their job (Shoaib Akhtar excelling with 4 for 37) and England had been bowled out for 206. Against an innocuous English attack and for a batting side in such fine touch, this was a straightforward task, but we ended up being all out for 144.

I was livid. This was no way to be warming up for the World Cup. This kind of inconsistency has always kept Pakistan from being a first-rate team alongside the likes of Australia and South Africa. I really had very little patience for it, and I didn't hide my disappointment from the boys.

It was a pathetic performance in cricketing terms, which was bad enough, but with all the talk of betting syndicates in international cricket, and with match-fixing allegations swirling around major cricket centres like Sharjah, I was also concerned that our performance may have had little to do with cricket.

It wasn't easy for me to shake off this idea. Once England had been dismissed for 206, I was elated and confident of victory. During the dinner interval of that day/night match, I received some telephone calls from people who said they were certain my team would not overhaul England's total and would end up collapsing for a low score. This was very disturbing. I called the boys in for an urgent meeting and confronted them with the rumour. I made them swear on the Holy Quran; they said that they knew nothing.

It ended up being a turbulent team meeting during which some of the 'senior' players were especially riled up. I didn't let the friction get to me. Instead, I outlined a simple strategy to overtake the modest English total and alerted everyone to play according to plan. The way our innings proceeded, though, it was as if I hadn't said a word to anyone. As the wickets began to fall, I still kept giving explicit technical instructions to each of the batsmen just before he was due to go in, but no one followed any of the instructions I had given. They played like undisciplined amateurs, getting out to irresponsible shots.

After that match against England, I had a frank exchange with the players. I talked to them about trust and honesty, and then I tried to calm everyone down and get them focused on the cricket again. We had reached the tournament final and would be playing against India on 19 April 1999. It was a Friday and the match would be a day/night affair. On the morning of the final, I had a final chat with the team to go over last-minute strategy and wished them luck. Then we all went together for Friday prayers. When the match began, everything felt right for us.

India won the toss and chose to bat. Wasim Akram opened the bowling for Pakistan and had India reeling at 0 for the loss of 2 wickets in the very first over. It was the kind of start from which few teams can recover, and India were blasted away in that final by Pakistan.

When we returned to Pakistan from Sharjah, I was still very upset at the events surrounding our batting display in that game against England. I had no proof of any wrong-doing, but there had been the suggestion that perhaps a game other than cricket was afoot and it distressed me.

What really disturbed me—and ultimately forced me to quit—was the way this whole affair played out in the public arena in Pakistan. Allegations were leaked to the press that I had fought with the players over my share of the prize money from the Sharjah tournament. This was ridiculous—I had wanted none of the prize money. The idea had no basis in reality and yet still it found credence in the Pakistani media. The net result of all this was that, as had happened often over the course of my career of service for Pakistan, I was being made to look like a villain again.

I had had enough of this heartache and didn't need it any more. So I resigned my position as the Pakistan coach. I resented being misunderstood and miscast to the public yet again, and felt there was little point in continuing.

I felt bad about the timing of my resignation, with the World Cup just before us. I know it was a shocking disappointment to many Pakistani fans, but I really had little choice. The team was not listening to my advice any more, and I had better things to do with my time than to try coaching an outfit that refuses to be coached.

At the time, I had no idea I would be back as coach in less than a year.

After my resignation in April 1999, Mushtaq Mohammed returned as coach. Pakistan went on to do quite well in the World Cup—up to the final. In that 1999 final, of course, they were no better than a high school team and ended up losing an extremely one-sided match by eight wickets to hand Australia their second World Cup title.

I happened to be in England during that World Cup, but only in a private capacity, vacationing with my wife and children. I had no contact with our team, although I followed the matches closely. I think the World Cup could really have been ours but we let it slip out of our grasp. There is no way to know if my presence as a coach would have made any difference to the eventual outcome of that wretched final match, but I do know there were some things I would have done differently.

For example, I probably would have advised Wasim to field first that day. Conditions at the start of the match were overcast, which our seamers could have exploited. I also would have sent in messages during our batting trying to guide the players through the survival tactics that became necessary after Australia had cheaply dismissed both openers.

After the 1999 World Cup, Pakistan undertook a demoralizing tour of Australia in which they lost all three Tests and were also outplayed by Australia in the Carlton and United Triangular limited-overs series. In the second Test at Hobart, Pakistan lost even after setting Australia a daunting fourth innings target of 368. Despite facing a bowling arsenal that included Wasim, Waqar, Saqlain, Shoaib and Azhar Mahmood, Australia were able to reach their target for the loss of six wickets, in the process recording the third-highest fourth innings total ever made to win a Test match.

Pakistan's commitments in the Australian season had stretched from October 1999 into early 2000. After returning home, the team hosted Sri Lanka for three Tests in Pakistan beginning in February. Prior to that series against Sri Lanka, Pakistan had lost its last three Test series at home in a row. There were the losses to Australia and Zimbabwe the previous season, and before that, in 1997-98, there had been a 0-1 loss in a three-Test series against South Africa. There was a lot of pressure to do well against Sri Lanka now. Certainly, a fourth consecutive series defeat at home was to be avoided at all costs.

Predictably, heads had rolled after the devastating losses in Australia. Intikhab Alam was now the coach, and the captaincy was taken from Wasim Akram and handed to Saeed Anwar. Saeed had been captain before, and had failed to inspire. It was no different this time around. Pakistan lost 0-3 the limited-overs series that preceded the Tests. Then Pakistan lost the first Test, at Rawalpindi, by two wickets. In the second Test, at Peshawar, Pakistan were set 294 to win in the second innings, but were short by 57 runs.

The fourth successive home series loss had come to pass.

I now received a call from the Pakistan Cricket Board chairman General Tauqir Zia asking me to return as the national coach. I asked for a long-term mandate and he agreed. He said he wanted me to see Pakistan through to the 2003 World Cup. He also said he hoped I would be the Pakistan coach at least for as long as he remained in office as the Board chairman. So I decided to take over, and returned to coach the team for the third Test of the series against Sri Lanka. (Apparently the Board had neglected to inform Intikhab Alam, the present coach, about their decision asking for my return. Intikhab expressed his anger at being kept in the dark until the last minute, which is understandable, though it had nothing to do with me.)

Along with my reappointment, the captain also changed for this third Test and Moin Khan took over. We bounced back to post a convincing win in that match, winning by 222 runs inside four days.

I oversaw a busy schedule during my second coaching tenure. In April-May 2000 we went to West Indies. After two drawn Tests, the hosts took the final Test by one wicket. Television replays are witness that Pakistan were the deserving winners in that match.

Moin Khan and I worked well together during that series. He sought advice freely and I helped as best I could. Sometimes I would spot a weakness in a batsman that I thought the players may not have picked up on the field. I would send in instructions about what field to set and what kind of delivery to bowl, which Moin would follow to the letter and the batsman would often succumb. Each time the ploy worked, it never failed to impress our manager, Brigadier Nasir Ahmed, who always asked for an encore!

I spent a lot of time working on batting technique with the players. I used to illustrate my instructions by putting on pads and demonstrating with my own batting. Sometimes, to firm up the batsmen's reflexes, I would stand on a chair in the middle of the pitch and throw balls at them. I tried to work on everyone, but the players I found most receptive were Inzamamul Haq and Yousuf Youhana, and to some extent also Younis Khan.

While in the West Indies, we received word that the Qayyum Report had been made public. This report was the result of an official one-man commission comprising Pakistan's Justice Malik Qayyum, who had investigated the allegations of match-fixing by Pakistani cricketers. Some of the players named in that report were in our touring party, and they took the news hard. The whole team was under a pall of gloom.

Rumours about match-fixing have been around for a long time. During my active playing days, we often heard about it, and people had their suspicions. There was never any proof, until South Africa's Hansie Cronje confessed to accepting bribes to alter the course of a match. This demonstrated the presence of match-fixing in cricket beyond any shadow of a doubt.

A good deal has been done to investigate the full dimensions of this mess and to identify the guilty players. Inquiry commissions have been constituted in Pakistan, India, Australia and South Africa. The ICC has also launched a major initiative against match-fixing, headed by a man with a background in law enforcement. While these efforts have produced some gains, a good deal more needs to be done.

Cricket is a team sport, and a highly sophisticated and complicated one. At any given time, the state of a cricket match is the net result of intricate interplay between several individuals from both sides. It is not the sort of thing just one or two people can easily influence. So it is important to realize that the dimensions of match-fixing in cricket go well beyond the handful of players who have been found guilty and have received bans, suspensions or reprimands.

People often want to know my views about match-fixing. Like most followers of the game, I too have had my suspicions, but there has never been any proof. Once during a limited-overs tournament in Sharjah sometime in the late 1980s, there were strong rumours that some of the Pakistan players were trying to throw a game. Imran was captain then and he and I discussed the rumours and Imran then took it up with the rest of the team. No one owned up of course and nothing came of it. That's the closest that the issue of match-fixing was ever discussed during my active playing days for Pakistan.

Everyone wants proof of match-fixing but it is impossible to get proof from what happens on the field. One can analyse suspicious matches in detail for evidence that a match has been thrown—like doing a post-mortem examination—but conclusions from such an exercise would still be based on judgement. 'Proof' is a much stronger and definitive word. Everybody makes mistakes and there is no way to know if a particular mistake is unintentional or a case of deliberate under-performance. Although I played many matches alongside Saleem Malik, who was found guilty of match-fixing by the Qayyum Commission and banned for life from playing for Pakistan, I saw nothing during our days playing together that could convince me he was trying to fix a match.

Particular matches are often cited as examples of match-fixing, like the Pakistan versus Bangladesh game in the 1999 World Cup (which Pakistan lost against all odds). This, however, is nothing more than speculative armchair talk. By simply following the cricket, no one can say for certain if these games were actually fixed. Scrutiny of on-field performances may raise suspicions, but it can never amount to any kind of proof. That's the nature of the beast.

One has to turn to off-the-field activities for a better chance of proof, but this is no easy matter either. I doubt any documentary evidence will ever be found because probably none exists. These arrangements must always be verbal, nothing ever recorded. One might stumble across a telephone conversation, like the incriminating evidence on Hansie Cronje in which he was taped talking to a notorious Indian bookie, but that's a rare case of the investigators getting lucky and is unlikely ever to happen again.

After the West Indies tour in April-May 2000, we went to Dhaka to play in the Asia Cup, a limited-overs tournament involving Bangladesh, India, Sri Lanka and ourselves that we had been participating in since 1983-84 but which we had never won. We moved unhindered through our three preliminary games, subduing Bangladesh by 233 runs, India by 44 runs, and Sri Lanka by 7 wickets. Then in the final, we comfortably defeated Sri Lanka by 39 runs.

Later in the summer of 2000, I accompanied the team to Sri Lanka for three Tests and a limited-overs triangular series involving Sri Lanka, Pakistan and South Africa. We lost the limited-overs games but took the Test series 2-0 with some commanding performances, notably from Wasim Akram, Waqar Younis and Abdur Razzaq. Some of the players began grumbling during this tour that they had been playing too much cricket and were 'exhausted,' to which I gently suggested they take up something more to their liking, like cross-stitch embroidery or flower arrangement.

In the 2000-01 season, England visited Pakistan for three Tests. We lost the series 0-1 mainly due to some irresponsible batting on the final day of the third Test at Karachi. Following that series, in early 2001, we went to New Zealand, where we drew a two-Test series 1-1.

After we returned home from New Zealand, I realized I could no longer continue as the coach with the team in its current composition. The cadre of 'senior' players had created an unhealthy attitude within the team and this was interfering with my ability to advise and guide the whole outfit. Another issue was that the media had managed to somehow make me directly responsible if the team performed poorly. The Board had also fallen in with this mind-set. My view was that performances came from the players, not the coach. The ones who produce the performances are the ones who need to be held accountable.

I stepped aside reluctantly, as my contract from the Board had been through 2003, and I had ideally hoped to coach the team even beyond that. Now it had become clear that the boys were not prepared to put in the hard work into their cricket that I demanded of them. Instead, I was being misunderstood and my well-meaning attitude towards the players was being misconstrued. The atmosphere was therefore not conducive to my continued involvement with the team.

One of my differences with the players was the timing of practice sessions. This conflict was typical of the differences in our approach towards cricket. I used to insist on having practice sessions in the mornings, starting at 10 a.m. after a light breakfast and going on until early afternoon. I saw many advantages in this. Morning light is the best light in which to get your eye set. You can also usually find some moisture on the surface at that time, which can create testing conditions. It is also the time when the body is at its most fresh and receptive. Most importantly, the majority of matches start in the mornings and one's preparations must reflect that. The players, however, wanted practice sessions to be held in the late afternoon and early evening. They preferred to sleep late and laze around for most of the day, and they would then invariably scoff down a heavy afternoon meal which made them slow and sluggish. Predictably, one gained very little from these late afternoon practice sessions.

It saddens me that during my coaching tenure for Pakistan, players were not able to go along with my coaching philosophy. I approached coaching as a teacher might approach a course of education, and I approached my players as a teacher would approach his students. I have always felt that while a teacher or coach should be generous with advice and instruction, they should be reserved with praise. In practice this meant that when someone did well, such as make a century perhaps, I tended to be tight-lipped with my commendation because I hoped my reticence would motivate them to do even better. Well-meaning and sincere as this approach was, I think the players misunderstood it and resented it.

These, however, are the training methods I was brought up with, and these are the training methods I believe work best. I regret that the players couldn't see that what I was doing was in the hopes of elevating their own performance. They wanted me to admire their performances constantly, but as a coach I do not see it as my job to admire and eulogize my apprentices. My job is to make sure they keep doing better and better and that they stay hungry for success.

After all, how can a teacher ever allow himself to be satisfied with a student's performance? Once that happens, it means the teacher has become satisfied with his own performance, which to me means that one has then ceased to be a teacher. It is sometimes said about my coaching that I fell out with the team because I couldn't manage them. I see it differently: In my opinion, many of the players lacked the calibre and discipline to avail of what I had to offer.

The goal of coaching cannot be constant victory. No coach in the world can guarantee constant victory for his team. That's an impossible goal and if one insists on aiming for it, long-range possibilities are seriously compromised. Rather, the goal of coaching is to impart a measure of depth and quality to the team that makes it a consistent performer season after season.

There is no quick-fix medicine in cricket. If there were, every coach would be using it. Instead, a coach has to be methodical and patient to achieve consistency in his team's performances.

I always insist that my players strive for continuous improvement—that is the important goal. Winning is secondary. You've got to perform better today than yesterday, and even better than that tomorrow. If a player can just be faithful to this philosophy, everything else will fall nicely into place. I would tell the boys to imagine that they are advancing in school based on how well they do with their game. Keep performing better and better, and you keep jumping up a class. Keep advancing steadily through the classes of skill and competence, and before you know it you've become a grandmaster.

As a grandmaster, you're in the stratosphere of accomplishment where even the most outstanding performances become for you a matter of routine. That is the place to strive for.

CHAPTER 21

Cricket in Pakistan

C ricket is Pakistan's premier sport, and one in which the country has excelled. Although Pakistan has been outstanding at other sports as well, notably squash and field hockey, cricket has the largest following. It remains a paradox that the organization of the game within Pakistan has not been able to match the public's love for it.

Cricket in Pakistan has yet to acquire the kind of solid and deep foundation that the sport enjoys in countries like England and Australia. Until this happens, the country's true cricketing potential will never be realized. I put the blame squarely on Pakistan's cricket administration. The primary reason behind this is that Pakistan's cricket boards have traditionally been appointed rather than elected, which has allowed malpractices like nepotism and favouritism to flourish. It is a real tragedy, because without a stable cricket administration the country can never hope to optimally realize its true cricketing potential.

In Pakistan, our cricket boards serve at the pleasure of, and are answerable to, whatever federal government happens to be in power. Usually, these are people with little or no knowledge of cricket, and the results are before us to see. This is the way cricket is administered in Pakistan.

Because of these traditional limitations, cricket administration in Pakistan has failed to become an empowered institution, even after operating for over fifty years.

I would dearly like to see the Pakistan Cricket Board be an independent, elected body based on representation from the regional cricket associations throughout Pakistan. Such a body should be independent of government and bureaucratic influence, and it should be answerable to individuals who are devoted to cricket.

It is extremely important that, once elected, the board should be allowed to serve out a full term. In my opinion, a minimum term of three years is necessary if the board is expected to accomplish anything substantial.

The way the Pakistan Cricket Board's affairs have been managed up till now, with politically motivated appointments of office-bearers and terms of office that start and end abruptly on the whims of government ministers and bureaucrats, it is remarkable that the country has been successful at cricket at all.

In addition to being independent of national politics, it is also crucial that the board not be held hostage to Pakistan's short-term cricketing fortunes. Our cricket-following public takes defeats very hard and often reacts by blaming those in charge of the team. All too often the Pakistan Cricket Board is reshuffled after the national team has performed unsuccessfully. Sometimes things have got so farcical that the board has been changed two or three times within the space of a few months. This is no way to manage the cricket affairs of a major Test-playing nation.

Victory and defeat are a part of cricket, like in any sport, and losing a Test or a limited-overs series does not necessarily reflect on the board's management skills. The most important thing is to provide the board with protection to pursue their work. This will allow them to act according to a strategic plan and a vision. While the board is ultimately accountable for the nation's cricketing health, this accountability must be measured over the long-term, at least over two or three years if not longer, and certainly not over the course of one or two rubbers.

The converse is also true. So if the national team does well, it doesn't automatically mean that the board is also doing the right job. The board could be pursuing a strategy that is effective in the short-term but that may eventually be detrimental. Or the team could be winning despite the board's supervision, not because of it. Again, the point is that the board's performance cannot be judged in terms of how well the team performs from series to series.

During my days of being associated with Pakistan cricket, both as a player and as the national coach, I have seen several cricket board chiefs come and go.

Pakistan's most famous cricket chief executive was probably Abdul Hafeez Kardar. He was Pakistan's first Test captain and went on to become an influential cricket administrator. As the cricket board chief, Kardar laid the foundations of Pakistan's domestic first-class cricket structure. He was a highly successful administrator, but I never really had a chance to interact with him as he was close to stepping down when I entered international cricket in 1975.

Pakistan's first chief cricket administrator, Justice A.R. Cornelius, is also hailed as a fine cricket executive, but of course that was in another time altogether (he took office in 1949) and I have no firsthand knowledge of his management tenure.

Another venerable administrator, and one with whom I did get to work closely as the Pakistan captain, was Air Marshal Nur Khan. Nur Khan's excellent management skills had worked wonders when he was chief of the Pakistan Hockey Federation, which oversaw field hockey in Pakistan, but his cricket tenure was too short-lived and he never got a chance to implement any lasting policy decisions.

The military-appointee General Tauqir Zia, who took over in late 1999, has been one of the few PCB chiefs who has been able to articulate and implement a long-term vision for Pakistan cricket at the grassroots level, which has obvious implications for elevating the game in the long run.

The General's initiatives have included efforts to promote the game in all corners of Pakistan, as he has built proper cricket facilities and set up cricket academies throughout the country. Better late than never, but in fact Pakistan's cricket administration should have taken these steps long ago. It is these kinds of capacity-building investments that are necessary to guarantee the national health of any sport.

None of the other Pakistan Cricket Board chiefs that I saw made any kind of lasting impact. It is hardly surprising since they knew next to nothing about cricket and, in any case, were unsure of their mandate, being appointed and removed arbitrarily.

A core mandate for the cricket board of any country is to identify, develop and channel talent into the national side. This is achieved by establishing organized cricket facilities in all parts of the country. By the time a player is inducted into the national team, he must already have gone through a grooming process that makes him an accomplished cricketer with a solid foundation in the basics of the game.

A major failure of Pakistan's cricket administration has been that players have been coming into the national team with inadequate preparation. It is not that the players have lacked in natural talent. Far from it, in fact. While talent is necessary for top-level cricket, talent alone will never be enough for sustained dominance. The problem rather is that, breathtakingly talented as many Pakistani players are, they have never been schooled in the game's fundamentals. These players will have great natural gifts for timing a cricket ball but they'll come into Test cricket still harbouring some fundamental weakness like going across too far or never knowing where their off stump is. Bowlers will have ferocious speed yet have little or no grasp of how and when to vary speed and line. And all too frequently, the players will have an inadequate command of the Laws. The comical result is that the Test side has become a nursery where Pakistan's national players finally get a chance to pick up the basic principles of cricket, something they should have learnt years ago.

A quick glance at the cricket facilities in Pakistan makes it clear that world-class players are emerging from Pakistan in spite of—not because of—the system. School and college cricket, the fountain source of any country's cricket talent, remains shabbily organized in Pakistan and has never managed to develop into an institution with core traditions and values. Because of the limited availability of proper grounds, many school and college matches are played on concrete wickets, which is the absolute worst way to raise an international cricket team. Even when a turf pitch is available, it will often be incorrectly prepared. Regardless of the kind of pitch, the outfield will usually be uneven and littered with all kinds of rocks and pebbles, hardly the place to learn the rudiments of fielding. These barbaric facilities are no way to groom cricketers.

By the time a player is ready to be inducted into the national side, he must be properly equipped—mentally, physically, and technically—to handle the big time. The only way to ensure this is through the organization of a sophisticated cricket infrastructure throughout the country that encourages and identifies talent at the grassroots level; nurtures, grooms and prepares it; and finally channels it into the Pakistan team. Such nation-wide organization of cricket is part of the Pakistan Cricket Board's mandate and the Board must be held accountable to it. There simply is no excuse for talented players still harbouring glaring technical gaps by the time they are picked to play for their country. The national team can hardly afford to be the place where players learn some of the basics. A Test side cannot serve as a cricket nursery, and these handicaps keep Pakistan from being a frontline cricket nation alongside Australia and South Africa.

For decades, Pakistan's cricket authorities could afford to overlook the need to invest in world-class cricket facilities. They got away with it because so many of Pakistan's Test players were being properly groomed in England, masking the gaps in our own training set-up at home. Many of Pakistan's leading players—myself included—have at one time or another been contracted to play in the English county championship, which has acted like a finishing school for polishing our raw talents. When restrictions on overseas players made opportunities in the county championship scarce, our players started looking like what they were: unfinished products, and the flaws in our local system became painfully obvious.

Finally, it must be acknowledged that the ultimate ingredient in making a quality cricketer is the player himself. The Pakistan Cricket Board can go all out and put up the best possible cricket facilities, but the real motivation to excel has to eventually come from the individual himself. We must hope for intelligent players with a mature outlook who approach the game thoughtfully and analytically, and who have a burning drive to succeed. Such attitudes can be taught, but I believe that to a great extent they are inborn. Any cricketing nation that can combine intelligent and ambitious raw talent with sophisticated infrastructure and facilities will remain at or near the top of world cricket, season after season.

As with any Test-playing nation, crucial to Pakistan's cricket fortunes is the health of the game in domestic competition. The organization of domestic first-class cricket in Pakistan has come under a good deal of criticism. Certainly it is not an ideal system, but I believe some of the criticism has been undeserved. There are important aspects of the system that need to be retained.

We play a good deal of cricket in the domestic first-class season in Pakistan. The Quaid-e-Azam Championship and the Patron's Trophy together account for in excess of one hundred first-class games. For several years we have also had a flagship limited-overs tournament. These games have been the breeding ground for the Pakistan Test and One-Day International sides and they have served us well.

A common complaint against our domestic cricket is the lack of public interest that it generates. Many of the teams competing in Pakistan's domestic first-class competitions represent government-sponsored corporations and businesses, like Pakistan Railways, Pakistan International Airlines, Habib Bank and National Bank. While there is representation from regional teams like Lahore, Karachi, Peshawar, Gujranwala, etc., the teams from the public corporate sector dominate the season. Compared with domestic tournaments in other parts of the cricket world, where regional teams are the norm, this is an unusual feature. Many Pakistani observers—including some experienced cricketers—have pointed to it as the reason behind the malaise in Pakistan's domestic cricket.

I take a different view. In my opinion, the corporate teams have been critical in sustaining Pakistan cricket over the years. In a nutshell, they have allowed a class of professional cricketers to be sustained indigenously. These corporate teams provide players with employment and a livelihood, to an extent far greater than can be provided by the regional cricket associations. Since I don't see the financial fortunes of our regional teams changing significantly in the foreseeable future, I would advocate that the current involvement of departmental and corporate entities in Pakistan cricket be persisted with.

The system of corporate or departmental teams was introduced towards the late 1960s by the late Abdul Hafeez Kardar. A towering figure in the annals of Pakistan's cricket administration, Kardar was a shrewd cricket analyst. He induced the corporate system to improve the financial health of the game in Pakistan. In my opinion, given all the constraints of a developing economy like Pakistan's, he could not have come up with a better system.

An important benefit of having numerous corporate first-class teams in addition to regional teams is the greater opportunity afforded for new talent to be recognized, displayed and nurtured. Regional teams are the top of the cricket pyramid for the towns and districts they represent. If our domestic competitions were left only to the regional teams, many talented players—especially from densely populated areas like the large cities—would be unable to find a spot and go unrecognized. In the existing set-up these players are free to try out for the corporate teams, get a chance to play in the premier tournaments, and be in the spotlight for national selection.

In some ways, players from the smaller towns are even greater beneficiaries of this system. Provincial teams from the small towns tend to do poorly against teams from the big cities, and even brilliantly talented players are at risk of getting overlooked if they are limited to playing in the small-town 'weaker' teams.

If there were no departmental teams in Pakistan cricket, opportunity to be in the limelight for national selection would be perpetually lost to many gifted players from the peripheral towns and districts. Were it not for the opportunity and grooming made available by corporate teams, amazing talents like Imran Nazir and Younis Khan, who hail from the provincial towns of Gujranwala and Mardan, respectively, may never have received national attention; and a world legend like Waqar Younis, who comes from the remote Punjabi village of Vehari, may well have languished in the rural districts. So I feel there is definite merit to retaining many aspects of the current first-class cricket structure in Pakistan.

The main criticism of corporate teams has been that they do not engender a loyal fan base or a passionate following, something that contests between regional teams like Lahore and Karachi can easily evoke. While I agree with this, I believe it is a minor flaw and easily outweighed by the benefits of corporate involvement in terms of far better player salaries and playing facilities.

There is also another matter. Greater fan interest and passionate player motivation are often cited as the advantages of a system based on regional teams, but it is worth pointing out that passion is not always a good thing. Ethnic and regional tensions are common in Pakistani society and there is every reason to believe these feelings will find an outlet in high-profile domestic cricket matches that pit one part of the country against another.

As it is, the tolerance of Pakistan's cricket fans towards defeat is minimal to non-existent. Pakistani crowds have been known to respond to poor national performances by pelting players' houses with stones and garbage. In this climate, it is easy to see a Lahore versus Karachi final turning very ugly. Worse still, emotions fuelled in domestic cricket could spill over into the Test side and create fractious groupings. So I fear that first-class cricket based exclusively on regional representation has the potential to exacerbate ethnic divisiveness in Pakistan cricket, which could well extend to the country as a whole.

In any case, the power of region-based teams to generate interest with the fans is in my view overestimated. One only has to look at the Quaid-e-Azam Trophy to realize this. Normally contested only by regional teams, Quaid-e-Azam Trophy matches remain unable to even partially fill stadiums.

The impression that corporate teams are unable to attract crowds is also a fallacy. In the days when I was active in

Pakistan's first-class cricket, our team at Habib Bank used to have a number of star players from the Pakistan Test side. I am a witness that the Habib Bank team in those days often attracted big crowds. Crowds may come for their teams at the international level, but at the domestic level they really come to watch their favourite individual players. Regional teams or commercial teams, in first-class cricket it is the high-profile players who pull crowds, not the teams they represent.

Far from doing away with corporate teams, I would in fact urge their even greater involvement. All my thinking and analysis about Pakistan's domestic cricket affairs points to this conclusion. Many of these teams are backed by institutionalized organizations like banks and airlines that have great resources at their command. These resources can be channelled through the corporate teams to develop better cricket facilities. For example, each of the major teams could be encouraged to build its own first-class stadium and practice facilities. Even the corporate teams would then have 'home' grounds, which itself would add an extra competitive flavour to our domestic season. These corporate stadiums—which would have the potential to mature into formal cricket academies—could be spread all over Pakistan. With around twenty such teams in Pakistan, imagine the tremendous advancement in our national cricket infrastructure this sort of initiative would bring about.

We have to remember that Pakistan is still a very poor country where most people live at or below the poverty line. Cricket around the world is not in general considered an expensive sport, but in Pakistan it certainly is, where cricket gear for one person can cost several times the average monthly household income. The corporate teams bring money into the domestic game in Pakistan and sustain a large body of professional cricketers. Given the economic realities of Pakistan, regional cricket just cannot match this largesse.

An appropriate question to ask is, if the benefits of the corporate system are so clear, what's in it for the corporations themselves? In a word, publicity.

During the Pakistan cricket home season, the names of these corporations regularly dominate the news, both in the print as well as the electronic media. These organizations also earn publicity and goodwill by holding training camps and coaching clinics that make sophisticated cricket set-ups accessible to large numbers of eager youngsters.

If the team does well and makes it to the mature stages of one of the major tournaments, the resulting television coverage is simply priceless advertising for the corporate parent—the sort of publicity even money can't buy. It is a classic win-win situation: the commercial organizations exploit the enormous following cricket enjoys in Pakistan, and in turn they sustain the sport by keeping its professional ranks healthy during Pakistan's domestic season.

All these arguments aside, in the end you have to see how the national team—the eventual product of the domestic system—has done over the years. By any standards, the system has given rise to a quality product: a one-day international team that's reigned as world champions and a Test side that's been a dominant force in world cricket for years. That, ultimately, is the best evidence in favour of Pakistan's existing domestic cricket structure.

Of course all this is not to say that Pakistan's is a perfect system, which it clearly isn't. Reforming it isn't as simple as breaking the hold of the commercial organizations and sending everyone back to play for whatever town they came from. A new scheme is needed that incorporates the virtues of both corporate teams as well as regional ones—something like the blend of commerce and regional loyalty that the United States has achieved in the system of team franchising in their major sports of baseball, basketball and American football.

This much is certain: any changes to be wrought in Pakistan's domestic cricket affairs must be undertaken cautiously and after great thought and deliberation—and in keeping with our culture. It is a matter not just of many people's livelihood but also, ultimately, of the fortunes of the national team.

CHAPTER 22

Some of the Very Best

I n my opinion, international cricket in the twenty-first century lacks the class of older times. Things were different when I started playing cricket. It may be a cliché, but it is also true. In the 1970s and 80s, competition in cricket was of a different calibre altogether. There was not the great disparity of talent that we see amongst international teams today. These days, competing against the newer Test teams makes it possible for average players to accumulate above-average statistics. You couldn't have done this in the old days, when there were no 'easy' opponents and every match was an honest fight.

The high level of competition in my era brought out the best in the players and pushed them to great heights of performance and achievement. I feel privileged to have played at a time when international cricket enjoyed the services of so many gifted players with rare ability.

In this chapter, I have recounted some of the best players of my time, whom I have been honoured to compete against, or to have played alongside in the same team. I saw these players up close, and can speak of the brilliance of their skill and character. The sport of cricket has benefited from the services of some outstanding talents over the years, the great players of my time amongst them. These are some of the very best.

BOWLERS

I have had the opportunity to face some truly outstanding bowlers in my time. When I was playing international cricket, every team had at least two and often more bowlers of genuine class. In my opinion, there has been no better bowling side than the famous West Indian battery of the 1970s and 80s, which included names like Michael Holding, Andy Roberts, Colin Croft, Joel Garner, Malcolm Marshall, Wayne Daniel, Sylvester Clarke, and Winston Benjamin. Later, Curtley Ambrose and Courtney Walsh were added to this phenomenal list. I have played all of them, and rank them with the best.

I was particularly uncomfortable against Colin Croft, who had an unusual bowling action in which the bowling arm whipped around over his head before delivery. He was a tall man with long arms and this unwieldy action made him very awkward to face.

Other bowlers had their own menacing qualities. Holding and Roberts had smooth run-ups and easy, effortless bowling actions; all very deceptive, because the ball came at you like a thunderbolt. Garner had the special advantage of having exceptional height, which always gave his deliveries extra lift.

Malcolm Marshall ran in like a rocket and bowled with great nip and bite; of all the bowlers I have faced, he was the fastest off the pitch. A big part of his bowling success was his rhythm, which never wavered. He kept up a steady tempo in his run-up and delivery from start to finish. He would run in with the same super speed whether he was bowling at the start of a day or towards the end of it. When you were facing Marshall, you knew there would be no let up. He was also an exceptionally clever bowler. I pride myself on being able to outthink bowlers and predict their deliveries, but I always had a hard time trying to figure out what Marshall was up to. He was so good mentally that he could trick you into thinking you had his bowling plan figured out, and he would then invariably surprise you.

Some of the West Indian bowlers were more successful in their careers than others, but as a batsman it is hard for me to choose amongst them. They each had their special qualities, but on their day, they were all equally good.

If I could choose one bowler that I would like to have avoided playing against, it would have to be Australia's Dennis Lillee.

He is one of history's greatest bowlers. The recipe for quality fast bowling has many ingredients—speed, swing, line, length and human psychology—and Dennis had mastered all of these. He could swing the new ball better than anyone I know. And he was brilliant at outthinking the batsman. On his best days, he was simply lethal.

Dennis's greatest asset, I believe, was consistency. His ability to deliver at the peak of his craft never wavered. He always sent down top-notch stuff, giving nothing away. Whenever I think back on batting against Dennis, I remember how frustrating he could be. Delivery after delivery, he would pitch at a perfect length on middle and off and move the ball away with speed and lift. There was hardly ever a chance to go forward and attempt a drive, or find room for a cut. He always had the batsman pegged back, never giving an inch.

Australia enjoyed the services of many other good bowlers in those days. Bowlers like Max Walker, Len Pascoe, and Gary Gilmour, had great command over swing and were never easy to get away. Rodney Hogg was also an exceptionally talented fast bowler with a natural hostility for whom I had great respect; his 123 career Test wickets do not do justice to his capabilities. In later years, Geoff Lawson and Terry Alderman were the leading Australian bowlers in my view; Lawson was the quicker of the two, but Alderman could bowl a terrific outswinger.

England had a number of talented bowlers at that time. Of these, Bob Willis and Ian Botham stand out from the rest. Their great strength was that they could bowl well anywhere in the world, under any conditions. Other English bowlers from that time, such as Chris Old, Geoff Arnold, Mike Hendrick and Peter Lever, depended on English conditions to be effective; their reputations had been built on the county circuit, not internationally.

I also have the greatest regard for England's John Snow. We never faced each other in Test cricket, but I tasted Snow's bowling many times in the nets during my days at Sussex. He was a class bowler, one of England's very best. As a fast bowler,

Snow was also a mentor to Imran Khan, and I admire him for being willing to pass on the skills of his craft to an able pupil.

The two English bowlers who impressed me in later years were Graham Dilley and Neil Foster. They were both aggressive and accurate bowlers, but Foster was quicker and had more nip.

New Zealand, of course, had Richard Hadlee, an outstanding bowler by any standards. Hadlee's greatest asset was his accuracy. He always aimed at the stumps, and forced the batsman to play every ball he bowled. He became even more effective after he shortened his run-up, which gave him laser-accuracy without appreciably diminishing his speed. I especially admired Hadlee for his composure; he never showed overt hostility or used abusive language. The only hostility one felt was the bowling itself, fast and deadly. Even when he was being hit about, Hadlee always managed to remain icy cool. It was quite remarkable.

Another New Zealand bowler who impressed me was Ewan Chatfield. Chatfield came as close to a bowling machine as any human I know. He would pick a spot and keep pitching on it, delivery after delivery. He was tireless and remained seemingly unmoved by the proceedings of the game itself. He would just come in to bowl, then go back up to the top of his run-up and come in again to repeat the identical delivery, all very machine-like. He was a good-natured fellow and I used to joke with him about this. 'Come back with me to Pakistan, I need a bowling machine,' I would say to Chatfield, and he would laugh.

India's bowling strength has traditionally been, and continues to be, spin. Each member of their celebrated quartet from the 1970s—Bedi, Chandrasekhar, Prasanna and Venkataraghavan—was a giant in the world of slow bowling. Two seamers from India also impressed me. Kapil Dev was a very good bowler, as is self-evident from his 434 career Test wickets. Later, Javagal Srinath became the most effective Indian seamer, capable of generating a fair amount of pace, bounce and nip.

Pakistan's most successful bowlers have been the quick bowlers Imran, Wasim and Waqar. They are in the category of the all-time greats, and there is very little to argue in that. These three bowlers mastered swing bowling—especially reverse-swing—better than anyone else.

The secret of reverse-swing lies in the difference of smoothness between the two sides of a cricket ball. The rougher one side is, and the smoother the other side, the better the chances of getting reverse-swing. This is why reverse-swing is best seen with an older ball—you need one side of the ball to have been roughed up quite a bit. The theory behind reverse-swing is straightforward, but it remains an art that not everyone can practice. By the late 1970s, Imran Khan was practising reverse-swing quite skilfully. In our 1982-83 home series against India, Imran used reverse-swing to great effect and kept knocking Indian wickets over like nine pins. Towards the late 1980s, Wasim Akram and Waqar Younis became masters of this art and dominated world cricket. Had the great West Indian and Australian fast bowlers understood reverse-swing the way the Pakistani bowlers did, they might well have ended up with over a thousand career wickets.

One highly talented and effective Pakistani seamer whose contribution often tends to get overlooked is Sarfraz Nawaz, who was for many years Imran's new-ball partner. Though not genuinely fast, Sarfraz was very nippy and could be very awkward to bat against. He once bowled an amazing spell taking seven wickets for one run (innings analysis of 9-86) in a Test against Australia at Melbourne. A highly intelligent bowler who bowled according to a thought-out plan, Sarfraz could swing the ball both ways, and could also bowl reverse-swing. If he had had a little more speed, he would have been as deadly with reverse-swing as Imran, Wasim and Waqar.

Pakistan has a strong tradition of producing quality spin bowlers as well. During my career, the two best spinners from Pakistan were Iqbal Qasim and Abdul Qadir. They were both big-hearted and tireless, and bowled accurate, tight spells that frustrated the best batsmen. Qasim, a left-arm orthodox finger spinner, also had a lethal arm ball; and Qadir, who bowled right-arm wrist spin, was a master of the flipper and googly. On their day, they could run through any batting side—and they often did. Qadir, in fact, was so good, I think he was even better than Shane Warne. I have never played against Warne but have observed him closely. There is no doubt he is one of the game's great leg-spin bowlers, but unlike Qadir, he has had the advantage of bowling against relatively weak opposition. Since Qasim and Qadir's retirement, Pakistan's best spinner has emerged to be Saqlain Mushtaq. A highly talented off-spinner, Saqlain has perfected the *doosra* (Urdu for 'the other one')— the delivery that keeps its line and spins away from the right-handed batsman. He is well on his way to becoming one of the highest wicket-takers in international cricket.

Even though Saqlain is an outstanding talent, he is still not the best spinner of his time. That honour belongs to Sri Lanka's Muttiah Muralitharan. Muralitharan is the only Sri Lankan bowler with over 300 Test wickets. You get an idea of his prowess when you realize that Sri Lanka's next most successful bowler, Chaminda Vaas, doesn't even have 200 Test wickets yet. Muralitharan is certain to join the 500-wicket club alongside Courtney Walsh, and deservedly so. The secret of Muralitharan's success is simply his fantastic ability to turn the ball. He is able to extract prodigious turn even from flat tracks that don't take spin from other bowlers. Every ball he bowls looks like a potential wicket-taker. Like Saqlain, he has also mastered the *doosra*, the off-spinner's googly equivalent that spins away from the right-handed batsman after pitching. I would go so far as to say that Muralitharan is one of the very best spinners in cricket history, and certainly the very best off-spinner. I never saw the other famed off-spinners such as Lance Gibbs and Jim Laker, but it is hard to imagine they had anything over Muralitharan.

BATSMEN

I played at a time when there were many fine batsmen in international cricket, many of whom are amongst the finest batsmen in history.

Viv Richards was the number one batsman of my time. I never saw the greats of yesteryear, like Bradman, Trumper,

Hobbs or Hammond, but Richards would have to be alongside them as one of the greatest batsmen ever. There were other outstanding West Indian batsmen from that era, but Viv was head and shoulders above them.

Viv was lovely to watch, except when you were on the fielding side. He could destroy any bowler's line and length. He had the power to hit any ball, anywhere and at any time, such was the measure of his quality. You can't say this about any other batsman except for Bradman. Of his teammates, probably Gordon Greenidge comes closest to matching Viv's talents and ability. The most aggressive opening batsman of my time, Greenidge butchered the best bowling attacks in the world and pounded even the most hostile bowlers into submission. Even so, Viv was in another class. Clive Lloyd was another tremendous West Indian batsman. I never saw anybody hit a cricket ball harder than he did. Desmond Haynes and Alvin Kallicharran were other West Indian batsmen from my time who impressed me.

In Australia, the Chappell brothers Ian and Greg, along with Allan Border, stand out from the rest. I never saw much of Doug Walters first-hand, but the little I did, earned my respect. The same is true for Ross Edwards and Rick McCosker, both fine, capable batsmen whose career statistics do not do justice to their actual talents. Other Australian batsmen that impressed were Dean Jones, David Boon and Geoff Marsh, and later of course the Waugh brothers Steve and Mark.

In England, the top batsmen from amongst my contemporaries were David Gower, Geoffrey Boycott and Graham Gooch. Compared to the other English batsmen, these three are in a class by themselves. Gower was the natural strokemaker with a gift for timing, Boycott was all method and application, and Gooch was somewhere in between. It is no surprise that each of them has over 8,000 career runs in Test cricket, and so far they are the only Englishmen to have done so.

Around the time when I first started playing international cricket, New Zealand were lacking a truly world-class batsman. Glen Turner retired in 1976 and left a vacuum that was not easily filled. John Wright anchored the New Zealand batting for a few years, but it was eventually in Martin Crowe that New Zealand found a batsman of surpassing merit. He is easily the best batsman ever produced by New Zealand, and for a few seasons was arguably the best batsman in the world.

India has had a rich tradition of producing quality batsmen. Top of the list is Sunil Gavaskar who, along with Viv Richards, became a legend in his own time. After Gavaskar, the Indian batsman everyone talks about is Sachin Tendulkar. Tendulkar is certainly one of the genuine greats, but in my view Gavaskar was superior.

There was something else about Sunil Gavaskar. A short fellow with a refined bearing, Gavaskar consistently got hundreds and double-hundreds against top-class bowling. Compared with Tendulkar, he made his runs against a better quality of opposition. Gavaskar's supremacy was clear from very early on. In his debut Test series, on a tour to West Indies in 1970-71, he made 65, 67, 116, 64, 1, 117, 124 and 220. He had the rare gift of making runs when they were most needed. The highest fourth innings total ever made to win a Test is 406-4 by India against West Indies at Port-of-Spain in 1975-76, a score that was set up by a pivotal 102 from Gavaskar. On another occasion, India once got to 429-8 needing 438 to win in the fourth innings of a Test against England at the Oval in 1979; Gavaskar led the charge with an unblemished 221.

In fact, if I were to pick one person who to my mind personified cricket greatness, I would—without hesitation—point to Sunil Gavaskar. A man of character, a gentleman, a cricketer with incredible skill and tenacity, and yet a humble man, down-to-earth, honest, sincere and utterly fair.

After Gavaskar, the best Indian batsman I played against has to be Mohammed Azharuddin. I followed his career from the very beginning, when he scored a hundred in each of his first three Tests (against England in 1984-85). With a dynamic, wristy technique and a gift for timing, Azharuddin's promise was obvious right from the start, and he lived up to it in his career. Azharuddin also became the first Indian batsman to master the craft of limited-overs batting and played some fine one-day innings at Sharjah and other venues.

Of my contemporaries, the other Indian batsmen who impressed me were Gundappa Vishwanath and Dilip Vengsarkar. Vishwanath was the more natural player, but Vengsarkar had the capacity to show remarkable determination. Another Indian batsman who was memorable for his batting technique was Ravi Shastri. Though more of an all-rounder rather than a frontline batsman, Shastri was technically very sound and capable of impeccable defence.

The best Pakistani batsmen of my era were Zaheer Abbas, Majid Khan, Mushtaq Mohammed and Asif Iqbal. I also had very high regard for Sadiq Mohammed. Zaheer is probably the most purely talented batsman so far produced by Pakistan. When he was in rhythm, he was second to none. In later years, Pakistan's best batsmen have been Inzamamul Haq and Yousuf Youhana, both enormously talented, world-class players.

Saleem Malik was another highly talented Pakistani batsman and one of the sweetest timers of a cricket ball, but throughout his career he remained shaky against genuine pace. Saeed Anwar is also a superb timer of the ball and has played some fine innings for his country, but his batting has some basic technical flaws, such as an inability to negotiate fast, rising deliveries outside the off-stump, that keep him from being truly world-class.

An excellent Pakistani batsman who remained under-appreciated throughout his career was Shoaib Mohammed. Shoaib had rock solid technique and a determination to match. He played forty-five Tests for Pakistan with a career average of 44.34, which is the sixth-best average in Pakistan's Test batting annals, ahead of names like Majid Khan, Zaheer Abbas, Mushtaq Mohammed, Asif Iqbal and even Saleem Malik. Shoaib's 'misfortune' was that he was born to the immortal Hanif Mohammed, Pakistan's legendary batting anchor from the country's inaugural Test years. Regrettably everyone—selectors, captains and fans alike—always judged Shoaib's performances against the greatness of his father. If he did well, he was just playing according to expectations; if he failed, he was castigated for being an undeserved selection. It is remarkable Shoaib was able to achieve what he did—he must have had nerves of steel.

Sri Lanka became a Test-playing country in 1982 but even in their short Test history, they have been able to produce a couple of world-class batsmen. P. Aravinda de Silva made his Test debut on a trip to Pakistan in 1985-86. He faced Imran in full cry without the slightest hint of anxiety and once, in one of the one-day games, stared him down with a couple of sixes that impressed us all. Sanath Jayasuria made his debut in 1991-92 and has now become arguably the best opening batsman in the world. His batting helped Sri Lanka win the 1996 World Cup and also enabled them to record the highest innings in Test cricket (952-6 declared in a Test against India, of which Jayasuria's contribution was 340). His aggressive batting style right from the word 'go' evokes comparisons to famous sloggers like Gordon Greenidge and Roy Fredericks.

Of the other Sri Lankan batsmen from my time, Roy Dias, Arjuna Ranatunga and Duleep Mendis performed creditably, but in my opinion, after de Silva and Jayasuria, the best Sri Lankan batsman I played against was Anura Tennekoon. Tennekoon never got to play any Tests because he retired before Sri Lanka received Test status. In fact, Sri Lanka should have become a Test-playing country much earlier than they did. They were held to a higher standard for Test entry than the two more recent entrants Zimbabwe and Bangladesh, and it cost Tennekoon the opportunity to become a Test player. With his subtle technique and solid temperament, he would have made a fine Test batsman.

BEST WICKETKEEPERS

Wicketkeeping is a hard job. It is the most specialized position in a cricket team and few players understand what is really involved. I have very high regard for wicketkeepers, having myself kept wickets for Pakistan in both Tests as well as in One-day Internationals.

The best wicketkeeper I ever saw was Pakistan's Wasim Bari. He was a real natural, and a perfectionist in his glovework. Bari played at a time when there were some outstanding wicketkeepers in world cricket, including Alan Knott and Bob Taylor from England, Rodney Marsh and Ian Healy from Australia, and Jeffrey Dujon from West Indies. In my opinion Bari was better than all of them.

Following Bari's retirement in 1983-84, Pakistan has continued to enjoy the services of some excellent wicketkeepers. I believe Rashid Latif leads the pack, in both glovework as well as temperament, although Saleem Yousuf and Moin Khan have also served Pakistan with great credit. Like Bari, Rashid is also a real natural at the job. It is as if he was born to keep wickets.

New Zealand's Ian Smith was also a first-rate wicketkeeper, and certainly the best wicketkeeper ever produced by that nation.

India's best and most successful wicketkeeper has been Syed Kirmani, who toured Pakistan three times and made many good friends in the Pakistan team. Whatever Kirmani may have lacked in glovework skill, he made up for with spirit and commitment.

THE GREAT ALL-ROUNDERS

The era in which I played international cricket is well known for being the age of the great all-rounders. The four greatest all-rounders in the history of the game—Imran Khan, Ian Botham, Kapil Dev and Richard Hadlee—had more or less contemporaneous careers, and it elevated the cricket of my era to exceptional heights.

The term 'all-rounder' has become a corrupted appellation in cricket. With the rise of limited-overs cricket, players who can slog a few boundaries in the late middle-order and serve as the fifth bowler in a one-day bowling line-up are considered 'all-rounders'. Far from being all-rounders, such players are better described as so-called 'bits-and-pieces' players, as the press appropriately refers to them. Imran, Botham, Kapil and Hadlee are in a separate class altogether. These four are genuine all-rounders, each of whom could have made it into their national Test side as either batsman or bowler. The only other all-rounder who was in the same league as these four was Gary Sobers. In the entire history of the game, no one else comes close.

It is very hard to choose between these four great cricketers to try and decide who was the very best. They were each spectacular in their own way, and each of them has a career record that places them in the upper stratosphere of cricket achievement. If one were forced to pick the single best all-rounder from these four, I believe the title would go to Imran Khan.

Imran was second to none as a bowler but, beyond that, he was really the only one of these four who truly batted like a batsman. Kapil, Botham and Hadlee were all fine, attacking batsmen with the ability to turn around a game, but Imran was a better batsman than any of them.

Imran was highly effective in attack, but he was also the only one who truly had a batsman's instincts and was able to think like one. Unlike the other three, Imran preferred ground strokes to lofted shots, a classic batsman's instinct. He was also capable of flawless defence and had the mental stamina for long innings.

Botham and Kapil Dev were both excellent strikers of the ball, capable of tremendous attacking batting. Botham even had some fine ground shots in his repertoire, but unlike Imran, these two lacked proper defensive technique.

Hadlee was probably a better defensive bat than either Botham or Kapil, but his overall range of shots was limited. I never saw Hadlee hit a cover drive or play a leg glance the way a regular batsman would. The others could do this. The differences in batting ability are reflected in the career Test batting averages of these all-rounders: Imran leads with 37.69 runs per innings, followed by Botham (33.54), Kapil (31.05) and Hadlee (27.16).

THE FUTURE

Cricketers come and go, but the best cricketers leave behind a legacy that enriches the game. I have mentioned some of the cricketers of my time who left their mark on the game. These players were gifted with great skill, but skill alone isn't enough—one needs that as well as the right mental attitude to become truly great.

Cricket is growing all over the world. The addition of newer Test nations like Zimbabwe and Bangladesh is undoubtedly good for the game. The new teams have a long way to go before they can be considered frontline Test sides, but I am certain that one day their time will come. Zimbabwe have already produced a world-class player like Andy Flower who can take the fight to any opposition. The day will also come when a Bangladeshi cricketer will rise to be counted amongst the game's greatest. Inspired by the heroes who have come before them, cricketers from all parts of the world will keep on striving to greater heights. Cricket has a rich future and great players will continue to come and serve this beautiful game that we all love.

CHAPTER 23

Picking the Gaps

I n telling the story of one's life, there are things you'd like to say, things that can't always be brought up when the main story is flowing. In this chapter I have collected some of these thoughts.

PAKISTAN

It is hard for me to explain what Pakistan means to me. Pakistan is in my blood. It is my identity and I have always felt great honour in representing that identity. I love Pakistan and am deeply grateful to it, the country that gave me the opportunity to make something of myself. If ever I was struggling out in the middle, pushing for victory or staving off defeat, the sight of the Pakistan flag fluttering defiantly would warm my heart and keep me going. Whenever we played in Sharjah, I used to run laps around the ground before the start of a match. People would start coming in around 6 a.m., after *fajr* prayers, and our team would arrive an hour or two later, around 7:30 or 8 a.m. By the time I began my laps, the entire stadium would be filled with Pakistani fans, waving our flag and shouting encouragement. Every now and then, they would erupt with shouts of *nara-e-takbeer,* which always brought tears to my eyes and sent a chill down my spine. The atmosphere was full of passion for Pakistan, and it would uplift us. It is this passion, this purely Pakistani passion, which has fuelled my cricket and has motivated me to do whatever I have been able to do.

Everything I have done in cricket, I have done for Pakistan. If I was aggressive and contentious, it wasn't for the sake of being so. I was aggressive because I wanted to see Pakistan succeed. Defeat was unacceptable.

Ups and downs are part of cricket, but whenever I under-performed, I took it very personally. If I had let Pakistan down, it was always a source of terrible embarrassment and shame for me. If we lost a game, I wouldn't feel like facing the public for days. My own performance was not as important as the team's. The only thing that could mitigate a poor individual personal showing from me would be victory for the team and glory for my country.

FAITH

Faith in Allah has been my ultimate source of strength in life and in cricket. My mother had wished for me to be a *Hafiz-e-Quran*, and I trained for it during my early years, which imprinted the words of Allah on my young mind. Although I later had to give up the *hifz* as it was starting to interfere with my schooling, the point to be made is that I was brought up in a house deeply rooted in faith. We didn't impose our faith on anyone else, but made every effort to live by it ourselves. So the ways of Islam—honesty, hard work, fasting, prayers—shaped me from an early age. These were the traditions of the family into which I was born; I have accepted them without question and they have served me well. Islam and the rituals of Islam were followed in our house as a matter of course, without making an issue of it. This background has shaped the ethic of my life. I have tried to put in an honest effort in everything I have done and believed that Allah would give me what I deserve.

If I have achieved anything in life, it is only because Allah has willed it. If I have got anywhere, it is only because Allah has heard the pleas of my well-wishers, of my elders, my family, my friends, my fans, all those who have been kind enough to include me in their prayers.

Today I am a content person because I do not believe I have ever been unjust to anyone or knowingly committed a wrong. My intentions and my heart have always been clean. This, to me, is the simple recipe for life-long happiness. If Allah has been kind enough to bestow on me any natural gifts, I have tried to use them, as I believe He would expect me to: for the betterment of others, for my family, for my country. Allah's purpose is behind everything. If in a country of 140 million people only one is chosen to receive some unique capability, it is to serve some divine purpose in Allah's grand scheme. To do justice to one's gifts, one should try to understand the purpose behind those gifts and then follow through with that purpose as faithfully as one can.

I have had some disappointments, but I have accepted them as Allah's will. It was an ambition of mine to get 10,000 runs in Test cricket. A number of factors conspired to keep me from doing so but I don't blame anyone and bear no ill will on the matter. Had Allah wanted me to reach that target, nothing could have stopped it. If I was unable to get to that goal, it is because it was not Allah's will, and I accept it. Oftentimes, even situations that appeared to be disappointments have eventually proved to be great positive events. I know Allah is always watching over me and will look after me.

WIFE AND FAMILY

I got married in 1981, to someone who is for me the best person in the world. I come from a culture where marriages are often arranged and the wedding occurs before the bride and groom may have had a chance to get to know each other. It is a fine system that has endured for generations and works well, as long as the bride and groom's backgrounds are more or less similar and the process has their ultimate consent. In my own case, however, things were quite the opposite of 'arranged'.

I first met Tahira at Lahore's Gaddafi Stadium where she had come to watch a cricket match. A little later I ran into her again at the home of a mutual acquaintance. She was the best thing in the world from all that I could tell, and I wanted to be with her forever. It was pointed out to me this is the state of 'being in love.' I was set on making her my life partner and asked her to marry me, and was completely bowled over when she said yes.

Then things got a little interesting. When we broke the news of our wedding plans to our respective families, it didn't go down too well at all. When I had first met Tahira, I had no idea about her family background. I soon learned, though, that she came from the well-known Saigol clan, a very wealthy family with great influence in Pakistan. I suppose a brash cricketer wasn't the sort of match Tahira's father had expected her to make.

Of course we weren't going to let anything stand in the way of our love for each other.

That day is one of the truly special days of my life. It was March 1981, and we had come towards the end of the first-class season in Pakistan. I was in Lahore, playing my last match for Habib Bank in one of our domestic competitions. I was leaving soon for Swansea to spend the summer playing for Glamorgan. Tahira and I decided to get married before I left for Wales.

A friend of mine arranged for a small ceremony to take place at his house in Lahore. As soon as the match I was playing for Habib Bank ended, I went straight to my friend's house. Tahira had also arrived, and was with her close friends. The Maulana arrived to solemnize our *nikah*. I was still in my cricket whites— it all happened so fast that I had not even had a chance to change. Our hosts—my dear friend Akbar and his wonderful wife Faiza—had thought of everything. Akbar gave me his *shalwar kameez* to wear and Tahira wore one of Faiza's formal dresses. We recited our vows after the Maulana and two of our friends signed their names as witnesses, and we had tied the knot.

Expectedly, it was something of a bombshell for our families. My mother nearly collapsed on hearing the news and it took me a long time to earn her forgiveness. Tahira's father—my father-in-law—took the news even harder and got quite worked up. In that tense situation, Tahira and I felt it would be best to get away from Lahore for a while and we flew down to Karachi, where we had a larger ceremony and invited several friends.

Up to that point we had tried hard to keep it all in the family, but some reporters found out and the story of my marriage appeared in the papers, with all the saucy details about the opposition from our families. We had nothing to hide and we were confident that our families would eventually come around, but still we resented the journalists' intrusion into our private lives.

We wanted to spend a quiet few days hoping for things to settle down. We took a brief trip to Dubai—our honeymoon— where Tahira could catch up with her shopping. We then went to Lahore to spend a few days with friends, before leaving to spend the summer in Wales.

After the English cricket season ended, in the autumn of 1981, Tahira and I returned home to Lahore. Time had passed and we were hoping for a reconciliation with the family. We didn't know it then, but my father-in-law had mellowed by this time. He was a very special man. A real firebrand, his close associates had nicknamed him 'Tiger'. Tahira was especially dear to him and she had always known that he could not stay angry with her for long.

Soon after we had come back to Lahore, I was approached by some of my father-in-law's friends—the Commissioner of Lahore among them—who tried to gauge my mood. I wanted nothing more than to put all differences aside and become friends with my father-in-law, and told them as much. Soon afterwards, Tahira received a telephone call from him asking to speak with me.

At the time, I happened to be playing in a match in Lahore against a visiting International XI, and Tahira and I were staying in a hotel with the rest of the team. Tahira told me about her father's telephone call when I got back to the hotel after the day's play. Rather than simply returning the call, I decided to go and see him at his home.

We had an emotional meeting. He held me close for a long time and the occasion overwhelmed us both. Forget about the part that says grown men don't cry—we did. From that point on, we were friends, and he accepted Tahira and me back into his life with great warmth and affection. A few days later, he threw a big reception for us and we had a grand time.

Allah has blessed us with three wonderful children. Our son Junaid is the eldest, followed by our son Jahangir, and then Maria, our daughter.

INTERLUDE IN BRUNEI

Soon after retiring from Test cricket, I received an offer from the Sultan of Brunei. I didn't know much about Brunei when the offer came. I had to look it up on the map and found it to be part of the island of Borneo in the Far Eastern tropics, surrounded on one side by the South China Sea and on all other sides by the Malaysian state of Sarawak.

The offer asked me to be part of a group of sportsmen being assembled by Prince Abdul Hakeem, the Sultan's nephew, who happened to be a sports fanatic. Pakistani squash legend Jahangir Khan had already become part of the group and urged me to join. The job called for spending a total of six months out of the year coaching cricket and playing sports in Brunei with Prince Hakeem and his group.

It isn't totally accurate calling this position a 'job', because there was really no sense of 'work' associated with it. It was like being part of a big, happy family. The Prince had managed to assemble a number of other sports personalities—Viv Richards and Ian Botham were two other cricketers—and we all played all kinds of sports together, those we were good at and even those at which we were terrible. In addition to playing cricket in Brunei, I also played a lot of soccer, tennis, squash, badminton, rugby and American Football.

My arrangement in Brunei lasted from 1994 through 1997. The experience makes me feel I have sampled a little bit of paradise on Earth. Brunei is a tiny country—population around 250,000—that sits on huge reserves of petroleum and natural gas. The natural wealth makes it one of the richest countries in the world and the Sultan of Brunei is generally regarded as one of the richest, if not the absolute richest, person in the world. With such resources, the Brunei royal family is really able to make their guests fabulously well cared for.

We had no worries or cares in Brunei. Living conditions were lavish, to put it mildly. The days would consist of getting together with Prince Hakeem and with the other sports personalities from around the globe at a state-of-the-art sports complex and engaging in sports activities—either playing or coaching, sometimes a bit of both. The dress code was comfortable and casual—we mostly wore shorts and T-shirts. We were given private chauffeur-driven cars for transport, and the food was outstanding, the menu limited only by one's imagination.

Some of the cricket we played in Brunei was top quality and would have been worthy of any of the major international cricket centres around the world, but the focus of our activities wasn't on competition; it was really about having fun and enjoying oneself through sports.

The great thing was that you didn't even have to be playing yourself to share in the fun. For a while during my time in Brunei, I was nursing the knee injury I had acquired in the cricket training camp in Lahore in August 1994. It had forced me on to crutches and made playing any sports impossible. It wasn't a problem, though, because I became a sports referee and continued to stay involved. I especially enjoyed umpiring tennis games involving Prince Hakeem. He often used to play doubles teaming up with one of his friends against the pair of Jahangir Khan and Viv Richards. Jahangir, especially, was an outstanding tennis player, and Richards wasn't that bad either. Some of the other personalities around would serve as linesmen. It was all so relaxed and informal, just like being in a family.

Apart from cricket and the other field sports, we also indulged in a lot of water sports (my favourite was jet-skiing.) The fun wasn't just limited to sports, though. Every now and then entertainment celebrities would be flown in to give what really amounted to private concert performances for us.

What I found most amazing was how despite all this unbelievable wealth, members of Brunei's royal family remain such warm, affectionate, down-to-earth people. I became especially close to Prince Hakeem and his father—the Sultan's brother—who is popularly known as Prince Geoffrey. They were extremely kind and considerate, polite to a fault, and looked after me with such attention that it often embarrassed me. The Sultan, too, was very considerate and every bit a man of his people. He offered Friday prayers in public and greeted and mixed with the other worshippers and made it clear that he was one of them.

The royal family had genuine sporting talent to match their unbounded love for sports. The Sultan himself was an accomplished polo player and his brother, Prince Geoffrey, an excellent golfer with an almost professional handicap. Prince Hakeem was an especially gifted marksman. He qualified to represent Brunei in the rifle shooting competition at the Atlanta Olympics in 1996. I went with him to Atlanta and we had a truly memorable time.

UNCLE KERRY

Cricket originated in England, but I think it is fair to say that modern cricket has originated in Australia. It was the Australian business tycoon Kerry Packer and his commercial extravaganza World Series Cricket that brought cricket into modern times. Many of the things we now take for granted in international cricket—coloured clothing, white balls, floodlights, portable wickets—were all introduced by World Series Cricket. Kerry Packer also revolutionized cricket's television coverage, with multiple camera angles and high-resolution slow motion replays.

These developments expanded the game's following and have been a lasting service to cricket. I believe the greatest contribution to the game has been Packer's treatment of the cricketers themselves. World Series Cricket employed players at a level of financial, and therefore emotional, security that cricketers had never known before. Because of this fact, I credit Kerry Packer with being the first person to acknowledge players' rights in cricket in a meaningful way.

The various national cricket boards had already banned the so-called Packer players from playing for their national teams and participating in Test cricket. Packer's enterprise was taking such good care of us, we used to wish all our other employers—the county clubs and the first-class teams in our own countries—would ban us as well. The Packer players had just wanted to play for Uncle Kerry. The contracts he had offered were several-fold—in some cases up to ten-fold—over what players were earning in county cricket. No one had ever been so good to the players before.

The largesse benefited not just the players. World Series Cricket also employed Test-level umpires and compensated them handsomely. It led to a significant improvement in umpires' salaries around the world.

Kerry Packer and I used to get along really well. I was the youngest player in World Series Cricket and I used to call him 'uncle,' which he found really amusing. Tony Greig, who was like an elder brother to me, was Packer's right-hand man in the cricket set-up. These were the late 1970s and I was just this little-known middle-order batsman from Pakistan, but because of Tony and Uncle Kerry, I enjoyed a great sense of belonging in World Series Cricket. I was also on very good terms with Uncle Kerry's business assistants Lynton Taylor and Andrew Caro.

Packer had been pushed to launch World Series Cricket after he had become embroiled with the Australian cricket establishment over television rights to cricket matches played in Australia. Not long after World Series Cricket began, he won this dispute, yet he didn't abandon the players. All the guarantees made to the players in his employ were honoured. It speaks of his character.

Ultimately, Kerry Packer's great contribution has been to modernize the game. Not everyone will be happy with the commercialism that has come into cricket as part of its modernization. It cannot be denied, though, that the commercialism has been a boon for players, and the modernization of the game has given cricket a new life with many new followers.

HABIB BANK

One of the most important relationships I have had with any institution has been with Habib Bank, my employer in Pakistan's domestic cricket. Habib Bank is not just any ordinary institution in Pakistan—it is a mega-institution, the country's oldest and largest bank.

Of all the people I got to know at Habib Bank, I owe a special debt of gratitude to Mr A.R. Wadiwalla, who used to oversee the Bank's sports affairs. The Bank had formed a cricket team in the 1970s, after reforms introduced by Abdul Hafeez Kardar had allowed corporate entities to field teams in Pakistan's domestic first-class competitions (Chapter 21). Mr Wadiwalla was a senior vice-president who had been made responsible for recruiting and organizing the team. He was a great lover of the game and oversaw the team's affairs with affection and a keen personal interest.

I joined Habib Bank the same year that they formed their cricket team—1975. The Bank president at the time was a gentleman named Amir Siddiqui, who was also a cricket enthusiast. He and Mr Wadiwalla had a famous working relationship and it was common knowledge that the President never turned down any cricket-related request from Mr Wadiwalla.

The offer from Habib Bank came through my father, who was an office-bearer of the Karachi City Cricket Association and whom Mr Wadiwalla knew in that capacity. I was representing my province of Sindh in the Quaid-e-Azam Trophy

at the time. A number of other corporate teams had also approached me in that 1975-76 season, and I was fortunate to have the luxury of choosing from several options. My father advised me to accept the offer from Habib Bank. He said he had a good feeling about it, which was good enough for me.

I became very close to Mr Wadiwalla. I respected him as an elder and he always looked after me like a son. One of the earliest words of advice he gave me was to never leave Habib Bank. Good things will happen if I stayed with Habib Bank, he would say. I continued to receive offers from other corporate teams during my first-class career in Pakistan. One of the most tempting was from Pakistan International Airlines (PIA), communicated to me in 1979 through no less a personality than Air Marshal Nur Khan, who was then the celebrated chairman of the Pakistan Cricket Board. The Air Marshal asked me to take over the PIA captaincy and was offering me superior remuneration and the added perk of free air travel. Mr Wadiwalla's words had touched me in a special way and I never left Habib Bank.

After I took over the Habib Bank captaincy, Mr Wadiwalla and I built a team that dominated Pakistan's domestic circuit for years. Players like Abdul Qadir, Saleem Malik, Mudassar Nazar, Ijaz Ahmed and Mohsin Khan played with me in that Habib Bank team. It finished top of our first-class competitions for many seasons. It was, in fact, a team that on its day could even have given a tough time to the Pakistan Test side.

I don't see my relationship with Habib Bank as an employer-employee association. I see it as a relationship based on warmth and affection. I left Habib Bank only after leaving active cricket, but Habib Bank hasn't left me. I will always be a Habib Bank man.

UMPIRING

On several occasions, I have been at the receiving end of what in my judgement was biased umpiring. Nowadays with

sophisticated video replays and neutral umpires, this has been greatly minimized. Even so, much room for improvement remains and neutral umpires at both ends as well as a greater involvement of video technology are absolutely necessary for the health of the game.

Even as far back as my first series in Australia—the 1976-77 tour—I remember being shocked when Australian players were judged not out even though they had been caught at the wicket. You clearly heard a noise, while the ball had travelled nowhere near the body and the bat had touched neither the ground nor the batsman's clothing, so it had to have nicked the bat. Yet the batsman would not be given out.

Umpiring in the West Indies was often worse, especially if there was a crucial lower-order partnership underway. If their last-wicket partnership was putting up a fight, even obvious catches would sometimes be denied. I witnessed this on the 1976-77 tour and also on the 1987-88 tour.

In the series-deciding third Test at Barbados in 1987-88, we had the West Indies 207-8 after setting them a victory target of 268, but we were put at a disadvantage through some one-sided umpiring and the West Indies managed to save the game. It happened yet again on our tour to the West Indies in April-May 2000 when I was the Pakistan coach. During a tenth-wicket partnership in the third Test's final moments, Courtney Walsh was given not out off a Saqlain Mushtaq off-spinner even though he had been caught off a thick edge on to the pads. The scorebooks show the West Indies winning that Test by one wicket. Incorrect umpiring kept us from winning that Test.

In New Zealand too the umpiring confers an advantage on the home team and we have received some very surprising umpiring decisions while on tour there. (I have already commented on umpiring in England and India in earlier chapters.)

Our own umpiring in Pakistan hasn't been perfect, but it has certainly not been what some other countries make it out to be. In my opinion, the overall umpiring in Pakistan is quite good and certainly comparable to anywhere else in the world with the possible exception of England. Our umpires do tend to come under pressure by the home side, but their intent is not to be biased against the touring side. The problem is that they fear making a mistake against the home side much more than they fear making a mistake against the visitors. Recognizing this reality, Pakistan led the campaign for neutral umpires in world cricket and, indeed, we are the first nation to unilaterally use neutral umpires at both ends in a Test series (West Indies tour to Pakistan, 1986-87, Chapter 14).

A major fallout from home umpiring is that losing teams are able to use it as an excuse. Certainly many teams losing in Pakistan have invoked this explanation for poor performances. Neutral umpires at both ends are absolutely essential to put an end to this. In every other major sport, this is a given practice.

The matter of neutral umpires had been delayed in cricket because countries like England and Australia, who have dominated world cricket affairs, have been loath to adopt this practice, feeling this would be an implicit concession that their own home umpiring had been biased. This has been a sad misreading of the situation. The point to be understood here is that it is impossible to distinguish unintentional human error from deliberate bias in the case of home umpires. Obviously umpires can and do make honest mistakes, but a genuine mistake by a home umpire against a touring side will never be seen as such by the aggrieved party; it will simply be seen as cheating and, therefore, as a justification for failure. In the absence of neutral umpires, any high-level cricket contest commanding world attention is meaningless, as there is always a suspicion of bias.

In addition to totally neutral umpires officiating in all international cricket matches, mechanisms must exist to maintain the quality of umpiring. To this end, the ICC should constitute a committee to monitor umpiring standards throughout the world. Such a committee would comprise ex-cricketers of stature drawn from all the Test-playing nations and it would observe, investigate and pass judgement on any situation where the umpiring has been controversial. To be truly effective, the committee must be empowered to censure umpires. The committee would function over and above the match referee, who is but one person and cannot provide the same collective wisdom as a multinational committee of experts.

Umpiring ultimately determines the conduct of cricket because the laws of the game invest umpires with the responsibility of being the sole judges of fair and unfair play. I have seen my share of bad umpiring in my career but I have seen some excellent umpires as well. Top of everyone's list has been England's Dickie Bird, and he tops my list as well. I also have high regard for Umpire David Sheppard from England and Umpires Shakoor Rana, Mehboob Shah and Shakeel Khan from Pakistan.

THE OXBRIDGE COMPLEX

There has been a tendency in Pakistan cricket in which players with an Oxford or Cambridge background have been overvalued, and players far removed from such a background have been undervalued. It is an injustice that was part of our cricket from the earliest days, and was kept alive well into my playing years.

I personally think an Oxbridge education is a sad waste if you cannot complement it with character, humility, warmth, and generosity towards your fellow beings.

If someone took the trouble to go to Oxford or Cambridge, they did it just for themselves. It wasn't a favour to anyone else. Anyway, what's the big deal? In many cases, an Oxbridge education gets you little more than unemployment and a spot in the welfare line.

I know that one of the criticisms against my captaincy had been that I lacked a complete education and didn't have a college degree. This was an irrelevant argument because I was extremely well educated in cricket. If some university awarded degrees in cricket, I would qualify for a Ph.D. without much difficulty, I should think.

Let's talk about formal education for a minute. I used to be a very good student, but a serious cricket ambition takes you away from formal schooling. By the time I was in my twelfth year at school, I was forced to choose between academics and cricket.

You don't have the luxury of allowing yourself to be distracted by courses and examinations once you find yourself on the fast track to international cricket. Players like Imran Khan who managed to graduate are in a sense lucky that their early performances were not up to the mark. In fact, Imran was able to read for a BA at Oxford because he was actually a Test discard in his early days. Had Imran done well in his debut Test against England in 1971, he would have found a permanent place in the Pakistan side and that could well have been the end of his formal studies. As it turned out, he was a failure in that initial Test and wasn't selected to play again for Pakistan until 1974.

In recent times the Oxbridge Complex in Pakistan cricket continues to exert its influence, albeit in a different form. The modern version exists in the value placed on the ability to speak English. It is no secret that English-speaking skills are an important consideration in appointing the Pakistan captain. This is a sad and deeply misplaced attitude. In choosing a captain, priority must be given to cricket acumen and leadership skills; English-speaking ability should be secondary. Granted that an international cricket captain has a media presence and is required to give interviews around the world, but if he can't speak English, he can simply use a translator or interpreter. There is no shame in a Pakistani not knowing English. It is not their mother tongue after all. Certainly, an inability to speak English should never be considered as a reason to deny someone the Pakistan captaincy.

THE FUTURE?

I have devoted my life to cricket, and I want to continue to do so as long as my physical capacities will allow. One of my dreams is to one day set up a cricket academy that will continue to help Pakistan realize its true potential in world cricket. I would even hope that the academy attracts aspiring youngsters not just from within Pakistan, but from all over the world. I feel that I have come to know and understand a thing or two about the game, and I would like nothing better than to pass this on to receptive young talent. I like to think I can help talented youngsters make the most of their cricket abilities and to go on to make a lasting impression on the game. It would be a contribution to cricket that I would be extremely proud of.

CAREER STATISTICS

Muhammad Javed Miandad Khan
Born: Karachi, 12 June 1957

COMPILED BY
Abid Ali Kazi
Philip Bailey

TEST MATCH CAREER FIGURES
Test Debut: Pakistan v New Zealand at Lahore 1976-77

SERIES BY SERIES TEST MATCH FIGURES

Season	Series	M	I	NO	R	HS	Ave	100s	50s	Ct	St	Balls	M	Runs	Wkts	Ave	Best	5WI	10WM
1976/77	P v NZ	3	5	1	504	206	126.00	2	1	4	0	492	11	207	8	25.87	3-74	0	0
1976/77	A v P	3	5	0	148	64	29.60	0	2	2	—	434	9	200	5	40.00	3-85	0	0
1976/77	WI v P	1	2	0	3	2	1.50	0	0	0	—	130	7	53	1	53.00	1-22	0	0
1977/78	P v E	3	5	3	262	88*	131.00	0	3	2	—	88	0	36	0	—	—	—	0
1978	E v P	3	5	0	77	39	15.40	0	0	2	—	18	0	14	1	14.00	1-14	—	0
1978/79	P v I	3	5	3	357	154*	178.50	2	1	2	—	60	2	26	1	26.00	1-7	0	0
1978/79	NZ v P	3	5	2	297	160*	99.00	1	0	5	—	—	—	—	—	—	—	—	—
1978/79	A v P	2	4	1	183	129*	61.00	1	0	1	—	32	0	20	1	20.00	1-8	0	0
1979/80	I v P	6	11	1	421	76	42.10	0	4	8	—	—	—	—	—	—	—	—	—
1979/80	P v A	3	4	1	181	106*	60.33	1	0	1	1	54	0	35	0	—	—	—	0
1980/81	P v WI	4	7	0	230	60	32.85	0	3	7	—	—	—	—	—	—	—	—	—
1981/82	A v P	3	5	0	205	79	41.00	0	2	1	—	36	0	29	0	—	—	0	0
1981/82	P v SL	3	5	0	176	92	35.20	0	1	4	—	6	0	1	0	—	—	0	0
1982	E v P	3	6	1	178	54	35.60	0	2	4	—	—	—	—	—	—	—	—	—
1982/83	P v A	3	3	0	176	138	58.66	1	0	3	—	6	0	2	0	—	—	0	0
1982/83	P v I	6	6	1	594	280*	118.80	2	1	2	—	12	0	11	0	—	—	0	0
1983/84	I v P	3	3	0	225	99	75.00	0	3	1	—	6	0	1	0	—	—	0	0
1983/84	A v P	5	9	0	302	131	33.55	1	1	2	—	48	0	26	0	—	—	0	0
1984/85	P v I	2	2	0	50	34	25.00	0	0	0	—	6	0	4	0	—	—	0	0
1984/85	P v NZ	3	6	2	337	104	84.25	2	1	3	—	—	—	—	—	—	—	—	—
1984/85	NZ v P	3	5	0	138	79	27.60	0	1	5	—	18	1	7	0	—	—	0	0
1985/86	P v SL	3	3	1	306	203*	153.00	1	1	3	—	—	—	—	—	—	—	—	—
1985/86	SL v P	3	4	0	63	36	15.75	0	0	3	—	—	—	—	—	—	—	—	—
1986/87	P v WI	3	6	0	176	76	29.33	0	1	0	—	—	—	—	—	—	—	—	—
1986/87	I v P	4	7	1	302	94	50.33	0	4	3	—	—	—	—	—	—	—	—	—

Season	Series	M	I	NO	R	HS	Ave	100s	50s	Ct	St	Balls	M	Runs	Wkts	Ave	Best	5WI	10WM
1987	E v P	5	5	0	360	260	72.00	1	1	3	—	24	2	10	0	—	—	0	0
1987/88	P v E	3	3	0	88	65	29.33	0	1	4	—	—	—	—	—	—	—	—	—
1987/88	WI v P	3	5	0	282	114	56.40	2	0	4	—	—	—	—	—	—	—	—	—
1988/89	P v A	3	5	0	412	211	82.40	2	0	1	—	—	—	—	—	—	—	—	—
1988/89	NZ v P	2	2	0	389	271	194.50	2	0	3	—	—	—	—	—	—	—	—	—
1989/90	P v I	4	5	0	279	145	55.80	1	1	2	—	—	—	—	—	—	—	—	—
1989/90	A v P	3	5	0	190	65	38.00	0	2	1	—	—	—	—	—	—	—	—	—
1990/91	P v NZ	3	4	0	150	55	37.50	0	1	0	—	—	—	—	—	—	—	—	—
1990/91	P v WI	2	3	0	23	9	7.66	0	0	1	—	—	—	—	—	—	—	—	—
1991/92	P v SL	3	4	1	37	20*	12.33	0	0	1	—	—	—	—	—	—	—	—	—
1992	E v P	5	8	2	364	153*	60.66	1	2	5	—	—	—	—	—	—	—	—	—
1992/93	NZ v P	1	2	0	104	92	52.00	0	1	0	—	—	—	—	—	—	—	—	—
1992/93	WI v P	3	5	0	120	43	24.00	0	0	0	—	—	—	—	—	—	—	—	—
1993/94	P v Z	3	5	0	143	70	28.60	0	1	0	—	—	—	—	—	—	—	—	—
Total		124	189	21	8832	280*	52.57	23	43	93	1	1470	32	682	17	40.11	3-74	0	0

RECORD AGAINST EACH COUNTRY IN TEST MATCHES

Opponents	M	I	NO	Runs	HS	Ave	100s	50s	Ct	St	Balls	M	Runs	Wkts	Ave	Best	5WI	10WM
Australia	25	40	2	1797	211	47.28	6	7	12	1	610	9	312	6	52.00	3-85	0	0
England	22	32	6	1329	260	51.11	2	9	20	—	130	2	60	1	60.00	1-14	0	0
India	28	39	6	2228	280*	67.51	5	14	18	—	84	2	42	1	42.00	1-7	0	0
New Zealand	18	29	5	1919	271	79.95	7	6	20	—	510	12	214	8	26.75	3-74	0	0
Sri Lanka	12	16	2	582	203*	41.57	1	2	11	—	6	0	1	0	—	—	—	—
West Indies	16	28	0	834	114	29.78	2	4	12	—	130	7	53	1	53.00	1-22	0	—
Zimbabwe	3	5	0	143	70	28.60	0	1	0	—	—	—	—	—	—	—	—	—
Total	124	189	21	8832	280*	52.57	23	43	93	1	1470	32	682	17	40.11	3-74	0	0

ONE-DAY INTERNATIONAL CAREER FIGURES

One-Day International Debut: Pakistan v West Indies at Birmingham 1975

RECORD AGAINST EACH COUNTRY IN ONE-DAY INTERNATIONALS

Opponents	M	I	NO	Runs	HS	Ave	100s	50s	Ct	St	Balls	M	Runs	Wkts	Ave	Best	5WI
Australia	35	33	3	1019	74*	33.96	0	7	10	1	60	0	72	1	72.00	1-28	0
Bangladesh	1	1	0	15	15	15.00	0	0	0	0	—	—	—	—	—	—	—
Canada	1	—	—	—	—	—	—	—	—	—	—	—	—	—	—	—	—
England	27	27	6	991	113	47.19	1	10	12	0	160	1	87	0	—	—	—
Holland	1	—	—	—	—	—	—	—	—	0	—	—	—	—	—	—	—
India	35	34	11	1175	119*	51.08	3	6	13	0	—	—	—	—	—	—	—
New Zealand	24	20	3	702	90*	41.29	0	4	6	0	48	0	31	2	15.50	2-31	0
South Africa	3	3	0	145	107	48.33	1	0	1	0	—	—	—	—	—	—	—
Sri Lanka	35	31	10	1141	115*	54.33	2	8	12	0	84	2	49	3	16.33	2-22	0
UAE	1	—	—	—	—	—	—	—	1	—	—	—	—	—	—	—	—
West Indies	64	64	7	1930	100*	33.85	1	12	14	1	84	0	58	1	58.00	1-46	0
Zimbabwe	6	5	1	263	89	65.75	0	3	2	0	—	—	—	—	—	—	—
Total	**233**	**218**	**41**	**7381**	**119***	**41.70**	**8**	**50**	**71**	**2**	**436**	**3**	**297**	**7**	**42.42**	**2-22**	**0**

WORLD CUP CAREER FIGURES

World Cups	M	I	NO	Runs	HS	Ave	100s	50s	Ct	St	Balls	M	Runs	Wkts	Ave	Best	5WI
1975	2	2	1	52	28*	52.00	0	0	2	0	114	2	68	3	22.66	2-22	0
1979	4	3	0	46	46	15.33	0	0	0	0	—	—	—	—	—	—	—
1983	6	6	0	220	72	36.66	0	2	3	1	—	—	—	—	—	—	—
1987	7	7	1	274	103	45.66	1	1	1	1	18	0	5	1	5.00	1-5	0
1992	9	9	2	437	89	62.42	0	5	1	0	—	—	—	—	—	—	—
1996	5	3	1	54	38	27.00	0	0	3	0	—	—	—	—	—	—	—
Total	**33**	**30**	**5**	**1083**	**103**	**43.32**	**1**	**8**	**10**	**1**	**132**	**2**	**73**	**4**	**18.25**	**2-22**	**0**

FIRST-CLASS CAREER FIGURES

First-class debut: Karachi Whites v Pakistan Customs at Karachi 1973–74

SEASON BY SEASON FIRST-CLASS FIGURES

Season	C	M	I	NO	Runs	HS	Ave	100s	50s	Ct	St	Balls	M	Runs	Wkts	Ave	Best	5WI	10WM
1973/74	P	13	23	2	557	100	26.52	1	2	18	—	1175	20	545	22	24.77	5-44	1	0
1974/75	P	12	20	0	947	311	47.35	4	1	7	—	1642	22	791	25	31.64	6-93	1	0
1975/76	P, SL	11	19	3	677	131*	42.31	1	6	13	—	1166	18	577	23	25.08	5-94	1	0
1976	E	5	10	1	523	162	58.11	2	2	10	—	222	4	165	2	82.50	2-27	0	0
1976/77	P, A, WI	19	36	4	1382	206	43.18	3	7	20	—	2487	58	1158	34	34.05	6-123	1	0
1977	E	24	39	6	1326	111	40.18	3	7	28	—	942	28	602	16	37.62	4-10	0	0
1977/78	P	16	23	4	1369	172	72.05	5	7	34	2	1245	14	556	22	25.27	5-52	1	0
1978	E	21	32	6	983	127	37.80	2	6	10	—	408	6	238	5	47.60	2-55	0	0
1978/79	P, A, NZ	17	27	10	1409	160*	82.88	4	7	14	—	534	13	266	4	66.50	1-7	0	0
1979	E	3	6	2	76	30*	19.00	0	0	4	—	144	4	73	1	73.00	1-26	0	0
1979/80	P, I	18	27	7	1142	110*	57.10	3	6	16	1	234	2	127	2	63.50	1-6	0	0
1980	E	20	32	5	1460	181	54.07	3	6	7	—	204	8	132	2	66.00	2-25	0	0
1980/81	P	13	23	0	1039	130	45.17	3	8	16	—	372	11	202	12	16.83	7-39	1	0
1981	E	22	37	7	2083	200*	69.43	8	7	11	—	222	7	108	3	36.00	2-12	0	0
1981/82	P, A	13	21	2	1199	177	63.10	4	6	17	—	252	5	144	1	144.00	1-20	0	0
1982	E	18	29	8	1051	105*	50.04	1	9	24	—	628	31	309	7	44.14	3-52	0	0
1982/83	P	14	16	2	1124	280*	80.28	4	2	8	—	48	1	32	0	—	—	0	0
1983	E	5	6	0	114	89	19.00	0	1	5	—	12	0	11	0	—	—	0	0
1983/84	I, A	13	21	3	1177	141*	65.38	3	9	4	—	132	5	81	0	—	—	0	0
1984	E	8	15	2	832	212*	64.00	2	3	4	—	308	9	187	6	31.16	2-26	0	0
1984/85	P, NZ	10	16	2	677	112	48.35	3	2	10	—	84	2	51	1	51.00	1-16	0	0
1985	E	20	29	6	1441	200*	62.65	4	8	13	—	165	2	120	3	40.00	2-67	0	0
1985/86	P, SL	9	11	1	456	203*	45.60	1	1	6	—	—	—	—	—	—	—	—	—
1986	E	1	2	1	143	102*	143.00	1	0	0	—	—	—	—	—	—	—	—	—
1986/87	I, P	9	15	1	631	151	45.07	1	5	3	—	—	—	—	—	—	—	—	—

Season	C	M	I	NO	Runs	HS	Ave	100s	50s	Ct	St	Balls	M	Runs	Wkts	Ave	Best	5WI	10WM
1987	E	12	14	1	822	260	63.23	2	3	5	—	64	2	32	0	—	—	0	0
1987/88	P, WI	10	15	2	814	144*	62.61	4	2	12	—	—	—	—	—	—	—	—	—
1988/89	NZ, P	7	10	1	1009	271	112.11	5	1	4	—	—	—	—	—	—	—	—	—
1989/90	A, P	8	12	1	601	145	54.63	1	5	3	—	—	—	—	—	—	—	—	—
1990/91	P	7	10	0	244	55	24.40	0	2	5	—	—	—	—	—	—	—	—	—
1991	E	1	2	0	110	88	55.00	0	1	1	—	—	—	—	—	—	—	—	—
1991/92	P	3	4	1	37	20*	12.33	0	0	1	—	—	—	—	—	—	—	—	—
1992	E	12	17	3	809	153*	57.78	2	4	8	—	—	—	—	—	—	—	—	—
1992/93	NZ, WI	5	8	1	256	92	36.57	0	1	0	—	—	—	—	—	—	—	—	—
1993/94	P	3	5	0	143	70	28.60	0	1	0	—	—	—	—	—	—	—	—	—
Total		402	632	95	28663	311	53.37	80	138	341	3	12690	272	6507	191	34.06	7–39	6	0

FIRST-CLASS CAREER FIGURES FOR SUSSEX

Season	M	I	NO	Runs	HS	Ave	100s	50s	Ct	Balls	M	Runs	Wkts	Ave	Best	5WI	10WM
1976	5	10	1	523	162	58.11	2	2	10	222	4	165	2	82.50	2-27	0	0
1977	24	39	6	1326	111	40.18	3	7	28	942	28	602	16	37.62	4-10	0	0
1978	8	12	2	586	127	58.60	2	4	5	150	2	101	3	33.66	2-55	0	0
1979	3	6	2	76	30*	19.00	0	0	4	144	4	73	1	73.00	1-26	0	0
Total	**40**	**67**	**11**	**2511**	**162**	**44.83**	**7**	**13**	**47**	**1458**	**38**	**941**	**22**	**42.77**	**4-10**	**0**	**0**

FIRST-CLASS CAREER FIGURES FOR GLAMORGAN

Season	M	I	NO	Runs	HS	Ave	100s	50s	Ct	Balls	M	Runs	Wkts	Ave	Best	5WI	10WM
1980	20	32	5	1460	181	54.07	3	6	7	204	8	132	2	66.00	2-25	0	0
1981	22	37	7	2083	200*	69.43	8	7	11	222	7	108	3	36.00	2-12	0	0
1982	8	16	2	601	96*	42.92	0	6	10	610	31	293	7	41.85	3-52	0	0
1983	5	6	0	114	89	19.00	0	1	5	12	0	11	0			0	0
1984	8	15	2	832	212*	64.00	2	3	4	308	9	187	6	31.16	2-26	0	0
1985	20	29	6	1441	200*	62.65	4	8	13	165	2	120	3	40.00	2-67	0	0
Total	**83**	**135**	**22**	**6531**	**212***	**57.79**	**17**	**31**	**50**	**1521**	**57**	**851**	**21**	**40.52**	**3-52**	**0**	**0**

FIRST-CLASS CAREER FIGURES FOR HABIB BANK

Season	M	I	NO	Runs	HS	Ave	100s	50s	Ct	St	Balls	M	Runs	Wkts	Ave	Best	5WI	10WM
1976/77	3	6	0	311	88	51.83	0	3	2	—	719	10	315	14	22.50	6-123	1	0
1977/78	12	16	1	1071	172	71.40	5	4	32	2	1157	14	520	22	23.63	5-52	1	0
1978/79	2	2	0	156	94	78.00	0	2	3	—	40	0	32	0	—	—	0	0
1979/80	4	5	0	268	91	53.60	0	2	5	—	90	1	35	0	—	—	0	0
1980/81	8	14	0	663	123	47.35	2	5	9	—	366	11	196	12	16.83	7-39	1	0
1981/82	2	3	0	163	107	54.33	1	1	7	—	18	1	6	0	—	—	0	0
1982/83	5	7	1	354	115	59.00	1	1	3	—	30	1	19	0	—	—	0	0
1985/86	2	2	0	31	29	15.50	0	0	0	—	—	—	—	—	—	—	—	—
1987/88	3	5	2	270	144*	90.00	1	0	3	—	—	—	—	—	—	—	—	—
1990/91	2	3	0	71	55	23.66	0	1	4	—	—	—	—	—	—	—	—	—
Total	**43**	**63**	**4**	**3358**	**172**	**56.91**	**10**	**19**	**68**	**2**	**2420**	**38**	**1123**	**48**	**23.39**	**7-39**	**3**	**0**

LIST OF FIRST-CLASS CENTURIES (80)

100	Sindh v Balochistan	Karachi	1973-74
107	Sindh v Punjab	Lahore	1974-75
115	Sindh A v PIA	Karachi	1974-75
101	Sindh A v Punjab A	Karachi	1974-75
311	Karachi Whites v National Bank	Karachi	1974-75
131*	Pakistan v BCCSL President's XI	Kandy	1975-76
135*	Sussex v Hampshire	Hove	1976
162	Sussex v Kent	Canterbury	1976
138*	NWFP Chief Minister's XI v NZ	Peshawar	1976-77
163	Pakistan v New Zealand	Lahore	1976-77
206	Pakistan v New Zealand	Karachi	1976-77
109	Sussex v Surrey	Hove	1977
111	Sussex v Yorkshire	Hove	1977
109*	Sussex v Hampshire	Hove	1977
100)	Habib Bank v PIA	Lahore	1977-78
118)	Habib Bank v PIA	Lahore	1977-78
148	Habib Bank v Pakistan Universities	Lahore	1977-78
172	Habib Bank v Sargodha	Faisalabad	1977-78
136	Habib Bank v Muslim Commercial Bank	Lahore	1977-78
110*	Sussex v Glamorgan	Swansea	1978
127	Sussex v Middlesex	Hove	1978
154*	Pakistan v India	Faisalabad	1978-79
100	Pakistan v India	Karachi	1978-79
160*	Pakistan v New Zealand	Christchurch	1978-79
129*	Pakistan v Australia	Perth	1978-79
110*	Pakistanis v Central Zone	Jaipur	1979-80
100*	Pakistanis v South Zone	Hyderabad(I)	1979-80
106*	Pakistan v Australia	Faisalabad	1979-80
140*	Glamorgan v Essex	Swansea	1980
141	Glamorgan v Gloucestershire	Bristol	1980
181	Glamorgan v Warwickshire	Birmingham	1980
107)	Habib Bank v National Bank	Lahore	1980-81
123)	Habib Bank v National Bank	Lahore	1980-81
130	BCCP President's XI v West Indians	Rawalpindi	1980-81
105	Glamorgan v Warwickshire	Cardiff	1981
137*)	Glamorgan v Somerset	Swansea	1981
106)	Glamorgan v Somerset	Swansea	1981
152	Glamorgan v Gloucestershire	Bristol	1981
200*	Glamorgan v Somerset	Taunton	1981
153*	Glamorgan v Warwickshire	Birmingham	1981
200*	Glamorgan v Essex	Colchester	1981
105*	Glamorgan v Leicestershire	Cardiff	1981
177	Pakistan XI v International XI	Lahore	1981-82
138	Pakistanis v Queensland	Brisbane	1981-82

158*	Pakistanis v Tasmania	Launceston	1981-82
107	Habib Bank v United Bank	Lahore	1981-82
105*	Pakistanis v Somerset	Taunton	1982
138	Pakistan v Australia	Lahore	1982-83
126	Pakistan v India	Faisalabad	1982-83
280*	Pakistan v India	Hyderabad(P)	1982-83
115	Habib Bank v National Bank	Lahore	1982-83
106*	Pakistanis v Victoria	Melbourne	1983-84
131	Pakistan v Australia	Adelaide	1983-84
141*	Pakistanis v Tasmania	Hobart	1983-84
212*	Glamorgan v Leicestershire	Swansea	1984
171	Glamorgan v Hampshire	Cardiff	1984
104)	Pakistan v New Zealand	Hyderabad(P)	1984-85
103*)	Pakistan v New Zealand	Hyderabad(P)	1984-85
112	Pakistanis v Canterbury	Christchurch	1984-85
125	Glamorgan v Surrey	Oval	1985
107	Glamorgan v Somerset	Cardiff	1985
164*	Glamorgan v Lancashire	Manchester	1985
200*	Glamorgan v Australians	Neath	1985
203*	Pakistan v Sri Lanka	Faisalabad	1985-86
102*	DB Close's XI v New Zealanders	Scarborough	1986
151	Pakistanis v Indian Under-25	Bombay	1986-87
211*	Pakistanis v Sussex	Hove	1987
260	Pakistan v England	Oval	1987
144*	Habib Bank v United Bank	Lahore	1987-88
111	Pakistanis v WICBC President's XI	Kingston	1987-88
114	Pakistan v West Indies	Georgetown	1987-88
102	Pakistan v West Indies	Port-of-Spain	1987-88
211	Pakistan v Australia	Karachi	1988-89
107	Pakistan v Australia	Faisalabad	1988-89
101*	Pakistanis v Canterbury	Christchurch	1988-89
118	Pakistan v New Zealand	Wellington	1988-89
271	Pakistan v New Zealand	Auckland	1988-89
145	Pakistan v India	Lahore	1989-90
153	Pakistan v England	Birmingham	1992
142*	Pakistanis v Hampshire	Southampton	1992

Index